Kant's Transcendental Logic

KANT'S

TRANSCENDENTAL LOGIC
17266

by Thomas Kaehao Swing

New Haven and London
Yale University Press
1969

Published with assistance from
the foundation established in memory
of William McKean Brown.
Copyright © 1969 by Yale University.
All rights reserved. This book may not be
reproduced, in whole or in part, in any form
(except by reviewers for the public press),
without written permission from the publishers.
Library of Congress catalog card number: 69–154–61.
Designed by Marvin Howard Simmons,
set in Times Roman type,
and printed in the United States of America by
The Carl Purington Rollins Printing-Office of
the Yale University Press, New Haven, Connecticut.
Distributed in Great Britain, Europe, Asia, and
Africa by Yale University Press Ltd., London; in
Canada by McGill University Press, Montreal; and
in Latin America by Centro Interamericano de Libros
Académicos, Mexico City.

To
My Splendid Teacher
F. S. C. Northrop

Preface

In the *Critique of Pure Reason,* Kant distinguishes formal logic from material logic. He characterizes the former as the logic of the forms of knowledge and the latter as the logic of its contents. It is well known among the students of Kant that he recognizes formal logic as an established science and respectfully gives Aristotle the credit of having brought it to perfection. What is not so well known even among Kant scholars is that he claims the merit of making the first systematic attempt to construct the science of material logic. This new science he presents under the name of transcendental logic.

Not many Kant scholars have paid serious attention to his claim of having constructed the science of material logic. This is reflected in the bibliographical fact that the expression 'transcendental (or material) logic' rarely appears in the titles of the almost countless books and essays accumulating in the vineyard of Kant scholarship. As far as I know, there are only two commentators who have taken this claim of Kant seriously. These two are Hegel and Peirce, both of whom have devoted considerable portions of their major works to the investigation of Kant's transcendental logic as a system of material logic. My own study of their investigations has convinced me that neither of these philosophers has adequately grasped the profound nature of Kant's adventure. It is this conviction that has led me to write this volume.

My main thesis in this book is that Kant tried to execute not one but two programs for constructing transcendental logic. This fact appears never to have been clearly recognized by Kant himself. That he never resolutely separated his "twin programs" from each other is the principal source for the unwieldy complexity and the systematic ambiguity of the *Critique*. I have tried to sort out these programs and have named them the axiomatic and the postulational programs. I have tried to show that these twin programs yield not one but two different systems of material logic and that Kant came to devise them because he in truth entertained two views of pure reason, that is, the formal and the material view. I have argued that the formal view of reason is Kant's own innovation, while the material view is his legacy from the Leibnizians.

As my inquiry unfolds, I have progressively tried to place Kant's adventure in the broad historical context of the Cartesian tradition. I have argued that Kant calls his material logic transcendental logic chiefly because he intends it to be the logic of transcendence, that is, the material logic that enables the Cartesian subject to transcend its subjectivity and attain objective knowledge. Descartes himself practically assumed the necessity of such a logic of transcendence (the logic of clear and distinct ideas) throughout his *Meditations* and even made some fragmentary attempts to construct one in his *Discourse on Method*. In his program of *characteristica universalis,* Leibniz reaffirmed the need for such a logic and further expressed his dream for its systematic construction. Placed in this historical context, Kant's transcendental logic is the first fullfledged embodiment of the Leibnizian dream of the Cartesian logic. For this reason, I have tried to assess its ultimate value by testing its efficacy in resolving the Cartesian problem of transcendence.

THOMAS KAEHAO SWING

Austin, Texas
May 27, 1968

Acknowledgments

In the course of composing this volume, I have had fruitful discussions with many persons. I will try to record some of the memorable ones.

My good fortune was to have Milton Fisk and Richard Zaner for my colleagues and friends. They were the two young responsive souls to express early enthusiasm for my unorthodox way of reading Kant. Without their encouragement, perhaps, I could not have overcome the moments of despair which are known only to those entangled in the Kantian marshland.

I had known of the so-called second version of the ontological argument and formulated my own criticism of it even before coming to the University of Texas and working with Charles Hartshorne in the same department. However, through many enlightening conversations with him, I came to see much more clearly the points of his contention and accordingly revised my refutation of his thesis. Nevertheless this indomitable metaphysician still believes that my criticism is not fair to him and Norman Malcolm.

On many occasions, I had to consult logicians on technical issues in formal logic. When I was at Yale, I was fortunate to have had a liberal access to Alan Ross Anderson's always incisive advice. When I came to Texas, I was equally fortunate to rely on the unfailing counsel of John Bacon.

Being only an amateur in the field of Kant scholarship, I was in need of some professional aid. I was glad to find it in M. J. Scott-Taggart of England, indisputably one of the most learned experts on Kantian studies in our generation. He went over my manuscript with meticulous care and sent me many valuable suggestions for its final polish.

I wrote the final draft of my manuscript with a 1967 summer research grant from the University of Texas Research Institute.

Finally I wish to acknowledge my gratitude to the following publishers, authors, translators, and editors for permission to use the quotations reproduced in this volume:

Kant, *Dissertation on the Form and Principles of the Sensible and the Intelligible World,* trans. by John Handyside and included in *Kant's Inaugural Dissertation and Early Writings on Space,* Chicago, The Open Court Publishing Co., 1929.
   Critique of Pure Reason, trans. by Norman Kemp Smith, London, Macmillan and Co., 1953.
   Prolegomena to Any Future Metaphysics, trans. by Lewis White Beck, Indianapolis, The Library of Liberal Arts, The Bobbs-Merrill Co., 1950.
   Critique of Judgement, trans. by James Creed Meredith, Oxford, Oxford University Press, 1952.
Rabel, Gabriele, ed. *Kant,* Oxford, Oxford University Press, 1963.
Smith, Norman Kemp, *A Commentary to Kant's 'Critique of Pure Reason,'* New York, Humanities Press, 1962.
Heidegger, Martin, *Kant and the Problem of Metaphysics,* trans. by James S. Churchill, Bloomington, Indiana University Press, 1962.
Anselm, St., *Proslogium,* trans. by S. W. Deane and included in his *Saint Anselm: Basic Writings,* La Salle, Open Court Publishing Co., 1962.
Henle, Paul, "Uses of the Ontological Argument," *The Philosophical Review,* 70 (1961).
Descartes, *Meditations on First Philosophy,* trans. by Norman Kemp Smith, in his *Descartes: Philosophical Writings,* New York, Random House, 1958.
Spinoza, *Ethics,* ed. by James Gutmann, New York, Hafner Publishing Co., 1955.
Latta, Robert, *Leibniz, The Monadology and Other Philosophical Writings,* Oxford, Oxford University Press, 1951.

Contents

Part I

Transcendental Concepts

Chapter 1

Judgment-Forms and Categories

A priori concepts are the primitive elements for the construction of transcendental logic. Kant wants to assure himself that his collection of these concepts is complete. He recognizes Aristotle as the only one who has tried to discover all the primitive concepts but he finds fault with the haphazard method that Aristotle used in his attempt. Kant says, "It was an enterprise worthy of an acute thinker like Aristotle to make search for these fundamental concepts. But as he did so on no principle, he merely picked them up as they came his way." (A 81 = B 107)* He wants to devise a systematic method to bring to completion the worthy enterprise that Aristotle tried to execute with his unsystematic method.

Kant's allegedly systematic method for discovering all a priori concepts has been generally known as the Metaphysical Deduction, whose purpose was to derive the Table of Categories from the Table of Judgments. Here are the two tables:

*All references to the *Critique of Pure Reason* are cited in parentheses in the text. Unless otherwise noted, these textual references are to the German edition, edited by Raymond Schmidt, in Die Philosophische Bibliothek (Hamburg, Felix Meiner, 1956) and to the English translation by Norman Kemp Smith (London, Macmillan, 1953), which incorporates both the first (1781) and second (1787) editions of the *Critique*. Citations like the above (A 81 = B 107) refer to the marginal notations in both the German edition and the English translation, where A 81 and B 107 identify the source of the translation as page 81 of the first German edition and its equivalent passage on page 107 of the second edition.

TABLE OF JUDGMENTS

I
Quantity of Judgments
Universal
Particular
Singular

II
Quality
Affirmative
Negative
Infinite

III
Relation
Categorical
Hypothetical
Disjunctive

IV
Modality
Problematic
Assertoric
Apodeictic

TABLE OF CATEGORIES

I
Of Quantity
Unity
Plurality
Totality

II
Of Quality
Reality
Negation
Limitation

III
Of Relation
Of Inherence and Subsistence
(substantia et accidens)
Of Causality and Dependence
(cause and effect)
Of Community (reciprocity
between agent and patient)

IV
Of Modality
Possibility–Impossibility
Existence–Non-existence
Necessity–Contingency

Kant calls the Table of Judgments "the clue to the discovery of all pure concepts of the understanding." (A 67 = B 92) The nature and function of this clue is one of the baffling mysteries in the *Critique*. Kant's own account is so implausible that his prized clue has seldom been taken at face value. Even those who accept the result of Kant's Metaphysical Deduction usually tend to relegate his elaborate method of derivation to the limbo of his transcendental architectonism.[1] To pay no more than cursory attention to Kant's method of derivation has become a well-established custom, even a prejudice, in Kant scholarship. It would be, however, worthwhile to hold this custom in abeyance and inquire anew first into the nature and then into the function of Kant's clue.

How did Kant obtain the Table of Judgments?

The Table of Judgments is meant to be a systematic classification of all the forms of judgment. By the forms of judgment, Kant means the logical forms that judgments must have regardless of their content. (A 70 = B 95) Since the forms of judgment have nothing to do with the content of knowledge, he assumes, they belong to the province of formal logic, which he sometimes also calls general logic. He further assumes that formal logic achieved a complete systematization at the hands of Aristotle and has since taken not a single step either forward or backward. (B viii) On the basis of these assumptions, Kant apparently believes that the Table of Judgments is an established legacy from Aristotle's formal logic. In order to determine the accuracy of this belief, we have to review briefly *De Interpretatione,* where Aristotle makes two separate attempts to classify the different kinds of judgment forms. Although these two atempts produce two slightly different classifications, they jointly contain what has been generally known as the Aristotelian classification of judgments or propositions.*

---

*By 'judgment' *(Urteil)* Kant means 'the act of judgment' as well as 'the content of judgment.' Since he uses 'judgment' in the latter sense

Aristotle's first distinction is between affirmation and denial in a proposition.[2] His second distinction is between a simple and a composite proposition.[3] His third distinction rests on the distribution of the subject, the well-known distinction between a universal and a particular proposition.[4] His final distinction concerns the division of the modal propositions into the possible and the necessary.[5]

The combination of the first and the third distinctions produces the well-known Aristotelian square:

(A) Universal Affirmation	(E) Universal Denial
(I) Particular Affirmation	(O) Particular Denial

Since this square has long been a prominent feature of Aristotelian logic books, Aristotle's first and third distinctions have been better known than his second and fourth distinctions. This appears to have been the case in Kant's own day. In his criticism of the Leibnizian logic, for instance, he mentions the universal and particular, and the affirmative and the negative, as the standard forms of judgment: "Before constructing any objective judgment we compare the concepts to find in them identity (of many representations under one concept) with a view to *universal* judgments, *difference* with a view to *particular* judgments, *agreement* with a view to *affirmative* judgments, *opposition* with a view to *negative* judgments, etc." (A 262 = B 317) It is clear that the Aristotelian square of opposition cannot provide Kant with the elaborate table he wants to have for the derivation of categories. The forms of judgments in that square are just too few in number. It thus seems advisable to put together all four of Aristotle's distinctions—which yields the following table:

interchangeably with 'proposition' *(Satz)*, I will also use these two terms interchangeably except when 'judgment' means the act of judgment rather than its content. I will refer to the former by the specific expression 'the act of judgment.'

PART I TRANSCENDENTAL CONCEPTS

ARISTOTLE'S TABLE OF PROPOSITIONS

I

Affirmation
Denial (or Negation)

II

Universal
Particular

III

Simple
Composite

IV

Possible
Necessary

For the sake of convenience, let us call Aristotle's table the A Table and Kant's the K Table. We can see a certain isomorphism between the two: Both consist of four divisions. But there are some discrepancies, the most noticeable of which is that each division of the A Table contains two members, while each division of the K Table consists of three members. Kant admits that the third members in some divisions of his Table are his own additions. (A 71ff. = B 96ff.) The K Table must be either an expansion or transformation of the A Table. Let us now determine which is the case.

Kant's Quantity of Judgments resembles Aristotle's Judgments of Distribution (Universal and Particular). Kant introduces a third form, singular judgment. In the textbooks of traditional logic, 'singular judgment' usually means a judgment which has a singular term for his subject, such as "Socrates is mortal." Kant's 'singular judgment' does not share this traditional meaning. Aristotle himself does not include the singular-term judgment in his doctrine of the judgments of distribution on the ground that the singular-term subject cannot be distributed.[6] By 'singular judgment' Kant means a judgment whose subject is a universal term in the singular form, such as "The horse is an animal" or "A horse is an animal."* Since Kant offers an involved argument for designating singular judgment as the third form of the quantified judgments, we had better cite the argument in its entirety:

> Logicians are justified in saying that, in the employment of judgments in syllogisms, singular judgments can be treated like those that are universal. For, since they have no extension at all, the predicate cannot relate to part only of that which is contained in the concept of the subject, and be excluded from the rest. The predicate is valid of that concept, without any such exception, just as if it were a general concept and had an extension to the whole of which the predicate applied. If, on the other hand, we compare a singular with a universal judgment, merely as knowledge, in respect of quantity, the singular stands to the universal as unity to infinity, and is therefore in itself essentially different from the universal. If, therefore, we estimate a singular judgment *(judicium singulare)*, not only according to its own inner validity, but as knowledge in general, according to its quantity in

*Professor M. J. Scott-Taggart has pointed out to me that this assertion is dubious in view of the fact that Kant himself gives "Caius is mortal" as an example of a singular judgment in his *Logik* §21. Although Kant gives no example of a singular judgment in the Metaphysical Deduction, the long passage we are about to quote in our text indicates that he has decided to use 'a singular judgment' to mean exclusively the unquantified judgments in the Deduction rather than the judgments having for their subjects singular terms, that is, proper names or definite descriptions. In this passage he admits the formal identity of the singular and the universal judgments and recognizes the possibility of their distinction from each other only in terms of their content. This admission would make no sense, if Kant were to retain the traditional meaning of the singular judgment. He appears to have abandoned its traditional usage in the Deduction simply because he saw the implausibility of deriving the category of totality from the traditionally recognized form of the singular judgment.

comparison with other knowledge, it is certainly different from general judgments *(judicia communia),* and in a complete table of the moments of thought in general deserves a separate place—though not, indeed, in a logic limited to the use of judgments in reference to each other. (A 71 = B 96)

If Kant is correct in his observation, the logicians of his day treated singular propositions as equivalent to universal propositions. Singular propositions have logical ambiguity and can also be treated as equivalent to particular propositions. This ambiguity stems from the incomplete character of singular propositions. That they are incomplete becomes obvious when we translate "The horse is an animal" or "A horse is an animal" into such symbolic notations as *"Hx ⊃ Ax"* or *"Hx · Ax."* The incompleteness of singular propositions shows up in the form of the unbound variables of these notations. A singular proposition is a neutral matrix that can and needs to be quantified either with an existential or with a universal quantifier. So it is an awkward move to designate it as one more form of quantified propositions along with universal and particular propositions.

Kant wants to defend this awkward move on the ground that singular propositions differ from universal propositions (and presumably also from particular propositions) in the quantity of knowledge they contain. We will try to spell out his reasoning behind this somewhat obscure assertion. He seems to hold that singular propositions differ from universal and particular propositions in the number of the objects that fall under the subject-concept. For example, "A horse is an animal" or "The horse is an animal" involves only one horse; "Some horses are animals" involves more than one or many horses; and "All horses are animals" involves an infinite (Kant really means an indefinite) number of horses. Thus he believes that these three kinds of judgments differ in the quantity of the content of knowledge. Kant has surreptitiously converted the quantifiers into quantitative terms.

In order to reveal the nature of this conversion, we have to employ the logician's distinction between logical and descriptive terms or signs. Descriptive terms or signs represent individuals, classes, properties, and relations; they are such words as 'Kelso,' 'horse,' 'courage,' and 'love.' Logical signs include the logical constants of the propositional calculus ('and,' 'or,' 'not,' and 'if–then') and the quantifiers of the predicate calculus ('every' and 'some').* Their function is not to represent any objects but to bring together descriptive terms into propositions, and simple propositions into complex ones. Theirs is a connective function. The distinction between logical and descriptive terms was known during medieval times as that between categorematic and syncategorematic terms. If we want to express this distinction in Kant's language, we have to adopt the expressions 'formal term' and 'material term.' This distinction is made in the domain of words but can be transferred to the domain of concepts; that is, concepts can be classified into formal and material concepts.

*The distinction between the logical and the descriptive signs is by no means a matter of unanimous agreement among logicians. Some of them would regard this distinction as one of degree, while others would view it as one of kind. Some logicians may include the identity sign and even the class-membership sign in the list of the logical signs, while others would not do so. Logicians have not been able to provide a "real" definition of logical signs; they usually content themselves with a definition by stipulation or enumeration. None of these technical points has any direct relevance to our exposition. All we need is the general recognition of the distinction between two kinds of signs in propositions, whether it be a distinction of kind or degree. I am sure that some would not accept this distinction in any form. To them, Kant's entire enterprise would appear to have been ill conceived from the beginning because it could not take a single step without presupposing the distinction between the formal and the material reason, which is equivalent to Carnap's distinction between the logical and the empirical truths.

The quantifiers 'all' and 'some' are not material but formal terms. Aristotle makes this point: "For the word 'every' does not make the subject a universal, but rather gives the proposition a universal character."[7] In the proposition "Every horse is an animal," for example, the quantifier 'every' does not concern the subject term but rather the entire proposition. Compare this proposition with "Five horses are now racing" or "A horse is missing." 'Five' and 'a' concern not the propositions but the subject terms. 'Five' and 'a' are material terms; 'every' is a formal term. The latter is a logical sign; the former are descriptive signs.*

Quantitative terms have material functions; they are concerned with the content of knowledge. But *quantifiers* play no material functions; they do not concern the content of knowledge. Kant reveals his awareness of these points in the long passage we have quoted. There he recognizes that formal logic deals only with formal terms and has nothing to do with material terms because it abstracts completely from the content of knowledge. The conversion of quantifiers into quantitative terms in the K Table is the transformation of formal terms into

---

*Expressing his dissatisfaction with this distinction, Professor Scott-Taggart writes "But I certainly see no intuitive distinction between the two which would entitle the assertion that 'every' qualifies the whole proposition while 'five' qualifies only the subject term. We could quite easily generate a series of quantifiers of the form $(E_n x)$ meaning that there are n x's such that . . ."

I can offer the following reply: Whereas "There are five horses" is a well-formed sentence, "There is every horse" is not. This can be taken as an intuitive evidence for assuming that 'every' is a formal sign while 'five' is a material sign. Numerical terms may take on the appearance of logical signs, when they are expressed in the form of numerical quantifiers. Even then, their behavior is fundamentally different from that of such normal logical signs as the universal or the existential quantifier. The numerical quantifiers can be eliminated in favor of the concept of class membership and those of numbers: $(E_n x) Fx \equiv \hat{x}Fx \ \varepsilon \ n$. But the universal and the existential quantifiers cannot be so eliminated.

material terms. Consequently the First Division of the K Table lists three kinds of quantitative judgments rather than three forms of quantified judgments. The discrimination of judgments in terms of quantitative terms is a material and not a formal distinction; it can have no relevance to the classification of the *forms* of judgments.

The Second Division of the K Table is called the Quality of Judgments and resembles that section of the A Table which distinguishes between Affirmation and Denial. Kant adds his third form, the infinite judgment, and gives as an example the proposition "The soul is nonmortal." (A 72 = B 97) He says that this judgment should be distinguished from both the affirmative judgment "The soul is mortal" and the negative judgment "The soul is not mortal." He admits that the infinite judgment is not different from the affirmative judgment in its formal structure because both take the form of affirmation, and that the infinite judgment is distinguished from other judgments through the nature of its predicate. The infinite judgment is a judgment which has an infinite predicate.

'Infinite predicate' and 'infinite judgment' are not quite fortunate expressions; 'indefinite predicate' and 'indefinite judgment' may be more suitable expressions. Aristotle uses the latter expressions.[8] He is far more acute than Kant when it comes to understanding the function of indefinite terms. He observes that the indefinite predicate can be denied ("Man is not not-just") or be affirmed of the subject ("Man is not-just"). He also points out that the indefinite terms can be used not only as predicate terms but also as subject terms ("Not-man is just," "Not-man is not just," "Not-man is not not-just," and "Not-man is not-just"). Peirce reports that the Romans kept the distinction of the definite and the indefinite subject terms as well as that of the definite and the indefinite predicate terms.[9] He further reports that Wolff decided to limit the distinction to the predicate terms. For this reason, Kant might have not known the use of the indefinite subject terms and thus have come to consider only the judgments containing indefinite predicate terms in the formation of the K Table.

There seem to be two objections to Kant's designation of infinite judgments as the third form of the Quality of Judgments. First, if he wants to accept the affirmative indefinite judgment as the third form, he should accept the negative indefinite judgment as the fourth form. His 'infinite judgment' covers only the affirmative one and excludes the negative one. Kant can give no reason for this exclusion except that he wants to have only three forms in each Division of his Table.

Our second objection is more serious. The distinction between indefinite and definite judgments is based on not formal but material terms. The distinction between affirmation and negation has the ambiguity of referring not only to propositions but to their material terms. "The horse is brown" and "The horse is not brown" are, respectively, affirmative and negative propositions. 'Brown' and 'not-brown' are, respectively, affirmative and negative material terms. The word 'not' performs a formal function of negation when it operates on the entire proposition ("It is not the case that the horse is brown"), but does not perform the same function when it operates on a material term like 'brown' and forms 'not-brown' ("It is the case that the horse is not-brown"). In the latter case, 'not' becomes a part of a material term and performs a material function. Thus the distinction between indefinite and definite judgments is based on material terms.

Kant readily recognizes that the logical classification of judgments cannot be based on the nature of the predicate terms because their nature does not belong to the province of formal logic. As he puts it, "General logic abstracts from all content of the predicate (even though it be negative); it enquires only whether the predicate be ascribed to the subject or opposed to it. But transcendental logic also considers what may be the worth or content of a logical affirmation." (A 72 =

B 97) He is asserting that the content of knowledge belongs to the province of transcendental logic, whereas it does not belong to that of formal logic. Because of this peculiarity of his transcendental logic, he claims, he can make use of material terms (predicates) in his classification of judgments in the Second Division of the K Table.

Thus the three forms of the Quality of Judgments reflect three kinds of predicate terms; they, too, have nothing to do with the formal functions of judgments. Kant's 'affirmative judgment' means a judgment containing a positive predicate; his 'negative judgment' means a judgment containing a negative predicate; and his 'infinite judgment' means a judgment containing an infinite predicate. He has transformed the distinction in the *quality* of judgments into a classification of *qualitative* judgments.

The Third Division of the K Table is called the Relation of Judgment and resembles that section of the A Table which distinguishes between Simple and Composite Propositions. Kemp Smith suggests that Kant has probably adopted the following division of simple and complex judgments in the prevalent Wolffian textbooks:[10]

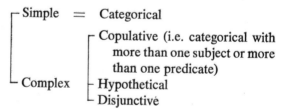

This chart is too complex; Kant cannot produce another triad by adding one more form. He first strikes out the distinction between the simple and the complex judgments and then eliminates the copulative (conjunctive) judgment. Thus he obtains the triad of the categorical, the hypothetical, and the disjunctive. Since he has decided to dispense with the distinction between the simple and the complex judgments, he has to find another common denominator for grouping the three members of his new triad under one heading. He has finally decided to adopt the 'relation of thought' as the common denominator. The 'relation of thought' is a rather unfamiliar expression to the science of logic, but Kant's explanation will help to clarify it:

> All relations of thought in judgments are *(a)* of the predicate to the subject, *(b)* of the ground to its consequence, *(c)* of the divided knowledge and of the members of the division, taken together, to each other. In the first kind of judgments we consider only two concepts, in the second two judgments, in the third several judgments in their relation to each other. (A 73 = B 98)

In this passage Kant distinguishes between two kinds of relations of thought: (1) the relation of terms in a proposition (the subject-predicate relation) and (2) the relation of propositions through logical connectives. Within this scheme of classification, the distinction between the hypothetical and the disjunctive judgment should stand as a subdivision of the second kind. Instead of a simple triad, in other words, Kant should have adopted the following classification:

The Relation of Thought in Judgments

┌─Relation of terms in a judgment = Categorical
│   ┌─Hypothetical
└─Relation of judgments   │
                                    └─Disjunctive

Even this classification is not perfect. In the first place, it leaves out the conjunctive judgment. We shall see that this omission forces Kant to make a dubious maneuver in deriving the category of community. In the second place, it is strange to find the 'relation of terms in a judgment' as a member of the third triad in the K Table. The forms of judgments which we have considered in the First and the Second Divisions of the K Table are none other than the various forms which can be taken by the relation of terms in a judgment. Affirmation and negation, and universal and existential quantifications are the four ways to characterize the nature of the relation which holds between the terms in a proposition. Such should be the case at least in the logic of terms.

Even if we take the first member of the third triad in the K Table as the categorical judgment rather than as the relation of terms in a judgment, we can still make the same point. The universal, the particular, the affirmative and the negative, and the singular and the infinite are the various forms of the categorical judgment. Some may hesitate to regard a negative judgment as categorical, but a negative judgment can be as categorically asserted as an affirmative one. So Kant should have made the first two Divisions of the K Table subdivisions of the categorical judgment. That, however, would have produced a radically different table from the K Table.

In spite of these irregularities, the third triad of the K Table seems to have at least one virtue. We have seen that Kant converts formal terms into material terms in the first two Divisions of the K Table. He does not seem to make the same kind of conversion in the Third Division. 'The categorical,' 'the hypothetical,' and 'the disjunctive' all seem to be the expressions of logical terms. Kant himself makes no claim that the content of judgments has been used in the classification of the three forms of judgments in this Division of the K Table. We shall take up this point in further detail when we examine Kant's derivation of the relational categories.

We now come to the final Division of the K Table. Whereas Aristotle recognizes only two pairs of modal propositions (Possible–Impossible and Necessary–Contingent), Kant presents three kinds of modal judgments. Furthermore, the expressions that Kant uses for his classification of modal judgments ('problematic,' 'assertoric,' and 'apodeictic') are not the

Aristotelian expressions. Kant may have decided to use his unorthodox modal expressions because he assigns to the modal terms functions different from their traditional ones.

To explain Kant's peculiar usage of the modal terms, we will employ G. H. von Wright's classification of modal functions. He recognizes four kinds of modal functions: alethic, existential, deontic, and epistemic.[11] The alethic modes are predicated of propositions: for example, "It is necessary that p," or "It is possible that p." The existential modes are regarded as properties of classes and belong to quantification theory. The deontic modes are used to describe the nature of obligations and rights. The epistemic modes describe the state of knowledge.

Of these four kinds of modal functions, Kant did not know of the deontic modes because these are the innovations of the deontic logic of our century. It is the alethic modes that have been known as the modal functions of traditional logic. The existential modes have been regarded as alternative expressions of the alethic modes, or rather these two sets of modal functions have been treated as equivalent to each other. Kant himself makes use of their equivalence in his claim that necessity (an alethic mode) and universality (an existential mode) are the two alternative criteria of a priori judgments. (B 4) In the Metaphysical Deduction, however, he repudiates the traditional modal concepts on the ground that modal concepts can really have nothing to do with the content of knowledge. (A 74 = B 99 f.) Thus he replaces the traditional modes with his epistemic modes. Whereas the former have been given the illegitimate function of characterizing the content of knowledge, he means to maintain, the latter will be given the only legitimate modal function of characterizing the modes of knowledge.

Kant recognizes three epistemic modes: the problematic, the assertoric, and the apodeictic. In order to clarify their meanings, we will try to translate these three modes into von Wright's modal expressions. The problematic judgment is one whose truth is unknown or undetermined; the assertoric judgment is one whose truth is known or verified; and the apodeictic judgment is one whose truth is guaranteed by the laws of thought alone.

Kant assumes that the three members of this triad are standing on the same level of classification. But this assumption is erroneous. A meticulous distinction of the three epistemic modes requires two stages of classification. All epistemic modes should first be classified into verified and unverified judgments. The unverified judgment is equivalent to Kant's problematic judgment. Kant's distinction between the assertoric and the apodeictic judgment can be obtained by the subdivision of the verified judgment because there are two ways of establishing the truths of propositions. That is, the second and third members of Kant's triad stand on the second level of classification while its first member stands on the first level of classification. Only by overlooking this point can Kant obtain his fourth triad.

In order to protect the neatness of this triad, Kant takes the radical step of rejecting the traditional functions of the modal terms. He tries to justify this radical step on the ground that modal terms contribute nothing to the content of judgments. (A 74 = B 100) It is difficult to determine the validity of this assertion because Kant does not explain what he means by 'the content of judgments.' Whether this contention is valid or invalid, he cannot dismiss the traditional modal functions because he uses them in specifying the criteria of a priori knowledge in the *Critique*. He maintains that necessity and universality are the two interchangeable criteria of a priori judgments. (A 2 and B 3) The necessity of a priori judgments may well be construed as an epistemic mode: Their truths are known with indubitable certainty. But this epistemic necessity cannot be secured without establishing the alethic necessity of those a priori judgments. The universality of a priori judgments cannot be accommodated in the epistemic modes because 'universality' is not one of Kant's three epistemic modal terms. The universality in question is clearly one of the existential modes. Thus the two modal functions of traditional logic turn out to to be the two pillars of Kant's doctrine of a priori knowledge. Hence he cannot reject them without razing his doctrine of a priori knowledge.

The epistemic modal terms can be called neither formal nor material. Formal and material terms are two kinds of constituents of propositions, but the epistemic modal terms are not the constituents of propositions. So we cannot say that Kant has converted formal terms into material terms in the Fourth Division of the K Table. The conversion in this Division is more drastic than in the first two Divisions of the K Table, because it is the conversion of intrapropositional terms into extrapropositional terms. The traditional modal terms are intrapropositional because they are constituents of propositions; the epistemic modal terms are extrapropositional because they are not such constituents. Kant picks up modal terms from the traditional logic and converts their intrapropositional functions into extrapropositional ones.

Let us summarize the results of our investigation. The K Table is not a mere expansion but a substantial transformation of the A Table. The notable feature of this transformation is the conversion of formal into material terms. We will now close our first question and open our second one.

How does the K Table function as a clue to the derivation of all pure concepts?

Kant never explains how the Table of Categories is derived from the Table of Judgments. He simply presents the two tables one after the other, apparently assuming that the derivation of one from the other is obvious. But it is one of the most baffling affairs in the *Critique*. In order to determine the relation between the two tables, therefore, we must carefully examine the derivation of each category.

Since Kant has transformed quantified judgments into quantitative judgments, he should have little trouble in deriving the quantitative categories, for quantitative categories are the essential constituents of quantitative judgments. But we find him making an unusually tortuous maneuver in this derivation. He derives *unity* from universal judgment, *plurality* from particular judgment, and *totality* from singular judgment. He thus seems to have confused the quantitative meanings of the singular and the universal judgments. It appears to be more sensible and natural to derive not *unity* but *totality* from universal judgment, and not *totality* but *unity* from singular judgment. Kemp Smith reports that Kant was not unaware of this more sensible line of derivation: "In *Reflexionen,* ii.563, Kant makes the more natural line of identifying totality with the universal, and unity with the singular."[12] We find evidence indeed to show that Kant had not forgotten this more natural line of thought at the time of the Metaphysical Deduction. He observes that "the singular [judgment] stands to the universal [judgment] as unity to infinity." (A 71 = B 96)

Why did Kant abandon this natural line of derivation? Kemp Smith concurs in Adickes' venerable conjecture: "Probably the reason of Kant's change of view is the necessity of obtaining totality by combining unity with multiplicity."[13] This conjecture seems to be however only a partial explanation. True, Kant wishes to hold the concepts of unity and plurality as a pair of opposing concepts and the concept of totality as their combination. (B 110–11) He could have achieved this objective simply by reversing the positions of the universal and the singular judgments:

Quantity of Judgments	Pure Concepts of Quantity
Singular	Unity
Particular	Plurality
Universal	Totality

By this simple procedure, Kant could have had *totality* as the third concept and yet derived it from universal judgment. Adickes' conjecture rests on the assumption that Kant could not see this simple solution.

We may obtain the other half of the probable explanation if we take Kant's "triadic" obsession to be a little more pervasive than Adickes assumes. Suppose that Kant wants to arrange in a triadic scheme not only the three concepts of quantity but also the three judgments of quantity. This is not an unreasonable supposition because the triad of judgments can be regarded as the reflection of the triad of concepts. If our assumption is correct, Kant should have wanted to see not only the first two concepts of quantity but also the first two judgments of quantity as a pair of opposites.

Universal and particular judgments are the best candidates for this pair because these two forms of judgment have been traditionally defined as a pair of opposites. Kant takes full advantage of this well-established tradition in placing universal and particular judgments as the first and the second judgments of quantity. Suppose further that Kant tried to place the singular as the first judgment of quantity. Then he would have to pair up the singular judgment with either the universal or the particular judgment. This would run counter to a two-thousand-year-old practice. To place the singular judgment as the third judgment gives Kant one more advantage. We have seen that the singular judgment, being unquantified, can be read either as a universal or as a particular judgment. This can reinforce the impression that the singular judgment is the combination of the universal and the particular judgments, just as the concept of totality is the combination of the concepts of unity and plurality. Let me repeat that this is only a conjecture. The only thing about which we can be certain is that Kant derives quantitative categories from quantitative judgments.

We have seen that Kant has transformed the quality of judgments into qualitative judgments. Since he distinguishes several forms of qualitative judgments by the nature of their predicate terms, he can be expected to make use of the predicate terms in deriving the concepts of quality. Since the affirmative judgment takes the positive predicate of "being so-and-so," he derives from it *reality,* the presence of a quality. From the negative judgment, which takes the negative predicate of "not being so-and-so," he derives *negation,* the absence of a quality. The infinite judgment presents a problem, because it takes the indefinite predicate of "being not-so-and-so." From this he should derive the category which represents some indefinite quality. The derivation of this category would indeed be the introduction of an unfamiliar entity into the domain of categories. Kant comes up with the category of limitation. In the second edition of the *Critique* he defines this unfamiliar category as "reality combined with negation." (B 111) Since this definition is offered as a part of his dubious attempt to maintain the general thesis that the third category in each triad is the combination of the other two, it is difficult to tell how seriously this definition should be taken. At any rate, the definition of *limitation* as the combination of *reality* and *negation* is ambiguous. By this definition he cannot mean the presence *(reality)* and absence *(negation)* of the same predicate in the same subject because that would be self-contradictory. He must mean the presence of one predicate and absence of some other predicate in the same subject; but this state of affairs cannot be described by an infinite judgment since its description requires at least two judgments. So there can be no plausible ground for believing that the category of limitation has anything to do with the infinite judgment. The derivation of *limitation* from the infinite judgment must be considered as another of the many mysteries in Kant's transcendental logical maneuver.

Let us now move on to the derivation of the relational categories. Kant derives *substance and accident* from the categorical judgment. He seems to have two steps of reasoning for this derivation. First, he assumes the categorical judgment to be the expression of the subject-predicate relation. (A 73 = B 98) Second, he further assumes that the subject-predicate relation in a judgment expresses the substance-accident relation. Neither of these assumptions is tenable.

The categorical judgment need not always take the subject-predicate form; it can also take the relational form. "The hare is faster than the tortoise" is as categorical as "The hare is fast." Kant could maintain his position on the ground that all the relational judgments can be reduced to the subject-predicate judgment. For example, he might argue that the judgment "The hare is faster than the tortoise" states the relation of the subject ("the hare") and the predicate ("being faster than the tortoise"). But this expanded definition of the categorical judgment would not allow Kant to derive only the category of substance and accident from the subject-predicate judgment. The expanded definition would allow him to derive all the other relational categories from the same judgment, because that judgment can express any kind of relation. Even the ingenious Kant would not know what use he could make of the other two members of his third triad, i.e. the hypothetical and the disjunctive judgments.

Even if the categorical judgment were defined as the subject-predicate judgment, Kant would still have difficulty in deriving *substance and accident* from that judgment. The 'subject-predicate' need not always express the substance-accident relation. The expression 'subject-predicate' states merely a grammatical relation of words; the expression 'substance-accident' states an ontological relation of objects. The former expresses a formal concept and the latter a material concept. There is no obvious or obscure link which connects the two. Kant could justify his derivation of *substance and accident* from the categorical judgment only by defining this judgment as the expression of the substance-accident relation. This definition of the categorical judgment, however, would amount to the conversion of a formal into a material definition.

Kant derives *cause and effect* from the hypothetical judgment. Very few may question the validity of this derivation, but even so it can be shown to be dubious on closer inspection. Kant defines the hypothetical judgment as the expression of the relation of the logical ground to its consequence. (A 73 = B 98) According to this definition, the hypothetical judgment is stronger than material implication and has the same force as logical entailment. Here are some examples that express the logical relation of ground and consequence: "If all horses are brown, then some horses are brown" rests on the rule of conversion, but it does not express a causal relation. "If A is faster than B and if B is faster than C, then A is faster than C," rests on the rule of transitivity and again in no sense expresses a causal relation.

True, the causal relation can be expressed in a hypothetical judgment (e.g. "If A, then B"). But this fact cannot justify the derivation of *cause and effect* (any more that it can justify the derivation of *transitivity)* from the hypothetical judgment. Furthermore, the hypothetical judgment has no monopoly on the expression of causal relation; the categorical judgment can express it equally well (e.g. *"A* is the cause of *B")*. So one can claim to derive the category of cause and effect from the categorical judgment as well.

Although the hypothetical judgment can express causal relations, the form of that judgment alone is never sufficient to indicate that the relation in question is a causal relation. By merely looking at "If A, then B," it is impossible to tell that A is the cause of B because the form of hypothetical judgment expresses only the logical relation of ground and consequence. 'Ground and consequence' expresses a logical relation; 'cause and effect' expresses a factual relation. The former stands for a formal concept; the latter stands for a material concept. Kant could justify his derivation of *cause and effect* from the hypothetical judgment only by defining it as the expression of a causal judgment. According to this definition, 'a hypothetical judgment' would be synonymous with a 'causal judgment.' That would be but another conversion of a formal expression into a material one.

Kant derives *community* from the disjunctive judgment. This category is the concept not of mere coexistence but of mutual causation. Kant tries to justify the derivation of this category on the ground that a disjunctive judgment presupposes a community of entities. For example, *"A is B, C, or D"* presupposes the community of *B, C,* and *D.* But this argument is not convincing; it would be easier to sustain an opposite argument. Since Kant takes the disjunctive judgment in its strong rather than its weak sense, it can be argued that the disjunctive judgment states the incompatibility or mutual exclusion of the disjoined members. The judgment "The horse is brown or black" has the function of stating the mutual exclusion of "The horse is brown" and "The horse is black." This would justify the derivation of *disunity* or *opposition* from disjunctive judgment.

The obvious candidate for the derivation of *community* is conjunctive judgment, but Kant has eliminated it from the K Table. Even if he were to retain conjunctive judgment in the K Table, however, it might justify the derivation of *coexistence* but not that of *community* or *reciprocal causation.* Kant can derive his category of community from disjunctive judgment only by defining it as the expression of mutual causation. Even Kant refrains from this drastic redefinition of disjunctive judgment.

In our examination of the construction of the K Table, we noted that Kant converted formal expressions into material expressions in the first two Divisions of that Table. We also noted that the Third Division was the only place where he seemed not to make this conversion. It now appears necessary for us to revise our initial impression of this matter. When Kant comes to the derivation of the relational categories, he operates as though he had made this conversion. By this I mean that his derivation of relational categories can be accepted only on that assumption.

Kant appears to admit such a conversion in a parenthetical remark in the course of explaining the unique nature of modal judgments: "The *modality* of judgments is a quite peculiar function. Its distinguishing characteristic is that it contributes nothing to the content of the judgments (for, besides quantity, quality, and relation, there is nothing that constitutes the content of a judgment)." (A 74 = B 100) Kant apparently holds that all the forms of judgments except the modal ones contribute to the content of judgments. This assertion cannot be made within the A Table because there none of the forms of judgment or logical terms has anything to do with the content of judgments. Kant can justify his claim only on the ground that the formal expressions in the first three Divisions of the K Table have all been converted into material expressions.

Kant apparently holds that every judgment consists of three terms: the subject, the predicate, and their relation. He believes that the quantity of a judgment is concerned with its subject, that its quality is concerned with its predicate, and that its relation is concerned with the relation of the subject and the predicate. Thus he assumes that quantity, quality, and relation exhaust the content of a judgment and leave nothing for the modal terms to contribute. We have seen that the quantity of a judgment in the K Table is concerned with the number of the subjects, and the quality of a judgment with the nature of the predicate. The only item that is left uncharacterized is the relation of the subject and the predicate, but Kant has apparently assumed all along that this relation is characterized by the relation of judgment. We thus have reasonable grounds to conclude that the Third Division of the K Table transforms the relation of judgments into relational judgments or judgments of relation.

Kant derives *possibility* and *impossibility* from the problematic judgment, *existence* and *nonexistence* from the assertoric judgment, and *necessity* and *contingency* from the apodeictic judgment. Here, however, he has derived too many categories because he obtains six from three forms of judgment. Moreover, he has no right to derive *impossibility* from the problematic judgment, *nonexistence* from the assertoric judgment, and *contingency* from the apodeictic judgment. The correct thing to do is rather to derive *possibility, existence, and necessity,* and then to add the other three categories as their opposites. In spite of this procedural flaw, Kant's derivation of the modal categories is the least questionable operation in the Metaphysical Deduction.

To restate our discovery: Kant's derivation of the categories becomes intelligible only on the supposition that the transformation of the A Table into the K Table rests on the conversion of formal terms (or concepts) into material terms (or concepts). We had already suspected the existence of this conversion while attempting to answer the first question posed in this chapter. Our examination of the derivation of the categories has substantially confirmed our initial suspicion.

We have yet to determine how Kant himself understood the nature of the K Table and its function in the Metaphysical Deduction. We must also assess the result of the Metaphysical Deduction. We will take up these questions in the following chapter.

Chapter 2

Categorial Deduction and Formal Reason

Having tried to determine the nature of the K Table and its function in the Metaphysical Deduction by examining the structure of the Table and its use in the derivation of the categories, we now must discover how closely or remotely our interpretation is related to Kant's own views.

*How has Kant himself understood the
nature of his Table of Judgments?*

On this question Kant is not only vague but also ambivalent. His pronouncements can be construed to assert either that his K Table is a slight expansion of the A Table or that his K Table is a complete transformation of it.

He expresses the former view in his assertion that his K Table lists the forms of judgment that exercise only logical functions. Of course, he does admit that the third forms of Quantity and Quality are his own additions. But he appears to be convinced that these additions do not damage the essential identity between his Table and the traditional one, for he says that his Table "appears to depart in some, though not in any essential respects, from the technical distinctions ordinarily recognized by logicians." (A 70 = B 96) When he assumes this fundamental identity of the two tables, he stresses the logical nature of his Table. In the *Critique,* he presents his Table in the section entitled "The Logical Function of the Understanding in Judgments." (A 70 = B 95) In the *Prolegomena,* he calls his Table "The Logical Table of Judgments." *(Prolegomena* §21)*

*All references to the *Prolegomena* are cited in parentheses in the text, as above. Unless otherwise noted, these textual references are to the English edition, translated by Lewis White Beck, The Library of Liberal Arts (Indianapolis, Bobbs-Merrill, 1950).

These and similar statements on the logical nature of the K Table have misled many to believe that Kant picked up the Table of Judgments from Aristotelian formal logic. Thus they have come to assume that Aristotle's logic, along with Euclid's geometry and Newton's physics, constitutes one of the pillars of transcendental philosophy. Some have even sententiously declared that the fundamental errors of Kant's philosophy stem from his naïve acceptance of Aristotle as much as from his acceptance of Euclid and Newton.

Kant expresses the 'transformation' view when he stresses the difference between the A and the K Tables. This he identifies as the difference between form and content (A 71 ff. = B 96 ff.). The classification of judgments in the K Table is based on the content of judgments, while the A Table's classification rests on the forms of judgments. One is the table of the logical functions of judgments, while the other is the table of their extralogical functions. When Kant is aware of this fundamental difference between the two tables, he calls the K Table not simply a logical table but "a transcendental table of all moments of thought in judgments." (A 73 = B 98)

If the simple expansion theory is correct, the K Table should be the table of the forms of judgment. If the complete transformation theory is correct, the K Table should be the table of the types of judgments.

I am introducing 'the types of judgments' in the light of the type-concepts. By 'type-concepts' I mean the concepts of the categorial types into which all the material concepts can be classified. It is in this sense of 'categories' that Aristotle regards his categories as the concepts of the ultimate genera. It is in the same sense of 'categories' that Kant calls his the concepts of an object in general. By 'the types of judgments' I mean the kinds of judgments that are classified in terms of the type-concepts to which the material terms of the judgments belong. For example, it is to specify a judgment-type to call a judgment a causal one because the judgment in question contains the causal category. If the K Table classifies judgments in terms of their material rather than their formal terms, then the Table must be the table of the types of judgments rather than that of the forms of judgment.

Let us call a formal table one that lists the forms of judgment and a material table one that lists the types of judgments. Depending on whether the K Table is a formal or a material table, it is going to have a radically different value as the clue to the discovery of all pure concepts. If it is really a formal table, the K Table can be of no use at all in the derivation of the categories, because formal concepts can never be a guide in the discovery of material concepts. To derive the categories from the forms of judgment is to derive material terms from formal terms. This is as impossible as the effort to draw water from a dry well. If the K Table is a material table, it can indeed be used for the derivation of the categories. To derive the categories from the types of judgments is to derive material terms from material terms. There is nothing ingenious about this procedure. It is as obvious as digging gold from gold mines.

Assuming that the K Table can function as Kant's clue only if it is a material table, let us determine its effectiveness in certifying the completeness of his categorial system. Kant adopted his Table of Judgments as a clue to the discovery of all and not merely some of the pure concepts of understanding. He knew very well that Aristotle had discovered quite a few categories without any elaborate method. But he wanted to find a method that would assure the discovery of all the categories, and he finally concluded that only a systematic method could fulfill this objective.

How effective is the K Table in ascertaining the completeness of Kant's categorial system?

The K Table must be systematically complete if it is to assure the completeness of the categorial system derived from it. Hence Kant has to find a method to test the completeness of the table itself. Here lurks the irony of the entire affair: The completeness of the K Table as a material table can be assured only by the completeness of the categorial system. We have defined a material table as a table of the types of judgments. The classification of the types of judgments can be made only in reference to the type-concepts. We can list as many types of judgments as we have categories. We can have a system of all the types of judgments only when we have secured a complete system of categories. Thus to use a material table as a method to test the systematic completeness of a categorial system is to put the cart before the horse.

In fact Kant's Table of Categories is far from complete. Its incompleteness is one of the main reasons that induced Hegel to spin out a host of categories in his *Science of Logic.* Kant himself makes a few statements that may reveal his own vague awareness of its incompleteness. Let us look at some of these statements.

Before concluding the Transcendental Analytic, he recognizes the need to give an account of the concept of nothing. (A 290 ff. = B 346 ff.) He maintains that this concept can be defined in terms of his categories, and he offers four different definitions of *nothing* that correspond to the four triads of his categorial system. This is a surprising move because Kant has already given us the impression that his Table of Categories contains the concept of nothing in the form of *negation.* He thus appears to have entertained the concept of nothing in two different ways. On the one hand, he understood 'nothing' in a narrow sense to be equivalent to 'privation' and identified this narrow sense of *nothing* with *negation.* On the other hand, he sensed that the primary concept of nothing is much broader than that of privation or absence. Thus he felt the need to give a few more definitions of nothing. And, indeed, his uneasy feeling about *nothing* is well founded. The category of nothing in its broad and pristine sense is not given a proper place in his categorial system.

Kant also seems to have entertained a similar ambivalent feeling about the concept of being. He understands *being* in a narrow sense to be identical with *presence,* which is listed in his Table of Categories as *reality.* He also feels that the primary concept of being is far richer than the concept of presence, for he equates *being* in its broad sense with the concept of an object in general. (A 290 = B 346)

How is the concept of an object in general related to his Table of Categories? Kant repeatedly calls the categories the concepts of an object in general. By this he means to assert that the categories are twelve ways of articulating the supreme concept of being or the concept of an object in general. If this is a correct view, then the concept of being is a more primitive concept than any of the twelve categories. Thus this most pristine of all pure concepts fails to get a place in his Table of Categories.* By taking note of this glaring mistake, Hegel begins his categorial deduction with the concept of being.

The Amphiboly of Concepts of Reflection is ostensibly meant to be Kant's formal criticism of Leibniz' monadism. But it can be argued that his hidden motive in the Amphiboly is to forestall the Leibnizians' charge that his categorial system is incomplete because it does not contain the Leibnizian categories. These categories are *identity* and *difference, agreement* and *opposition, the inner* and *the outer,* and *matter* and *form.* Hegel holds that Kant composed the Amphiboly in order to add the Leibnizian categories to his categorial system when he realized its incompleteness.[1] Although this is an inaccurate account of Kant's intention, he is right in assuming that one of Kant's main concerns in the Amphiboly is with the completeness of his categorial system.

In the Amphiboly Kant does not want to add the Leibnizian

*Kant appears to treat the concept of an object in general as a primitive concept when he says that time is the pure image of the concept of all sense objects in general. (A 142 = B 181) categories to his categorial system but tries to explain why these categories have been left out. He calls the Leibnizian categories the concepts of reflection and holds that their function is to compare concepts. (A 261 = B 317) If the concepts of reflection can perform only the function of comparison, they cannot be regarded as categories and be admitted into Kant's categorial system. For Kant defines categories as those primitive concepts which perform constitutive functions, the functions of constituting objects. Thus he appears to believe that the completeness of his categorial system cannot be affected by the omission of the Leibnizian categories.

My view that one of Kant's main concerns in the Amphiboly is the completeness of his categorial system is further reinforced by the fact that he also explains in the Amphiboly the relation of the concepts of being and nothing to his categorial system.

Hegel must have felt that Kant's omission of the concepts of reflection from the categories is unjustifiable, for he appropriates these Leibnizian outcasts from Kant's Table into his own opulent categorial system. It would not take much effort to show that Hegel is right in this restoration of the Leibnizian categories.

Let us leave the question of completeness at this point and return to the question of the feasibility of Kant's program in the Metaphysical Deduction. I hope to have made it clear that the K Table can be of no use in performing the task of the Metaphysical Deduction, whether it be a formal or a material table. If the K Table is a formal table, the Deduction becomes an impossible task. If the Table is a material table, the Deduction becomes a ludicrous affair. Thus the Metaphysical Deduction turns out to be an ill-conceived program. It now remains for us to reflect on the reasons that prompted Kant to undertake it at all.

Kemp Smith reports that the discovery of the categorial system was one of the most tortuous stages in the development of the *Critique of Pure Reason*. Let me briefly summarize his fine report.[2] As early as 1772, that is, nine years before the publication of the first edition of the *Critique,* Kant wrote Marcus Herz that he was seeking a method to establish a system of categories and that he was dissatisfied with Aristotle's unsystematic method. In the same letter Kant informed Herz that he would be in a position to publish the *Critique of Pure Reason* "within some three months." These "some three months" turned out to be nine years. Kemp Smith suggests that the difficulty in securing the categorial system was one of the main causes of delay in publication. In the same 1772 letter to Herz, Kant also expressed his conviction that only a systematically complete method could produce a complete system of categories.

Kemp Smith believes that Kant kept looking for the right method and kept reshuffling his table of categories for nine years. Kant's thought assumed many shapes in those nine years, but in general it took the form of two triads. The first triad was the triad of the method: The categories were acquired by reflection upon the three activities of the understanding in *comparing, combining,* or *separating.* The second triad was the triad of the. result: The categories were classified into three groups, *thesis, analysis,* and *synthesis.* We can easily notice a close relation between the triad of method and the triad of the result. It is not difficult to correlate the activity of *comparing* with the categories of *thesis,* the activity of *separating* with the categories of *analysis,* and the activity of *combining* with the categories of *synthesis.*

The proposed correlation is not Kemp Smith's but my own; he reports no evidence to show such a correlation to have been Kant's objective. My only object in proposing the correlation is to suggest that Kant must have been trying to establish an organic relation between the systematic method and the systematic result of discovering all the categories and that he was coming close to a definite resolution of the problem in the correlation of the two triads. In the final draft of the *Critique,* however, he drops the two triads and adopts the two tetrads, the Table of Judgments and the Table of Categories.

Why did Kant decide to adopt the Table of Judgments as the clue in place of the three kinds of judgment-activity?

Kemp Smith suggests that Kant's decision rested on his recognition that the ultimate form of thinking is judgment and that the categories are inseparably connected with the act of judgment.[3] This view nevertheless fails to resolve the question to our satisfaction. While it is true that Kant regarded judgment as the ultimate unit of cognition, it is also true that the three kinds of activity are none other than three aspects of the activity of judgment. Why then did Kant abandon the judgment-activities as the clue in favor of the judgment-forms?

An obvious answer to this question is that the judgment-activities had not yielded desirable results in the systematic derivation of the categories, although he had tried out the clue in almost every possible way. Here is one fairly representative example of his many steadfast trials, as reported by Kemp Smith:[4]

Thesis	=	The metaphysical concepts are, first, absolute possibility and existence; secondly, relative:
		(a) Unity and plurality: *omnitudo* and *particularitas.*
Analysis	=	(b) Limits: the first, the last: *infinitum, finitum.*
Synthesis	=	(c) Connection: coordination: whole and part, simple and compound; subordination:
		(1) Subject and predicate.
		(2) Ground and Consequence.

This rather haphazard table is far from Kant's dream of achieving a systematic tabulation of all categories. When Kant could not get any more satisfactory result than this after nine years of toil, he probably could not help losing faith in the efficacy of the judgment-activities as a clue. Thus he appears to have decided to abandon this clue and to seek a better one.

Why did Kant expect to find a more effective clue in the forms of judgment? To answer this question, we have to determine what essential difference he saw between the three kinds of judgment-activity and the twelve forms of judgment. We have some grounds to suspect that he thought their difference reflected the difference between formal and material reason: The forms of judgment pertain to the formal use of intellect while the judgment-activities pertain to its material use.

I will try to substantiate this suspicion. For this, we have to try to go back to a great controversy, which took place during Kant's formative days. This was the controversy among the Wolffians over the reducibility of the principle of identity or contradiction to the principle of sufficient reason.* The Wolffians inherited these two principles from Leibniz, who had held that the principle of identity governs the realm of essences and that the principle of sufficient reason governs the realm of existences. Hence any question about the relation between these two principles is a question about the relation between the realm of essences and the realm of existences.

The ultimate aim of the Wolffians' attempt to reduce the principle of sufficient reason to the principle of contradiction was to complete the Cartesian program of deducing the domain of the real from the domain of the mental or ideal. The Wolffians regarded the realm of essences as coextensive with the

*The principle of identity and the principle of contradiction were not distinguished as two separate principles but regarded as alternative expressions of one principle by Leibniz, Leibnizians, Wolffians, and Kant.

domain of the mental or ideal because the realm of essences could be exhaustively determined by the principle of contradiction alone or by pure conceptual operations. If the principle of sufficient reason could be reduced to the principle of contradiction, they believed, the mind could with certainty secure the knowledge of the actual world through its conceptual power alone. Thus the reduction of the principle of sufficient reason to the principle of contradiction would bring to perfection the Cartesian program. The subjective mind could attain the objective truth through its thoughts alone.

De Vleeschauwer says that the controversy became heated around the year 1750 and that many empiricists in England and France objected to the Wolffians' rationalistic program.[5] He also says that the most articulate German critic of the Wolffians was Crusius. Crusius distinguished between logical reason and real reason in the course of his disputations with the Wolffians. By 'logical reason' was meant the reason that operates with the logical principle of contradiction; by 'real reason' was meant the reason that operates with the real principle of sufficient reason. The former is concerned with the realm of essences and the latter with the realm of existences. Crusius adamantly maintained that real reason can never be reduced to logical reason. His position was exactly the same as Hume's: Contingency in matters of fact can never be reduced to the certitude of relations of ideas.

De Vleeschauwer reports that Kant became interested in this controversy and that he accepted Crusius' position.[6] His acceptance was announced as early as 1755 in *Dilucidatio*, which was published sixteen years before the *Critique*. In the *Inaugural Dissertation* of 1770 he reaffirms the distinction between logical and real reason.

This distinction remains the crucial line of thought along which the transcendental philosophy develops. In the *Critique*, Kant stresses the difference between the two functions of understanding and reason. Understanding has a logical use as well as a real use. (A 70 = B 95; A 79 = B 105) Reason performs a logical function as well as a real function. (A 299 = B 355) By the 'logical use' or 'logical function' of understanding and reason, Kant means the operations of these intellectual faculties in and by themselves, that is, in their self-contained realm. By the 'real use' or 'real function' of these faculties, he means their operations in the realm of real objects or existences.

In place of 'logical' and 'real,' Kant often uses 'formal' and 'material.' He appears to maintain the equivalence of these two sets of terms on the ground that the real functions of understanding and reason are concerned with the content or material of knowledge while their logical functions are confined to its forms. It is his fundamental principle that their formal functions can produce only analytic unity in cognition while their material functions can secure its synthetic unity. (A 79 = B 105) The analytic unity is the unity of an analytical proposition; the synthetic unity is the unity of a synthetic proposition. The truth of the former can be secured by the principle of contradiction alone, while the truth of the latter cannot; for the analytic unity is the unity of the self-contained thoughts, which need only to maintain self-consistency, but the synthetic unity is the unity of those thoughts which refer to objects whose existence is not guaranteed by the self-consistency of thought.

If we now look at the three kinds of judgment-activity that Kant had long tried out as a clue, we can see that they are in fact the material (real) use of reason. Comparison, separation, and combination involve the content of judgments; they cannot exclusively belong to the formal (logical) use of reason. To rely on the material use of reason as a clue is precisely Locke's "plain historical method." When the material use of reason gave Kant only unsystematic results, he probably located the source of trouble not in reason but in senses, which provide the contents of judgments. As a rationalist, Kant never lost his faith in the integrity and unity of reason. It is with the affirmation of this faith that he opens the Transcendental Analytic:

Pure understanding distinguishes itself from all that is empirical but completely also from all sensibility. It is a unity self-subsistent, self-sufficient, and not to be increased by any additions from without. The sum of its knowledge thus constitutes a system, comprehended and determined by one idea. (A 65 = B 89 f.)

Along with this faith in the systematic unity of reason, Kant also believed that reason could have a complete knowledge of itself.* He says, "For it is the very essence of reason that we should be able to give an account of all our concepts, opinions, and assertions." (A 614= B 642) If it is the very essence of reason to give a complete account of all its possessions, reason must be able to get hold of a complete knowledge of its a priori possessions—its pure concepts. Gottfried Martin says that this faith in the possibility of reason's complete self-knowledge is the unjustifiable optimism of the Enlightenment.[7] Martin is not quite correct in attributing this rational faith directly to the Enlightenment; it is rather a legacy of the Baroque age. Descartes, Leibniz, and their fellow rationalists assumed that reason can have a complete knowledge of its innate possessions. For them, innate ideas are precisely the kind of ideas whose possession can be an object of indubitable knowledge. In Kant, this rationalists' faith became the conviction that pure reason must be able to have a self-knowledge of its a priori possessions.

By combining his faith in the systematic unity of pure reason and his faith in the possibility of a complete knowledge of its a priori possessions, Kant must have concluded that pure reason must be able to produce an indubitable, systematic knowledge of its pure concepts. With this unshakable trust in the self-knowledge of reason, Kant is likely to have attributed

---

*Kant uses 'reason' in two different senses. In its narrow sense, 'reason' is distinguished from 'understanding.' In its broad sense, 'reason' includes 'understanding' and is synonymous with 'intellect.' I am here using 'reason' in this broad sense.

the failure of the material use of reason as a clue to its con-
tamination by the sensuous content. This suspicion appears to
be contained in the following observation with which Kant
opens the search for the clue in the *Critique:*

> When we call a faculty of knowledge into play, then, as
> the occasioning circumstances differ, various concepts
> stand forth and make the faculty known, and allow of
> their being collected with more or less completeness, in
> proportion as observation has been made of them over a
> longer time or with greater acuteness. But when the en-
> quiry is carried on in this mechanical fashion, we can
> never be sure whether it has been brought to completion.
> Further, the concepts which we thus discover only as
> opportunity offers, exhibit no order and systematic unity,
> but are in the end merely arranged in pairs according to
> similarities, and in series according to the amount of their
> contents, from the simple to the more composite—an ar-
> rangement which is anything but systematic, although to
> a certain extent methodically instituted. (A 66 f. =
> B 91 f.)

This whole passage appears to be Kant's recollection of his
frustrating search for the categorial system with the material
use of reason as a clue. To "call a faculty of knowledge into
play" is to make a material use of that faculty. In this search,
we have seen, Kant assembled a group of concepts that "exhibit
no order and systematic unity, but are in the end merely ar-
ranged in pairs according to similarities." He seems to have
concluded that the material use of reason is not a systematic
clue because it is connected with the sensuous occasions. Since
the sensuous is always contingent, he appears to have assumed,
the material use of reason is bound to be a helpless prey to the
contingency of the "occasioning circumstances." It is at this
point that the formal use of reason might have presented itself
to him as the only alternative and as the only scientific clue.

The formal use of reason does not involve the sensuous content; it involves nothing but reason itself. In its formal (logical) use, understanding is in no danger of being subject to occasioning circumstances and fortuitous opportunities. Thus Kant appears to have decided to adopt the formal use of understanding as his clue. The first section of The Clue to the Discovery of All Pure Concepts of the Understanding, is entitled The Logical Employment of the Understanding.

While to use the material use of reason in the discovery of pure concepts is to gain the knowledge of pure reason in reliance on the extrarational elements, to use the formal use of reason as the sole clue for the discovery of pure concepts is to gain the knowledge of pure reason in and of itself. Hence Kant's faith in pure reason's self-sufficiency and self-knowledge can be substantiated only by the success of the formal use of reason as the clue in the discovery of the categorial system.

At this point formal logic must have attracted Kant's attention. He believed that formal logic was an edifice constructed by pure reason alone. Since formal logic is constructed in a complete abstraction from the content of knowledge, he appears to have thought, it can have nothing to do with the material use of reason. Because formal logic is concerned only with the forms of reason, he seems to have concluded, it attained perfection as a science almost at the time of its birth. Thus formal logic as the culmination of reason in its formal function appears to have engaged Kant's attention as the long-sought clue. Even after settling upon formal logic as his final clue, he had yet to determine which part of formal logic he was to use and how he was to apply it.

There are three principal divisions in Aristotle's logical doctrines: the doctrine of terms, the doctrine of propositions, and the doctrine of syllogisms. The last two divisions have constituted what has been known as Aristotelian, or traditional, logic. The first of the three divisions contains nothing that can be called truths of logic, which Leibnizians and Kant assumed to be ascertainable by the principle of identity or contradiction alone.* It is in Aristotle's doctrines of propositions and syllogisms that the principle of contradiction or identity seems to play the central role in producing analytical or formal truths. For example, the mutual relations of A, E, I, and O in the Aristotelian square of conversion appear to be instances of the analytical relation. The syllogistic inferences are one and all supposed to be expressions of analytical relations. Thus the province of formal logic in the Aristotelian sense has been confined to the domain of these analytical relations and Kant had to seek his clue in this domain.

Why then did Kant single out the forms of judgment for the derivation of the pure concepts of understanding, and the forms of syllogism for the derivation of the pure concepts of reason? This was probably due to his peculiar conception of formal logic. We have observed that he conceived logic as the only pure formal discipline, that is, the only science of formal reason. He did not regard even arithmetic as a purely formal science because he believed it had some content as well as some formal components. When he conceived formal logic as a purely formal science, he apparently believed that formal logic is the science which investigates all the *forms* of thinking. He often calls these forms the logical forms. He distinguished between two kinds of logical forms: the forms of judgment and the forms of inference. He decided to use the former in the derivation of the pure concepts of understanding and the latter in the derivation of the pure concepts of reason.

We have so far explained how frustration with the material use of reason drove Kant to consider the formal use of reason as the clue, and why he considered the forms of judgment as

*Kant did not distinguish the principle of identity from the principle of contradiction but regarded them as alternative expressions of one logical principle. Throughout this chapter I treat these two principles as Kant did.

the crystallization of formal reason. We now come to the most intriguing question of the entire Metaphysical Deduction:

Why did Kant think that the forms of judgment might be the clue to the derivation of the categories?

The adoption of the judgment-forms as the clue cannot be justified simply by the failure of material reason to provide the clue. It can be justified only by establishing a definite connection between the forms of judgment and the pure concepts of understanding. Kant apparently believed that he saw a one-to-one matching relation between the two. He was driven to this belief by his peculiar view of the pure concepts of understanding. He held onto the view that the pure concepts serve two different functions in two different contexts: the formal functions in abstraction from objects, and the material functions in confrontation with objects. (A 79 = B 104 f.) He believes that the forms of judgment are the expressions of the formal functions of the pure concepts of understanding and that the categories as the concepts of an object in general are the expressions of their material functions. He expresses this double-function theory by his favorite double characterization of the categories: He sometimes calls them the logical functions of judgment and sometimes the concepts of an object in general.

If the judgment-forms and the categories were to be only functionally different expressions of the same pure concepts of understanding, there would be a one-to-one matching relation between the judgment-forms and the categories. This mapping relation could justify the use of the former as the clue in the derivation of the latter. This is the line of reasoning that must have governed Kant's Metaphysical Deduction. We have repeatedly noted that there is a generic difference between formal and material concepts. Kant mistook their generic difference for a mere functional one. The entire Metaphysical Deduction hinges on this mistake.

Why did Kant hold the implausible view that one set of concepts can discharge both formal and material functions? In order to answer this question, let me propose a somewhat radical hypothesis: Kant believed that all concepts, formal as well as material, were class-concepts. Since the idea of class-concepts was his only idea of concepts, he tried to assimilate formal concepts to class-concepts by viewing the former as a set of special functions of the latter. He never had the idea of formal concepts; he had only the idea of the formal functions of class-concepts. Let me try to present some extenuating circumstances for this erroneous conception of formal concepts.

Kant was bred in the ontological tradition that had taken the class-concept as the prototype of all concepts. The "forms" of Plato and Aristotle were generally conceived as the essences of classes, most of them being the essences of the monadic classes. It was this tradition of the monadic generic concept that made it difficult for the Scholastic philosophers to render an adequate ontological account of relations. Since our logical tools are a little more developed, we can easily dispose of this medieval problem by subsuming various relations under the class-concepts of the ordered couples, the ordered triples, the ordered quadruples, etc. But we know that we cannot find a proper way to regard logical concepts as generic ones. It is simply senseless, for instance, to postulate the classes of assertion, negation, conjunction, disjunction, etc. But Kant appears to have simply assumed these concepts to be generic concepts, due to his habit of thought, which had been hammered out on the anvil of class-ontology.

The only logic Kant knew was the logic of classes. We can find no evidence that he knew anything of propositional logic. He seems to have interpreted even the logical signs of propositional logic, such as those of disjunction and implication, within the context of class-logic. For example, he says that the function of logical disjunction is to divide a large class into smaller ones. (A 74 = B 99) In the *Inaugural Dissertation* he defines the logical use of intellect as the function of establishing class-relations. *(Dissertation* §5)* This reflects his view that the ultimate function of class-logic is to establish class-relations.

He expresses this view of logical function again in the Appendix to the Transcendental Dialectic. There he calls the principle of identity or homogeneity the logical principle of genera and the principle of diversity or specification the logical principle of species. (A 654 = B 682). He maintains that the function of the principle of identity is to bring the different species under one genus; that the function of the principle of diversity is to divide one genus into different species. He further holds that the logical principle of continuity mediates the functions of the other two principles. Thus he means to hold that the ultimate function of the logic of classes is to form classes and establish their mutual relations. This conception of logic is likely to have reinforced Kant's belief that all concepts are really class-concepts.

Thus, in Kant's view, there can be no drastic difference between formal (logical) and material (real) concepts. They are both class-concepts and their only difference lies in the degrees of generality. Formal concepts indeed occupy a unique position in the realm of concepts, but their uniqueness lies only in the fact that they stand at the apex of generic concepts. Because formal concepts are the most general abstract concepts and because the most abstract concepts are empty of all content, Kant seems to have thought, they have the special qualifications necessary to perform formal (logical) functions.

Since Kant conceives all concepts to be class-concepts, he characterizes the function of a concept as unification: "By 'function' [of concepts] I mean the unity of the act of bringing various representations under one common representation."

*All references to the *Inaugural Dissertation* are cited in parentheses in the text, as above. Unless otherwise noted, these textual references are to the English translation by John Handyside (Chicago, Open Court Publishing Co., 1929).

(A 68 = B 93) He believes that this function can be performed in two ways, formally and materially. When this function is material, he believes, it brings the manifold of sense under one concept. This is what is known as the function of synthesis or the function of synthetic unity. When the function is formal, he believes, it becomes a form of judgment. For example, the logical or formal function of the concept of reality is to provide the form of an affirmative judgment, which is the formal function of bringing one concept under another concept.

Kant appears to have been misled into accepting the belief that all logical concepts are class-concepts because he thought that all the logical functions can be performed by class-concepts. He apparently thought that the function of bringing one concept under another concept requires only two class-concepts. He did not realize that this logical operation requires the logical concept of 'bringing under' (subsumption) in addition to the two class-concepts and that this third concept cannot be a class-concept.

In any case, Kant clearly held that all logical concepts are class-concepts, and this led him to identify the logical concepts with the categories. Kant elaborated this identity in terms of functions: Logical concepts are nothing but the expressions of the formal functions of the pure concepts of understanding. Since he believed that these same pure concepts can also perform material functions, he came to conclude that the categories are the unique set of class-concepts, which has the following Janus-like nature:

> The same function which gives unity to the various representations *in a judgment* also gives unity to the mere synthesis of various representations *in an intuition;* and this unity, in its most general expression, I entitle the pure concept of understanding. The same understanding, through the same operations by which in concepts, by means of analytical unity, it produced the logical form of a judgment, also introduces a transcendental content

into its representations, by means of the synthetic unity of the manifold in intuition in general. (A 79 = B 104 f.)

If the forms of judgments and the categories are not really two sets of concepts but two sets of functions of the same pure concepts, Kant must have reasoned, then the forms of judgment should stand in a one-to-one matching relation with the pure concepts of understanding. Similarly, he must have concluded that this functional matching relation establishes the value of his clue. Thus Kant came to believe that the forms of judgment would be the only systematic clue to the discovery of the entire categorial system.

It would be helpful at this point to place Kant's Metaphysical Deduction in its historical context. To do this we must return to Descartes' deductive program. Let us note that his program can be carried out if our ideas form a deductive system. In fact, the Cartesian method and program rest on the implicit belief that at least our innate ideas do form such a systematic whole. Kant inherits this Cartesian faith. Descartes' faith in the systematic unity of innate ideas becomes Kant's faith in the systematic unity of pure reason. In the Preface to the first edition of the *Critique,* Kant proclaims, "In this enquiry I have made completeness my chief aim." (A xiii) He goes on to say that he could attain this aim of completeness because pure reason forms a perfect unity. In the Preface to the second edition he shows that all the criticisms of the first edition have not shaken his faith in the systematic unity of pure reason and his program:

> Now, *as regards this second edition,* I have, as is fitting, endeavored to profit by the opportunity, in order to remove, wherever possible, difficulties and obscurity which, not perhaps without my fault, may have given rise to the many misunderstandings into which even acute thinkers have fallen in passing judgments upon my book. In the propositions themselves and their proofs, and also in the

form and completeness of the [architectonic] plan, I have found nothing to alter. This is due partly to the long examination to which I have subjected them, before offering them to the public, partly to the nature of the subject-matter with which we are dealing. For pure speculative reason has a structure wherein everything is an *organ,* the whole being for the sake of every part, and every part for the sake of all the others, so that even the smallest imperfection, be it a fault (error) or a deficiency, must inevitably betray itself in use. (B xxxvii f.)

Descartes' deductive program however took a drastic turn in Kant's hands. The objects of the Cartesian deduction had been described in two interchangeable ways: *de re,* the external objects, or *de dicto,* the propositions about these external objects. Descartes wished to find the ways to deduce *(de re)* the external objects from the most perfect being, or *(de dicto)* the ideas (propositions) of the former from the idea of the latter. He admitted his failure in bringing about this deduction, but many of his followers tried to fulfill his dream. Kant was even more ambitious than Descartes and his followers; he wanted to extend the systematic unity from the domain of propositions to that of concepts. He was not of course the first one to think of this extension. Leibniz had certainly entertained this idea of establishing a systematic unity in the domain of primitive concepts as the first step in founding his *characteristica universalis.* But Kant was surely the first to have the audacity actually to undertake this extension. He thus became the father of the categorial deduction.

It is well known that Kant's dream of the categorial deduction has been one of the overriding concerns in Western philosophy during the past two centuries. Hegel wrote one of the longest and most intricate works in the history of philosophy in an effort to realize Kant's dream. Peirce, too, spent many of his formative years in such an effort. Even those who appointed themselves archenemies of the deductive program could not completely divorce themselves from its spell. Kierkegaard tried to secure a systematic unity of his existential categories, and Marx sought to establish a systematic unity of his dialectical categories.

Kant's dream came from sound reasons. Concepts are more fundamental units of cognition than propositions; the systematic unity of concepts is therefore indispensable to securing the systematic unity of propositions. This point has been fully acknowledged by those who have appreciated the analysis of formal systems.

Before the hidden wisdom of Kant's dream came to be fully understood, nevertheless, it had to go through a stage of sinister nightmares. This is the stage where it was believed that the systematic unity of a conceptual system could be established by the deduction of all concepts by the logical principle of identity or contradiction alone. Thus Hegel made the outrageous claim of having deduced everything by the magic force of the principle of contradiction alone. The seeds of this nightmare were sown by Kant himself.

We have seen that the possibility of deriving all the categories by the formal use of reason alone was entailed in Kant's assumption that pure reason must be able to gain an indubitable, systematic knowledge of its a priori possessions. If this assumption is correct, there should be no need to seek a clue to the systematic discovery of all pure concepts. If the pure concepts form a self-subsistent system, pure reason must be able to produce a systematic knowledge of them without relying on any clues. This is precisely the essence of Hegel's program in his *Science of Logic*. In his dialectical deduction of the categories, Hegel tries not only to present a complete categorial system but also to account for its systematic unity. He attempts to realize both of these goals by employing only the logical principle of identity or contradiction which governs, in Kant's view, the formal use of reason. In these terms of premises and expectations, Hegel's *Science of Logic* is a far more faithful attempt to realize Kant's dream of vindicating pure reason's self-knowledge than Kant's own Metaphysical Deduction. Since Hegel attempted to be more faithful to Kant's implausible dream than Kant himself, he was driven to undertake far more tortuous logical maneuvers than Kant's own.

With the development of the logical calculus, however, we know more now than Kant or Hegel ever knew about what the principle of identity or contradiction can and cannot do. We know that it is impossible to deduce what is not contained in the premise by means of this logical principle. If one begins with the concept of being, one has the certitude of deducing the concept of being and any other concepts contained in it. The concepts of nothing and becoming can be deduced from the concept of being only if the former are contained in the latter. So the whole question depends not only on the principle of contradiction but also on what kind of concept of being is presupposed.

Hegel makes the incredible claim that the concepts of nothing and becoming can be deduced from the concept of pure being, which does not contain the other concepts. He attempts to give this claim plausibility by his figurative assertion that the concept of pure being "moves over" to the concept of pure nothing and that the concept of becoming is the movement "back and forth" between the concept of being and the concept of nothing.[8] These metaphorical descriptions can be accepted, however, only by obliterating the distinction between the agents of thought and the instruments of thought.* But the concepts are not the agents of thought; they are its instruments; they can neither "move" nor "stand still." It is only the agent of thought that has motive force. If there is any

---

*Hegel uses 'thought' to mean both 'the agent of thought' and 'the instrument of thought.' He delights in taking advantage of the ambiguity of this dual usage.

motion from one concept to another, the motion must belong not to concepts but to the agent of concepts. We sometimes encounter expressions (e.g. "the development of a conceptual system") that imply the motion of concepts. But this sort of expression is just as elliptical as 'the growth of a factory.' A conceptual system cannot be an agent of growth any more than a factory can.

The agent of thought in its movement need not be shackled by the logical principle of contradiction. Kant is correct in holding that conceptual activities can be synthetic as well as analytic. Although he recognized this freedom of thought in the domain of judgments, he failed to do so in the domain of concepts because of the mistaken belief that concepts are only *discovered* whereas judgments are *made*. He saw the possibility of freedom in the activities of making but not in the activities of discovering. Hegel not only recognizes but emphasizes the synthetic function of thought while disparaging its analytical function. He proudly admits that his *Science of Logic* is meant to be a scientific account of the synthetic (dialectical synthesis) function of thought. But he erroneously believes that thought needs to employ the single logical principle of contradiction in performing its synthetic functions. This self-contradictory idea governs the entire program of his dialectical idealism.

The systematic unity of a conceptual system should be understood in quite a different way from the way it was understood by Kant and Hegel. It is not the logical unity which is bound together by the principle of contradiction. The unity of any conceptual system is like the unity of a game. Wittgenstein's theory of language-games applies readily to this point. Although all the chess pieces and the rules for their moves form a system, it is impossible to deduce one piece from another. By the deduction of one piece from another, I mean to infer what kind of moves one piece can and cannot make from the knowledge of the moves the other piece can and cannot make. The unity of the game of chess is synthetic; so, too, is a conceptual unity.

"To know a chess piece" is far from univocal. We have said that to know one chess piece is to know the moves it can and cannot make, but we can also say that to know one chess piece is to know all the other pieces. It is impossible to understand fully the role of the king without understanding the roles of the queen, the bishops, the castles, and all other pieces. 'The knowledge of a chess piece' in this strong sense is equivalent to 'the knowledge of the entire game.' If 'the knowledge of a chess piece' is taken in this strong sense, it is possible to deduce from one chess piece any other piece. There is nothing miraculous about this deduction, because it is the deduction of the constituents of a game from the entire game or the deduction of the parts from the whole.

Hegel, to be sure, sometimes takes his deduction to be this sort of innocuous affair. For example, he sometimes implies that his concept of being implicitly contains all other concepts. This is an acceptable assertion because no entity can escape the absolutely universal category of being. But this rich concept of being should not be called the concept of *pure being*. It is possible to deduce anything, even Herr Krug's quill pen, from this rich concept of being. Surely this sort of deduction can and must make use of the logical principles of identity or contradiction, which are indispensable for making tautologous assertions, but it cannot make room for dialectical conflicts and resolutions.

My intention is not to expose Hegel's logical errors, but to elucidate their nature as the best means to achieve an understanding of the nature of Kant's errors. Because Hegel's *Science of Logic* is a far more substantial attempt to realize Kant's dream of the pure reason's systematic self-discovery, Hegel's errors fully illuminate the implausibility of Kant's deductive program, which can be sensed only vaguely in Kant's own execution. The implausibility in both cases is the impossibility of discovering the synthetic functions of thought through its analytical functions alone. Kant has tried to deduce all the ultimate material concepts of synthetic reason from the logical forms of analytical reason; Hegel has tried to deduce all the material concepts of dialectical synthesis from the logical operation of contradiction. These implausible programs came to be conceived through Kant's mistaken idea that the unity of a conceptual scheme must be a deductive one.

Chapter 3

Pure Concepts and Their Schemata

The Metaphysical Deduction and the Schematism are the two brief sections of the *Critique* that perhaps harbor more opacities than any of the other sections. In the two preceding chapters, we have tried to unravel Kant's intentions and performances as they are vaguely sketched in the Metaphysical Deduction. We will devote the following two chapters to probing the enigmas of the Schematism.

Kant says that the problem of the transcendental schematism arises from the heterogeneity of the pure concepts of understanding and the percepts of intuitions. (A 137 = B 176) The heterogeneity of the pure concepts precludes the possibility of their direct application to the manifold of the senses. Transcendental schemata are designed to overcome this obstacle and mediate between the pure concepts and the sense objects. (A 138 = B 177)

Kant's doctrine of transcendental schematism has been an even more controversial topic than his doctrine of the categorial deduction, because some of his readers are not even convinced of the existence of the problem that is to be resolved by the doctrine of the transcendental schematism. Thus it has generated controversial issues on the very nature of Kant's problem as well as on his resolution of it.

We shall postpone discussion of these controversial issues until the following chapter because we cannot properly handle them without a substantial knowledge of transcendental schemata. In this chapter we will acquaint ourselves with the nature of transcendental schemata and their generation.

How does Kant conceive the nature of transcendental schema?

As a preliminary to understanding Kant's conception of transcendental schema, we must first clarify his conception of schema itself. 'Schema' was one of the new technical terms that had been introduced into transcendental logic, and Kant's explanation of it is difficult to grasp. As Paton points out, Kant makes the threefold distinction of concept, schema, and image.[1] The image is a particular, and the concept is a universal, while the schema is a "third thing," mediating between the particular and the universal. If the schema does stand between these two, we may want to inquire whether it is a universal or a particular. It is in this inquiry that we encounter conflicting answers from Kant's somewhat obscure account of the schema. Some of his remarks on its nature can be construed to mean that the schema is a universal, while others must be taken to mean that it is a particular.

We will first examine the reasons for viewing the schema as a universal. Kant says:

> No image could ever be adequate to the concept of a triangle in general. It would never attain that universality of the concept which renders it valid of all triangles, whether right-angled, obtuse-angled, or acute-angled; it would always be limited to a part only of this sphere. The schema of the triangle can exist nowhere but in thought. It is a rule of synthesis of the imagination, in respect of pure figures in space. (A 141 = B 180)

Kant is here contrasting schema with the image. While the image is a particular, the schema is a universal; the first exists in the senses, while the second exists in thought. When he calls the schema a rule of synthesis, he seems to give it all the requisite properties of a concept: A rule of synthesis is Kant's functional definition of a concept. (A 106) There can be no functional difference between the concept of a triangle and the rule for constructing a triangle. Thus Paton has ample reason to justify his identification of the schema with the concept.[2]

There may be an objection to a complete identification of a concept with its schema defined as a rule of synthesis. It may be said that the use of a concept cannot be limited to its function of synthesis. A concept can certainly have other functions; for example, it can be used for the function of recognition. But this reservation is insignificant in Kant's case because he holds synthesis to be the central function of a concept on which all its other functions hinge. For example, even the function of recognition is only the culmination of the synthetic function in Kant's doctrine of synthesis. (A 103 ff.)

The identification of a concept with its schema would then be impossible for any concept that cannot function as a rule of synthesis. If pure concepts are really heterogeneous from sensible intuitions, they cannot serve as rules of synthesis. So we have to distinguish concepts from their schemata only in the case of pure concepts. Except for this special case, a schema must be always identical with its concept because it is a universal and a rule of synthesis.

If a schema is indistinguishable from a concept, a schema cannot be a "third thing" to mediate between a concept and an image. The identification of a schema with its concept in fact does away with the need for the mediation which the schema is meant to fulfill. Since this is an awkward consequence, students of Kant usually seize upon another conception of the schema.[3] They commonly view the schema as a monogram or a schematic image, that is, an image which is used to *represent* a concept. Since the image is a particular, the schema can also be defined as a particular that represents a universal. This definition of the schema sounds almost like Berkeley's definition of an abstract idea.

Thus we reach two conflicting conceptions of the schema. In one view, the schema is a universal or a rule for the construction of particulars. In the other view, the schema is a particular representing a universal. It has become a customary practice in Kant scholarship to treat these two views of the schema as two features of one thing. Since the schema has a dual nature, students of Kant have held, it can be at once regarded as a universal and as a particular. This interpretation of schema sounds especially plausible because the dual nature of the schema appears to be well suited to its anticipated function of mediation between intellect and intuition. Thus the schema has come to be understood to be an image (or a particular) which represents a concept (or a universal) that functions as a rule of synthesis.

This venerable interpretation, however, is not acceptable. According to it, a schema is a mere symbol or monogram used to represent a rule of synthesis. But this symbolic function is not what Kant assigns to the schema; he speaks rather of the function of synthesis itself. Thus the traditional interpretation misrepresents the function of a schema.

How then should we understand Kant's conflicting definitions of the schema? Let us suppose that he has entertained two definitions of the schema rather than one. I shall try to show that this hypothesis produces a far more cohesive interpretation of Kant's doctrine of schematism than the traditional one.

On the hypothesis that Kant has offered two definitions of the schema, let us adopt two different names to designate them: 'image-schema' and 'concept-schema.' The 'image-schema' means the schema that is an image or particular, representing a concept or universal; the 'concept-schema' means the schema that is a concept or universal, functioning as a rule of synthesis. The former has about the same sense as Heidegger's "schema-image."[4] A particular triangle representing all triangles or the concept of triangularity is the image-schema of triangle; the rule for constructing all particular triangles is the concept-schema of triangle.

These two notions of the schema reappear in Kant's two

notions of the transcendental schema. He defines the transcendental schema both as a pure image or particular representing a pure concept and as a universal or a rule of synthesis embodying a pure concept. The first definition appears to be contained in the following observation:

> Obviously there must be some third thing, which is homogeneous on the one hand with the category, and on the other hand with the appearance, and which thus makes the application of the former to the latter possible. This mediating representation must be pure, that is, void of all empirical content, and yet at the same time, while it must in one respect be *intellectual,* it must in another be sensible. Such a representation is the *transcendental schema.* (A 138 = B 177)

The transcendental schema has to be sensible and yet devoid of all empirical content. Neither concepts nor sensations can meet this dual requirement; only the pure intuitions of space and time can. But even these may fall short of fulfilling all the specifications because they cannot be rightly regarded as *intellectual.* But this apparent shortcoming can be overlooked because Kant's use of 'intellectual' in its broad sense is synonymous with 'of a priori origin' or simply 'a priori.' It is in this broad sense of reason (intellect) that the *Critique of Pure Reason* covers the domain of pure intuitions as well as the domain of understanding and reason.

If we assume pure intuitions to be both sensible and intellectual, we could define the transcendental schema as a pure image or intuition which mediates the application of pure concepts to empirical intuitions. Since the pure image or intuition is a particular, this definition of transcendental schema is in line with the definition of the schema as a particular representing a universal.

PART I   TRANSCENDENTAL CONCEPTS

The definition of transcendental schema as a universal or a rule appears in the following statement:

> Now a transcendental determination of time is so far homogeneous with the category, which constitutes its unity, in that it is universal and rests upon an *a priori* rule. But, on the other hand, it is so far homogeneous with appearance, in that time is contained in every empirical representation of the manifold. Thus an application of the category to appearances becomes possible by means of the transcendental determination of time, which, as the schema of the concepts of understanding, mediates the subsumption of appearance under the category. (139 f. = B 177 f.)

The transcendental schema is here called the transcendental determination of time. 'Transcendental determination of time' is an unusual expression, but Kant does not define it. All he says is that it is like the category "in that it is universal and rests on an *a priori* rule." Defined as the transcendental determination of time, the transcendental schema is clearly not a particular but a universal.

At this point we should determine precisely what is meant by 'the transcendental determination of time.' Let us begin first with 'the determination of time *(die Zeitbestimmung).*' Kant appears to be using 'determination' in a traditional sense to show the relation of universal to particular. He says that the concepts of matter and form have traditionally represented the determinable *(das Bestimmbare)* and its determination *(dessen Bestimmung).* (A 266 = B 322) If judgment is viewed as an act of determining particulars (objects) by universals (concepts), particulars can be regarded as the determinable and universals as their determination. In this classical context of usage, 'time-determination' means the universal (or concept) that determines time or specifies the nature of time.

'Determination' is not the appropriate English correlative of 'determinable'; the appropriate correlative should be 'determinant.' *'Bestimmung'* itself is an ambiguous word, for it can mean the agent, the act, or the instrument of determination. 'Time-determinant' is a more accurate translation of *'die Zeitbestimmung'* than 'time-determination' because Kant's expression is used to mean the instrument of determination rather than the act of determination.

Even with this clarification, however, 'time-determinant (time-determination)' still has the ambiguity inherent in the notion of time. Kant uses 'time' in two senses: On the one hand, it is the pure intuition of time, the empty time which is the form of all intuitions; on the other hand, it is the inner sense which contains all human intuitions. Because of these two senses of 'time,' 'time-determinant' can mean either the universal (concept) determining the pure manifold of time or the universal (concept) determining the inner sense and all of its content.

Of these two senses of 'time-determinant,' Kant seems to adopt the latter sense. He says, "All increase in empirical knowledge . . . is nothing but an extension of the determination of inner sense, that is, advance in time." (A 210 = B 255) Here he seems to identify the determination of time with that of inner sense and all its contents. He also says that the rules for determining the time-series, the time-content, the time-order, and the scope of time are the time-determinants. (A 145 = B 184) These rules are meant to determine not only the pure intuition of time but also all contents of inner sense. In this broad sense, the determinant of time is equivalent to the determinant of the entire phenomenal world.

Having ascertained Kant's meaning of 'time-determinant,' we can now proceed to clarify that of 'transcendental time-determinant.' Kant says, "Now a transcendental determination [determinant] of time is so far homogeneous with the category, which constitutes its unity, in that it is universal and rests upon an *a priori* rule." (A 138 = B 177) A transcendental time-determinant is here characterized as a universal (or concept) that derives its conceptual unity from a category and that determines time. This characterization of transcendental schema is in line with the definition of schema as a universal or a rule for constructing particulars or images.

We have tried to substantiate at least provisionally our hypothesis that Kant has entertained two definitions of transcendental schema corresponding to his two definitions of schema. As before, let us use here two expressions—'transcendental image-schema' and 'transcendental concept-schema'—to distinguish between the two kinds of transcendental schemata. The former expression refers to the pure image or intuition which represents a pure concept; the latter expression designates the rule of synthesis which mediates between a pure concept and the domain of time.

With these definitions of transcendental schema, we can now study all Kant's transcendental schemata. This will require us to examine not only the short chapter in the *Critique* called the Schematism but also the long chapter called the System of all Principles of Pure Understanding, which is generally understood to present Kant's demonstration of his a priori principles. A large part of it, however, is devoted to his second attempt to schematize the pure concepts of understanding. This second effort produces a far more substantial result than his initial one in the Schematism. The two attempts jointly produce two transcendental image-schemata and eight transcendental concept-schemata. We must now examine these schemata and their production.

*What are the transcendental schemata
and how are they produced?*

Kant presents his two transcendental image-schemata in this one sentence: "The pure image of all magnitudes *(quan-*

torum) for outer sense is space; that of all objects of the senses in general is time." (A 142 = B 182) I am assuming here that 'the pure image' is synonymous with 'the transcendental image-schema,' because the latter has been defined as the pure image representing a pure concept. We can see no direct connection between these two image-schemata and Kant's Table of Categories, however, because the concept of magnitude and that of all objects do not appear there. The concept of magnitude comes on the scene only as the concept-schema of the pure concepts of quantity. So space as the image-schema presupposes the concept-schematization of the categories of quantity.

Time as the image-schema of the concept of all objects is also an anomaly because the concept of all objects appears neither in Kant's categorial deduction nor in his concept-schematization. We may assume that the concept of all objects is the same as the concept of an object in general. In the preceding chapter, we have seen that this concept is not recognized as a primitive one in Kant's categorial table, although it may be the most primordial concept. Moreover, we have seen that Kant regards the concept of an object in general as equivalent to the concept of being in general. We may therefore call time the "transcendental image-schema of being in general."

We shall now examine Kant's eight transcendental concept-schemata. At this point, it should be pointed out that Kant does not produce as many concept-schemata as the pure concepts of understanding. Every pure concept of relation and modality receives a corresponding concept-schema, but the first two triads of pure concepts (quantity and quality) are given only two concept-schemata.

In the Axioms of Intuition Kant uses the concept of extensive magnitude as the concept-schema of the three pure concepts of quantity. But he appears to give a different one for the same pure concepts in the Schematism, where he designates the concept of number as their schema. (A 142 = B 182) But the difference between these two schemata turns out to be only terminological. He equates *number* with *magnitude: "Numerus est quantitas phenomenon."* (A 146 = B 186) He defines number as "a representation which comprises the successive addition of homogeneous units." (A 142 = B 182) This definition of number is almost interchangeable with his definition of extensive magnitude: "I entitle a magnitude extensive when the representation of the parts makes possible, and therefore necessarily precedes, the representation of the whole." (A 162 = B 203) He gives as an example of extensive magnitude the representation of a line on the ground: that a line can be drawn by adding together its parts. (A 162 f. = B 203) The concept of extensive magnitude is therefore the concept of the whole that can be produced by a successive addition of homogeneous parts.

It is not certain that Kant's definition of extensive magnitude is correct. But let us provisionally accept it and then determine how the concept of extensive magnitude can be produced by the schematization of the pure concepts of quantity. These pure concepts are those of unity, plurality, and totality. Kant does not explain how the schematization of these three concepts produces the concept of extensive magnitude. We thus have to try to construct hypothetically what might have been in his mind.

Kant may have regarded the concept of extensive magnitude as the schema of the pure concepts of unity, plurality, and totality, on the ground that the last three concepts are used in the production of an extensive magnitude. The concepts of parts and whole are indeed prominent in Kant's definition of the extensive synthesis, the synthesis that produces an extensive magnitude. Kant seems to assume moreover that the successive addition of homogeneous parts in producing a whole is just the operation of the pure concepts of quantity. Let us therefore restate his definition of extensive magnitude in such a way as to indicate the use of the pure concepts of quantity: An extensive magnitude is a whole *(totality)* that is produced by the successive addition of the many *(plurality)* parts which are homogeneous units *(unity)*. Although it is not certain that Kant would accept this as an accurate account of the nature of the schematization of the pure concepts of quantity, it is about the best hypothetical reconstruction we can offer.

Still, even this hypothetical account is untenable. First of all, this account runs counter to Kant's entire doctrine of the schematism. The problem of schematism has arisen supposedly from the fact that the pure concepts are not immediately applicable to the sensory manifold. Since the schema is supposed to mediate the application of the pure concepts to the objects of intuitions, the production of the schema should *precede* the use of the pure concepts. But the use of the pure concepts of unity, plurality, and totality turns out to be prerequisite to the production of their schema. This plainly places the cart before the horse.

If Kant nevertheless wants to maintain that the concept of extensive magnitude is the schema of the pure concepts of quantity, it becomes necessary to revise his definition of schema and schematization. Schematization would first have to be defined as the production of a complex concept by the use of simple concepts, and then the schema would have to be defined as the complex concept thus produced. In fact, it seems fairly certain that this is the way Kant understood the relation between the concept of extensive magnitude and the pure concepts of quantity. Even within this new definition of schema and schematization, the concept of extensive magnitude cannot be properly regarded as the schema only of *unity, plurality,* and *totality,* because the production of extensive magnitudes requires a few more concepts than these three.

The concepts of quality and extension are as indispensable in the production of extensive magnitudes as any other concepts can be. Kant defines extensive synthesis as a successive addition of homogeneous units. The concept of quality is indispensable in determining the homogeneity of the homogeneous units. But this concept of quality is not one of the pure concepts of quality *(reality, negation,* and *limitation)* and is not even listed in the Table of the Categories.

That the concept of extension or the extended is also involved in the production of extensive magnitudes can be shown by Kant's definition of extensive magnitude. He defines it as the magnitude of a whole that is produced by the combination of parts. Since the word 'extensive' appears only in the *definiendum* and not in the *definiens,* the definition in question gives the impression that an extensive magnitude emerges in the process of combining extensionless parts. In that event, the concept of extension would not be required in the production of extensive magnitudes because the property of extension emerges only in the product of extensive synthesis. But this notion of extension is not Kant's; it is Leibniz' definition.

Since Kant cannot accept the idea that extension can emerge in the combination of extensionless parts, he needs to augment his definition of extensive magnitudes: Extensive magnitude is the magnitude of a whole which is produced by the combination of *extended* parts. Here, the concept of extension or the extended appears in the *definiens* as well as in the *definiendum.* That means that the concept of extension is also indispensable in the process of generating extensive magnitudes.

If an extensive whole can be produced by combining only extensive parts, however, Kant cannot maintain his thesis that the parts are prior to the whole in the production of extensive magnitudes. Since every part is extended, the parts are as much extensive magnitudes as their whole. The process of combining parts into a whole cannot have priority over the process of dividing a whole into parts. Since the parts are extensive magnitudes as much as their combined whole, the concepts of parts and whole really have nothing to do with the production or definition of extensive magnitude. Hence, Kant should not have allowed the concepts of whole and parts to add unnecessary complications to his definition of extensive magnitude. He should rather have simply defined extensive magnitude as the magnitude of the extended or of the extension.

We have observed that the concept of quality is an integral feature of the concept of extensive magnitude. Extension is a quality and the magnitude of this quality is extensive magnitude. The concept of magnitude (quantity) always presupposes the concept of quality (property) because magnitude is always the magnitude of some quality. But not every quality can have quantitative determination; only the variable qualities can have magnitudes. We can make use of Hegel's distinction between discrete and continuous qualities.[5] Length is a continuous quality; color is a discrete one. Whereas red cannot have more or less color than blue, two feet is shorter than three feet and longer than one foot. Colors do not admit of being *more or less,* as lengths do. By 'variable properties,' I mean continuous properties that are capable of quantitative variation—of being more or less. Thus magnitude always presupposes continuous or variable properties.

If extensive magnitude is defined as the magnitude of extension or the extended, the concept of extensive magnitude has nothing to do with the concepts of unity, plurality, totality, parts and whole, or numbers. Why has Kant then held the erroneous idea that these latter concepts are essential to the production of extensive magnitudes? This erroneous idea appears to reflect his confusion about the two kinds of quantity. Our quantitative questions generally take one of two forms: "How much?" or "How many?" The former may be called the question of magnitude and the latter the question of number. Kant indicates his awareness of these two kinds of quantity by his use of two different Latin quantitative terms, *quantum* (or *quantorum)* and *quantitas.* (A 142 = B 182; B 203; A 163 = B 204)

Kant appears to believe that the concept of extensive magnitude involves the concepts of both *quantum* and *quantitas.* But if so, he has confused the concept of extensive magnitude with that of metrical determination. The metrical determination of a property requires the unit of measurement and the total number of the units of the measured property. When the property to be measured is extension, its metrical determination will require the unit of extension and the total number of the units in the measured object. The unit of extension is *quantum* and the total number of the units is *quantitas*. The determination of the total units of the measured extension certainly requires what Kant calls the successive addition of homogeneous units, which in turn requires number, and Kant believes that this rests on the operation of the pure concepts of quantity. So Kant's extensive magnitude turns out to be the metrically determined quantity of extension.

Since the concept of extensive magnitude is independent of or prior to the concept of its metrical determination, to use these two concepts equivalently is bound to produce serious confusion.

The definition of extensive magnitude as the metrical determination of extension does not improve Kant's claim that the concept of extensive magnitude is the concept-schema of the pure concepts of unity, plurality, and totality. This new definition of extensive magnitude involves the concepts of extension, magnitude (the nature of the unit of measurement), and the numerical quantity. The first two have nothing to do with any of the pure concepts of quantity; only the third may have some connection with these pure concepts, because the concept of the numerical quantity involves the concept of number or counter which Kant seems to claim is generated by the use of the pure concepts of quantity. (Cf. A 143 = B 183; A 164 f. = B 204 f.) Even this tenuous connection between the pure concepts of quantity and their supposed schema, the concept of extensive magnitude, can be maintained only with the absurd consequence that pure concepts are used in the production of their schema, whose function is to mediate the use of pure concepts

Having tried various ways to test the claim that the concept of extensive magnitude is the schema of the pure concepts of unity, plurality, and totality, we must conclude that this claim cannot be permitted to stand within Kant's theory of schemata and their function. Under the name of schematization, Kant has simply substituted the concept of extensive magnitude for the pure concepts of quantity.

Kant presents the concept of intensive magnitude as the concept-schema of the pure concepts of quality. He appears to define intensive magnitude in contrast to extensive magnitude: "A magnitude which is apprehended only as unity, and in which multiplicity can be represented only through approximation to negation = 0, I entitle *intensive* magnitude." (A 168 = B 210) Whereas the successive *addition* of parts is prior to the generation of a whole in the case of extensive magnitudes, the successive *division* of a whole is prior to the generation of its parts in the case of intensive magnitudes. Here we need to point out that the concepts of parts and whole, plurality (multiplicity) and totality, and unity are as important to the generation of intensive magnitudes as to that of extensive magnitudes. The concept of intensive magnitude has as strong a claim to be called the schema of the pure concepts of quantity as the concept of extensive magnitude.

At the same time, let us not overlook two points of difference between the definitions of intensive magnitude and extensive magnitude. First, the former definition involves the pure concept of negation while the latter definition does not. Second, the order of whole and parts in one case is the reverse of what it is in the other. The concept of negation (privation) is really a gratuitous element in Kant's definition of intensive magnitude. What is essential to his definition is that an intensive magnitude is apprehended as a whole and that its parts can be represented by a successive division of it. The operation of successive division does not have any closer relation to the concept of negation than does the operation of successive addition. The successive division of a magnitude cannot reach the state of no magnitude if the successive addition of magnitude-less entities cannot produce any magnitude.

That the order of the whole and parts is different in the apprehensions of extensive and intensive magnitudes is also a dubious assertion. We have seen that the successive addition of parts can produce an extensive magnitude only if the parts themselves are extensive magnitudes, in which case each part must be apprehended as such. Kant may believe that each of these parts is an extensive magnitude because each of them is apprehended as a result of an extensive synthesis. But this notion will throw the apprehension of extensive magnitudes into an infinite regress. Thus it is necessary to assume that some extensive magnitudes are apprehended as wholes. Since Kant cannot hold that these wholes are indivisible, he has to maintain that they can be divided into smaller units. So the order of whole and parts is not permanently fixed in the apprehension of extensive magnitudes. This apprehension can take one of two forms: successive addition or successive division.

That the order of parts and whole is reversible reflects not only the nature of extensive magnitude but the nature of magnitude itself. Hence, the apprehension of a whole cannot always take precedence over that of its parts in the apprehension of an intensive magnitude. Kant seems to have noticed this point and, in the second edition, revises his definition of intensive magnitude accordingly: "[An intensive magnitude] is generated in the act of apprehension whereby the empirical conscious-ness of it can in a certain time increase from nothing $= 0$ to the given measure." (B 208) In fact Kant recognizes that both intensive and extensive magnitudes are *quanta continua:* "All appearances, then, are continuous magnitudes, alike in their intuition, as extensive, and in their mere perception (sensation, and with it reality) as intensive." (A 170 $=$ B 212) All con-tinuous (variable) magnitudes, extensive or intensive, can go through the operation of successive addition or that of successive division.

We have seen that the concept of magnitude always presupposes the concept of variable properties. This is as true in the case of intensive as in the case of extensive magnitudes. The only difference between the two lies in the nature of the qualities involved. Intensive magnitude is the magnitude of nonextended qualities; extensive magnitude is the magnitude of extended qualities. So the definition of intensive magnitude requires only the concepts of magnitude and variable nonextended qualities. Just as Kant's 'extensive magnitude' means the metrical determination of extensive magnitude, so his 'intensive magnitude' really means the metrical determination of intensive magnitudes. This is why he calls intensive magnitude degree or measure, which expresses the concept of measurement. (A 143 = B 182; B 208) The definition of intensive magnitude as the metrical determination of nonextended qualities would require the concepts of nonextended qualities, magnitude (the nature of the unit of measurement), and numerical quantity.

This definition involves precisely the same set of concepts that are required for the definition of extensive magnitudes, except for the concepts of extended and nonextended qualities (properties). There is nothing remarkable about this. Intensive and extensive magnitudes are simply two species of magnitude, and the concept of magnitude always presupposes concepts of qualities. The differentiae of these two species are extended and nonextended qualities.

Kant makes a few scattered attempts to show how the pure concepts of reality, negation, and limitation are uniquely involved in the generation of intensive magnitudes. (A 143 = B 182; B 208; A 168 = B 210) None of these attempts however is systematic and complete. He has not even made up his mind about whether he should call intensive magnitude the schema of *reality* or *limitation*. (A 143 = B 182 f.) Needless to say, none of his arguments is convincing. The assertion that the pure concepts of quality are used in the production of intensive magnitudes is as untenable as the assertion that the pure concepts of quantity are used in the production of extensive magnitudes. There is no need to criticize in detail the new assertion: every defect we have found in the early assertion will also be found there. As in the case of the schematization of the pure concepts of quantity, Kant simply substitutes the concept of intensive magnitude for the pure concepts of quality in the name of the transcendental schematization.

Kant's desire to establish a special association between the concept of extensive magnitude and the categories of quantity on the one hand, and between the concept of intensive magnitude and the categories of quality on the other may stem from the need to prepare the ground for the division of labor between the Axioms of Intuition and the Anticipations of Perception. Since Kant has assumed that the latter a priori principle has the function of determining the nature of sense *qualities,* he has perhaps decided to establish a special affiliation between the concept of intensive magnitude and the pure concepts of *quality.* Since he has assumed that the former a priori principle has the function of determining the *magnitude (quantity)* of extension, he has perhaps decided to establish a special affiliation between the concept of extensive magnitude and the pure concepts of *quantity.* But it is his error to assume the existence of a special connection between the concept of quantity and that of the extended and between the concept of quality and that of sense qualities. The concept of quality cuts across the boundary between extended and nonextended qualities; the concept of quantity also cuts across the boundary between extended and nonextended magnitudes.

In both cases, the transcendental schematization turns out to be the operation of simple substitution of concepts. As we have seen, Kant implies that the pure concepts in question are used in producing the schematized categories, but we have shown that this implication is incompatible with his original premise that the need for schemata is created by the inapplicability of the pure concepts to the objects of intuitions.

The two operations of substitution perform the salutary function of amending Kant's categorial table. One serious flaw in Kant's Table of Categories is that it fails to list the concepts of quality and quantity—which have been counted as two principal categories in Western ontology. In the Table of Categories Kant uses 'quantity' and 'quality' as two headings or labels for the first two triads of the pure concepts of understanding. Although 'quality' and 'quantity' are mere labels in Kant's original categorial table, the concepts of quality and quantity do perform principal roles in producing the concepts of intensive and extensive magnitudes. The transcendental schematization serves the function of surreptitiously elevating the concepts of quality and quantity from the labeling position to the categorial position.

We have seen that Kant gives only two transcendental image-schemata. Contrary to this observation, Heidegger says that Kant also gives the image-schema of the pure concept of substance. Let us cite his argument for this view:

> "The schema of substance is the permanence of the real in time." For the full elucidation of schematism of this schema, it is necessary to refer to the *First Analogy*. . . .
>
> Substance as a notion signifies first of all "that which underlies" (subsistent). Its schema must be the representation of subsistence so far as this schema is presented in the pure image of time. But time as the pure *now*-sequence is ever now. That is, in every *now* it is now. Time thus manifests its own constancy. As such, time is "non-transitory and abiding" "while all else changes." More precisely: time is not one permanent thing among others . . . it provides the pure aspect of permanence in general. As

this pure image (an immediate, pure "aspect") it presents the subsistent in pure intuition.[6]

Heidegger argues here that time is a pure image, which does not merely represent but exemplifies the concept of permanent subsistence. Thus the pure intuition of time meets the qualification of functioning as the transcendental image-schema of *substance*. Heidegger's argument is a perfect execution of Kant's general idea of transcendental image-schemata but is not a correct interpretation of Kant's own schematization of the pure concept of substance.

In order to support his argument, Heidegger is compelled to misread "The schema of substance is the permanence of the real" as "Time is the transcendental schema (the pure image) of substance." This amounts to confusing the permanence of *the real in time* with the permanence *of time*. "The schema of substance is the permanence of the real in time" is really an elliptical expression for "the concept-schema of substance means the permanence of the real in time." Thus Kant in truth gives only a concept-schema for the pure concept of substance. Here is the full text in which he presents this schema:

> The schema of substance is permanence of the real in time, that is, the representation of the real as a substrate of empirical determination of time in general, and so as abiding while all else changes. (The existence of what is transitory passes away in time but not time itself. To time, itself non-transitory and abiding, there corresponds in the [field of] appearance what is non-transitory in its existence, that is, substance.) (A 143= B 183)

It is clearly the parenthetical remark which prompted Heidegger's interpretation. In this parenthetical assertion, Kant indeed says that time is the exemplification of permanence. But he does not go on to conclude that, "Therefore, time is the pure image of substance." This is the missing conclusion that Heidegger is anxious to provide. To do so, however, is not to interpret but to rewrite Kant.

Although he gives no image-schema of the pure concept of substance, Kant does present two concept-schemata for that pure concept: the concept of the permanent and the concept of substratum. (A 143 = B 183) He appears to view these two concepts as two equivalent conceptions of substance. But these two concepts do not play equal roles in his definition of substance, for he seems to treat permanence as the defining property of substance. He calls permanence "our sole ground for applying the category of substance to appearance," and "an essential and quite peculiar characteristic of substance." (A 184 = B 227; A 205 = B 250) Kant does not explain how the concept of substratum enters into the schematization of *substance*. He appears to treat the concept of substratum as equivalent to the concept of the permanent, on the ground that only the substratum of appearances is permanent while their superstratum is always changing.

In the case of the pure concept of substance, Kant appears to understand schematization as a process of conceptual transformation—the unschematized concept of substance (which is the concept of a subject in general) becomes through schematization the concept of a subject in the phenomenal world. Kant seems to hold that the concept of permanence cannot be contained in the concept of a subject in general because permanence is exclusively a property of the phenomenal world in time. He also seems to conceive of the subject of the phenomenal world as what is permanent on the ground that only the permanent can be the ultimate subject for the predication of phenomenal properties. (Cf. A 205 = B 250) Thus the schematization of the pure concept of substance is tantamount to the transformation of the concept of the subject in general into the concept of the phenomenal subject.

Kant gives the concept of necessary succession as the schema of the pure concept of causation. (A 144 = B 183) Here again he seems to understand schematization as a process of conceptual transformation. The concept of succession, which is essential to that of causation in the phenomenal world, cannot be contained in the unschematized concept of causation because this is the concept of causation in general.* Schematization transforms the concept of causation in general into the concept of causation in the phenomenal world.

Kant gives the concept of mutual causation as the schema for the pure concept of community or reciprocity. (A 144 = B 183) He treats this third relational category not as a simple but as a composite concept. Since the concept of community is definable by that of causation, the schematization of one pure concept should be of the same nature as the other.

There is some terminological inconsistency, however, in calling the schema of *community* or *reciprocity* the concept of mutual causation. Since he has decided not to use 'causation' (but rather 'necessary succession') in the schematization of his second relational category, he has given the impression that the term 'causation' is used exclusively to designate the unschematized concept of causation and not its schema. So he should have avoided using the same expression in naming the schema of his third relational category, and he should have used the name of the schema of *causation* ('necessary succes-

*It may be argued that the unschematized concept is not the concept of causation in general but of ground and consequence. In fact, this is the position we will develop in the following chapter. The concept of causation in general is material; that of ground and consequence is formal. In Chapter 4 we will see that the concept-schematization is the process of transforming formal into material concepts. In this chapter, however, I have decided to ignore the distinction between the concept of causation in general and that of ground and consequence for two reasons. First, to take a full note of this distinction would require the conceptual framework that will be developed in the following chapter. Second, as it was pointed out in the last chapter, Kant himself regarded the formal concepts as identical with the generic concepts of the highest level.

sion') in defining the schema of *community*. That is, this schema should be called the concept of *reversible necessary succession* rather than the concept of *mutual causation*.

In quite parallel ways, the remainder of Kant's schematization can be seen to be in truth conceptual transformations. He defines the schema of *possibility* as the concept of conformity with the formal conditions of experience and the schema of *actuality* as the concept of the fulfillment of the material conditions of experience. (A 218 = B 265 f.) The schema of *possibility* is the concept of possibility in the phenomenal world; only those things that meet the formal conditions of intuitions and concepts are possible in the phenomenal world. The concept of possibility in general need not specify these conditions, which are unique to this phenomenal world. The schema of actuality is the concept of existence in the phenomenal world. The concept of existence is inseparable from the concept of intuitions—that which exists must be intuited by some kind of intuition. The concept of actuality in general is the concept of existence whose intuition is left unspecified. The concept of existence in the phenomenal world can be specified by the nature of human intuitions that are sensible or receptive. The schematization of both pure concepts of modality is of the same kind of conceptual transformation as the schematization of the relational categories.

In specifying the schema of *necessity,* Kant says, "That which in its connection with the actual is determined in accordance with universal conditions of experience, is (that is, exists as) *necessary." (*A 218 = B 266) This exposition of the schema of *necessity* makes this schema the joint product of the schema of *possibility* and that of *actuality*. In the course of his exposition of the Third Postulate, however, Kant calls the schema of *necessity* 'material necessity' and identifies it with causal necessity. (A 226 f. = B 279) This was an unfortunate blunder on his part. Kant might have identified the schema of *necessity* with the concept of causal necessity because the necessity in the phenomenal world has been traditionally understood as causal necessity. But he cannot afford to show any respect for this traditional notion of necessity, because his identification of the schema of necessity with causal necessity contradicts his original definition of that schema as the joint product of the schema of *possibility* and that of *actuality*.

Kant may have felt uneasy in leaving out the concept of causation from his conception of *necessity*. But that would be a needless misgiving. The schema of *necessity* as the joint product of the schemata of *possibility* and *actuality* is a far richer concept than the concept of causal necessity. Since the causal principle is one of the formal conditions of experience, it is already included in the schema of *possibility* which in turn constitutes only one half of the schema of *necessity*.

For the sake of architectonic integrity, Kant should stay with his original schematization of the pure concept of necessity. *Necessity* is the concept of that which meets the formal and the material conditions of experience. It is the concept of what is necessary in the phenomenal world. The concept of necessity in general is not bound by the conditions of experience in the phenomenal world; schematization transforms the concept of necessity in general into the concept of the phenomenal necessity. Thus the schematization of the pure concept of necessity serves the same function as the schematization of the pure concepts of possibility and actuality.

This concludes our examination of Kant's two transcendental image-schemata and eight transcendental concept-schemata. Before taking up some of the controversial questions on his doctrine of schematism in the following chapter, let us summarize the results of our investigation in the following chart:

TRANSCENDENTAL IMAGE-SCHEMATA

Unschematized Concepts	Image-Schemata
1. concept of all magnitudes	space
2. concept of all objects	time

TRANSCENDENTAL CONCEPT-SCHEMATA

Unschematized Concepts	Concept-Schemata
1. pure concepts of quantity	concept of extensive magnitude
2. pure concepts of quality	concept of intensive magnitude
3. pure concept of substance	concept of the permanent (substratum)
4. pure concept of causation	concept of necessary succession
5. pure concept of community	concept of mutual causation (reversible necessary succession)
6. pure concept of possibility	concept of the conformity with formal conditions of experience
7. pure concept of actuality	concept of the conformity with material conditions of experience
8. pure concept of necessity	concept of the conformity with both conditions of experience

Chapter 4

Material Reason and Material Concepts

Although every major topic in the *Critique* has been a source of controversy, the doctrine of schematism has attained a unique status even among those controversial topics. In the case of this doctrine, even the legitimacy of the problem itself has not been commonly acknowledged. Kant says that the problem of schematism arises from the inapplicability of the pure concepts of understanding to appearances, and that the function of the transcendental schemata is to resolve this problem by mediating between the pure concepts and the sensory manifold. Some have even tried to expose the absurdity of Kant's problem simply on the premise that to have a concept is to know how to use or apply it.[1] "To have inapplicable concepts" is therefore a contradiction in terms.

Even those who have conceded the legitimacy of Kant's problem are often convinced of its insolubility. If the pure concepts are really inapplicable to the sensory manifold, it is argued, their mediation cannot be executed by the transcendental schemata, because their status as mediators would be mercilessly vitiated by Aristotle's 'third man' argument against Plato.[2] If Kant's problem of the schematism is really either absurd or insoluble, there should be no need to scrutinize his involved, obscure doctrine. For this reason, we had best resume our inquiry by examining the nature of Kant's problem.

How has Kant understood the problem of schematism?

Kant propounds the inapplicability of the pure concepts in terms of *subsumption*. (A 137 = B 176) He holds that to make use of a concept in a judgment is to subsume an object under that concept. He further holds that there is a unique difficulty in the subsumption of appearances under pure concepts due to the peculiar nature of these concepts. Thus his doctrine of judgment as subsumption constitutes the theoretical framework within which he formulates the problem of transcendental schematism. It is this theoretical framework which provokes the first criticism regarding the legitimacy of Kant's problem. Kemp Smith maintains that this is not the right framework in which to pose the question of schematism:

> Schematism, properly understood, is not a process of subsumption, but . . . of synthetic interpretation. Creative synthesis, whereby contents are apprehended in terms of functional relations, not subsumption of particulars under universals that are homogeneous with them, is what Kant must ultimately mean by the schematism of the pure forms of understanding. A category, that is to say, cannot be viewed as a *predicate* of a possible judgment, and as being applied to a subject independently apprehended; its function is to articulate the judgment as a whole. The category of substance and attribute, for instance, is the *form* of the categorical judgment, and must not be equated with any one of its single parts.[3]

Kemp Smith is accusing Kant of misrepresenting the function of the categories. Whereas the function of generic concepts may be described as subsumption, he warns us, the function of the categories can be so described only at the risk of misrepresentation. This admonition is based on his frequently asserted conviction that there is a generic difference between generic concepts and categories: "A generic or abstract concept expresses common qualities found in each of a number of complex contents. It is itself a content. A category, on the other hand, is always a function of unity whereby contents are interpreted. It is not a content, but a form for the organization of content."[4] He emphasizes his claim that the relation of the categories to the objects of intuitions should be conceived not as the relation of class-concepts to their instances but as that of forms to their contents.

By characterizing the difference between the categories and the generic concepts as that between forms and contents, Kemp Smith attempts to specify the functional difference between them. Their functional difference as he conceives it can be regarded as the difference between the formal and the material function. The latter involves the contents of judgments, whereas the former does not. If the categories can perform only the formal functions, they cannot discharge the function of "synthetic interpretation," which Kemp Smith claims as the unique function of the categories. He has forgotten that formal functions can produce only the analytic unity and that only material functions can produce the synthetic unity. The synthetic function is inseparable from the contents of judgments. Thus Kemp Smith's characterization of the supposedly unique function of the categories turns out to be self-contradictory.

The applicability of the categories to the objects of intuitions has nothing to do with the formal functions of the categories. Formal concepts are not meant to apply to objects; only material concepts are meant to do that. Material concepts are in fact defined as those concepts which are meant to apply to objects. Formal concepts are defined as those concepts whose function is to articulate the forms of judgment. As far as Kant is concerned, the formal functions of the categories can never become problematic. He assumes that their formal functions are the most obvious features of our primitive conceptual system. This is why he has attempted to use their formal functions as the clue in his derivation of the categories.

When he brings up the question of applicability of the categories in the Schematism, he wants to determine how the pure concepts achieve their material functions, or rather how they develop into material concepts. Since only material concepts can by definition be used for subsumption, to use a concept for subsumption is to use the same concept as a material concept. Thus Kant's question "How can the pure concepts of understanding be used for subsumption?" is virtually the same question as "How can those pure concepts function as material concepts?"

The question of the schematism concerns, then, the material function of the categories. This type of question has never been raised with other categorial systems simply because all of them have been ab initio conceived as systems of the ultimate material concepts. As we will see more clearly in what follows, Kant's conception of a priori concepts does not allow him to take it for granted that his pure concepts of understanding are by their nature material concepts ready to be used for the function of subsumption.

We may as well resolve another misgiving of Kemp Smith's: that the function of subsumption is incompatible with the synthetic function of the categories. The function of synthesis is to bring the many into one, which Kant often calls the function of unity. The function of subsumption is also to bring the many into one: Many objects can be subsumed under one concept. The unity that is established by subsumption is the *unity of a class,* whereas the function of synthesis is rather to establish the *unity of an object,* that is, to combine sense representations for the construction of a unitary object. (Cf. A 77, 103, 118, 119; B 130, 151) Kemp Smith's apprehension appears to be well founded, for the function of synthesis seems incompatible with the function of subsumption because the former establishes the unity of an object whereas the latter establishes the unity of a class.

We will see that this apprehension is really groundless. Let us first note that a concept can perform a synthetic function only if it is an ontologically composite concept. By 'ontologically composite concept' I mean a concept that can designate a composite object. For example, the concept of triangle can be a rule for combining three straight lines into one figure because it is an ontologically composite concept. In contrast to this, the concept of a point cannot perform the function of combining many representations into one because it is not an ontologically composite concept. Neither can a formal concept perform the synthetic function because it designates no objects.

All the relational categories are well equipped to perform synthetic functions because all of them are ontologically composite concepts. Hence Kant has the relational categories chiefly in mind when he advocates the connective or synthetic functions of the pure concepts. The modal categories cannot perform synthetic functions, not because they are simple but because they are not ontological. ("They refer not to the objects of knowledge but to the state of knowledge.") For this reason, Kant assigns no synthetic functions to the modal categories. He expresses this point in claiming that the Postulates of Empirical Thought in General are not synthetic propositions but only the explications of the modal categories. (A 219 = B 266)

The pure concepts of quality and quantity (especially *unity* and *plurality; reality* and *negation)* appear to be ontologically simple concepts. If so, they could not perform synthetic functions. In order to insure the synthetic functions of the mathematical categories, Kant surreptitiously replaces the pure concepts of quantity and quality with the concepts of extensive and intensive magnitudes. Both of these concepts are ontologically composite concepts and hence are well suited for synthetic functions. I do not mean to say that Kant has intentionally done all these things; that would credit him with a far greater self-knowledge than he is entitled to. I merely say that the operation of the categorial substitution that is most likely to have been executed unconsciously dovetails with Kant's theory of the synthetic categorial functions.

What we have called an ontologically composite concept is

nothing more than a composite material concept. But since all material concepts are generic concepts, all composite material concepts must be able to perform the function of subsumption as well as the function of synthesis. In fact, this is the case. For example, the concept of triangle can bring many triangles under it and also combine three straight lines into one plane figure. There can be no conflict between these two functions.

There nevertheless appears to be some conflict between these two functions if the function of subsumption is understood to bring *many* instances under one concept. To bring many instances under one concept may sound like the operation of forming a class, but subsumption is not the operation of class-formation. Strictly speaking, subsumption is the operation of bringing an instance under a concept. In this strict sense, Kant is likely to say that the function of subsumption is inseparable from the function of synthesis in the case of the composite material concepts. For example, to bring a triangle under the concept of triangle is to combine three straight lines into one plane figure in accordance with the concept of triangle. Subsumption under a simple concept cannot involve synthesis, but subsumption under a composite concept does always involve an act of synthesis. Thus the function of synthesis is not incompatible with, but inseparable from, the function of subsumption; this should dispose of Kemp Smith's second misgiving.

He also voices a terminological displeasure with Kant's choice of the expression 'subsumption' for describing the function of judgment. He says that 'subsumption' has been traditionally used as a technical term to describe the relation between the major and the minor premises in the syllogistic inference, where the minor premise is said to be subsumed under the major premise. He produces a passage from Kant's *Logik* to show that Kant himself knew about this technical usage of the term in question and employed it precisely in this technical sense. Since 'subsumption' has been established as a technical syllogistic term, he maintains, Kant's use of it for the description of the function of judgment has the danger of associating judgment with syllogism rather than with proposition. As Kemp Smith puts it: "But there is a further complication. Kant . . . defines judgment as being [the faculty of subsuming under rules]. Now this view of judgment really connects with syllogism, not with the proposition."[5]

In order to determine the merit of this terminological complaint, let us first be clear about the meaning of 'subsume' and 'subsumption.' These two are fundamentally classificatory terms. 'To subsume (*subsumere*)' means to bring an entity under a category or to include it in a class. As a classificatory term, 'subsumption' is well suited for describing the function of propositions, especially as Kant has understood the term. In Chapter 2 we have seen that he most likely knew only the logic of classes. Within this logic, the function of a proposition is to specify the class-relations. '*S* is *P*' means that *S* falls under the class *P*; 'No *S* is *P*' means that the class *S* is excluded from the class *P*. Thus in 'subsumption' Kant has found a most appropriate term for describing the function of propositions and consequently also the function of judgments.

The use of 'subsumption' in syllogistic inferences can be regarded merely as a logical extension of its use in propositions. The function of syllogisms in the logic of classes is the extension of the function of propositions in specifying the class-relations. Whereas the function of propositions is to specify the class-relations with no mediation, the function of syllogistic inferences is to do so through mediation. "If all *A*'s are *B*'s and if all *B*'s are *C*'s, then all *A*'s are *C*'s," performs the function of subsuming the class of *A*'s under the class of *C*'s through the mediation of the class of *B*'s. The subsumption of the minor premise under the major premise should be understood in the spirit of this classificatory sense. So Kant's use of 'subsumption' need not introduce the misleading association and the unnecessary complication which provoke Kemp Smith's apprehension, as long as the nature of judgment or proposition in the logic of classes is distinctly comprehended.

We may thus conclude that the theory of subsumption is an appropriate theoretical framework in which to formulate the problem of schematism and, further, that 'subsumption' is a well-chosen technical term with which to characterize the function of judgment. Let us remember that the question of subsumption in the case of the pure concepts is a question concerning the ability of these concepts to perform their categorial functions as material concepts. With this in mind, let us now see how Kant understood the problem of transcendental schematism within the general framework of subsumption.

Kant lays down the conditions for subsumption as follows:

> In all subsumption of an object under a concept the representation of the object must be *homogeneous* with the concept; in other words, the concept must contain something which is represented in the object to be subsumed under it. This, in fact, is what is meant by the expression, 'an object is contained under a concept.' Thus the empirical concept of a *plate* is homogeneous with the pure geometrical concept of *a circle*. The roundness which is thought in the latter can be intuited in the former. (A 137 = B 176)

The last two sentences of this passage require some emendation: "Thus the empirical concept of a *plate* . . ." should read "Thus the empirical object (or representation) of a *plate* is homogeneous with the pure geometrical concept of *a circle*. The roundness which is thought in the latter can be intuited in the former." This emendation is required because the passage is concerned with the relation of a concept not to another concept but to an object, and because the roundness of a circle can be intuited not in the concept of a plate but only in a circular object.

With this slight emendation, the passage states a fairly simple doctrine. A concept is homogeneous with an object when the latter has the properties or relations connoted by the former. In such a relation of homogeneity, the properties and relations connoted by the concept can be discovered in the object through inspection. The first of these two assertions can be taken as the definition of *homogeneity* and the other as its test. The test stands on the premise that all properties and relations are open to direct intuition or inspection. This is a highly dubious premise, but we will not allow it to detain us any longer.

One strange feature in Kant's doctrine of homogeneity is his decision to introduce 'homogeneity' as a new technical term, although there appears to have been no real need to do so. He was fully familiar with a few well-established terms expressing the relation of the homogeneity of a concept to an object. (Cf. B xviii, 180, 291) These are such terms as 'conformity,' 'correspondence,' 'commensurateness,' and 'adequacy.' Instead of saying that a concept is homogeneous with an object, he could say that a concept is commensurate with the object, or that an object corresponds to a concept. Instead of saying that a concept is heterogeneous from an object, he could say that a concept is not adequate to an object, or that an object fails to correspond to a concept. Restated in these familiar terms, Kant's doctrine of homogeneity reveals itself as the obvious thesis that a concept should be commensurate with its object in a judgment. But this familiar thesis takes an unexpected turn when Kant brings it to bear on the relation of the pure concepts to the objects of senses:

> But pure concepts of understanding being quite heterogeneous from empirical intuitions, and indeed from all sensible intuitions, can never be met within any intuition. For no one will say that a category, such as that of causality, can be intuited through sense and is itself con-

tained in appearance. How, then, is the *subsumption* of intuitions under pure concepts, the *application* of a category to appearances, possible? A transcendental doctrine of judgment is necessary just because of this natural and important question. We must be able to show how pure concepts can be applicable to appearances. (A 137 f. = B 176 f.)

This formal presentation of Kant's problem has two grave defects. First, it fails to delineate the scope of the problem. It is not clear whether Kant is asserting the heterogeneity of the pure concepts "from empirical intuitions" only or "from all sensible intuitions." This ambiguity renders the scope of the problem unclear, that is, it is not determined whether the problem is that of applying pure concepts to empirical intuitions only or to both empirical and pure intuitions. Second, Kant does not even bother to substantiate the basic premise for his problem: The premise that the pure concepts are heterogeneous from the objects of intuitions.

Kant seems to take the premise in question as obvious. The first sentence of the passage which begins "But pure concepts of understanding *being quite heterogeneous* . . ." shows that Kant takes for granted the heterogeneity in question. The same attitude on his part is also reflected in his rhetorical assertion: "For no one will say that a category, such as that of causality, can be intuited through sense and is itself contained in appearance." In this rhetorical statement, Kant may be resting his case on Hume's demonstration that causal nexus cannot be intuited in impressions.

But Hume's demonstration is not sufficient to support Kant's claim that *all* the pure concepts are heterogeneous from appearances. Of course we know that Kant is proud of his master scheme to generalize Hume's problem, but it is surely too hasty a move to conclude from the heterogeneity of one pure concept that of twelve pure concepts. We have seen in the last chapter that Kant employs the pure concepts of quantity and quality in the production of intensive and extensive magnitudes. Surely, such a use of those pure concepts should prove their homogeneity with appearances. Whether he employs them or not, it is indeed unreasonable to maintain that the concepts of unity and plurality and of reality and negation are not intuitable in the field of appearances. Even Hume never questions their intuitability, hence their homogeneity with impressions. Thus the premise on which Kant's problem of schematism stands is an ill-founded assumption.

We have so far assumed that 'heterogeneity' and 'homogeneity' designate logical relations between concept and objects because Kant's own explanation of these terms gives only their logical senses. We may be able to make somewhat better sense of Kant's case if we take those terms in their genetic sense. The etymologies of 'homogeneity *(Gleichartichkeit)*' and 'heterogeneity *(Ungleichartichkeit)*' refer to 'kind,' 'breed,' and 'nature.' Thus these terms can be used to describe the genetic relation of concepts and objects. For example, the proposition 'Empirical concepts are homogeneous with empirical intuitions' can be used to assert that empirical concepts and empirical intuitions are of the same kind or from the same source. The genetic interpretation of these two terms helps us to understand why Kant takes for granted the homogeneity of mathematical concepts with pure intuitions and that of empirical concepts with empirical intuitions.

Because Kant intends to use 'homogeneity' and 'heterogeneity' in their genetic sense, he seems to feel the need for introducing these new technical terms instead of using such familiar terms as 'correspondence' and 'adequacy.' These familiar terms carry no such genetic meaning. Kant seems to have believed that the logical relation connoted by 'commensurateness' and 'incommensurateness' is grounded in the genetic relation connoted by 'homogeneity' and 'heterogeneity.' A concept would be commensurate with an object only if they have the same origin; and a concept would be incommensurate with an object if they do not have the same origin.

If the logical relation of fitness between concepts and objects is always determined by their genetic relation, the pure concepts of understanding cannot correspond to the objects of empirical intuitions. In order to establish their heterogeneity, Kant has only to prove that the concept and the object have different origins. He assumes that the empirical origin of sensations is too obvious to require proof. He claims to have proved the a priori origin of pure concepts by the Metaphysical Deduction: "In the *metaphysical deduction* the *a priori* origin of the categories has been proved through their complete agreement with the general logical functions of thought." (B 159) That the categories have been discovered by formal reason alone is taken by him as sufficient to prove their a priori origin. Since the pure concepts and the empirical intuitions are of different origins, Kant must have thought, the former could not be commensurate with the later. Thus he seems to have concluded that their incommensurateness creates the problem of transcendental schematism. The nature of this problem may be further illuminated if we compare Kant's doctrine of ideas with those of Leibniz and Hume.

Hume holds that all ideas are copies of impressions. This genetic theory of ideas guarantees that every idea will fit some impression. His genetic theory precludes the possibility of encountering any ideas which cannot fit any impressions. Therefore Hume's discovery that the idea of causation cannot be referred back to any impression invalidates his genetic theory of ideas. In order to cover up this consequence, he tries to deny the very existence of the idea of necessary connection by explaining it away as the operation of custom and habit. As long as his theory of ideas is correct, the application of concepts to objects will never become a problem.

The relation of ideas to objects in Leibniz' theory is the reverse of what it is in Hume's. The priority of the possibles to the actuals is assumed in Leibniz' thesis that the actual world is the best of all possible worlds. Since the possibles constitute the domain of essences or ideas, the ideas serve as the patterns for the creation of the domain of existences. This relation of the patterns with the patterned guarantees the correspondence of the objects to the concepts.

Although Leibniz and Hume hold exactly opposite theories, they agree in assuming that concepts and objects are related in their origin, or rather have a common origin. If they had no such genetic relation, it would be a plain miracle that concepts turn out to correspond to objects because there is no more reason to expect a concept to fit to an object than to expect a polar bear to fit into a rabbit's skin.

If Kant had accepted either Leibniz' or Hume's theory of the genetic relation of ideas and objects, he would never have encountered the problem of fitting objects to concepts. But he rejects both theories and maintains that pure concepts and objects of senses are of entirely different origins. This novelty in his genetic theory of concepts and objects creates the problem of transcendental schematism. So he was compelled to seek a new way to account for the relation of concepts and objects. In his 1772 letter to Marcus Herz (which has been heralded as the "Birth of Critical Philosophy"), Kant explains that this epistemological inquiry constitutes the program for a *Critique of Pure Reason*. Since this letter beautifully delineates the historical background for Kant's position, let us quote from it at some length:

> After your departure from Koenigsberg, in the intervals between business and the relaxation which I so urgently need, I looked once again over the outline of those trains of thought which you and I had discussed together; I tried to fit it into all philosophical and other knowledge and to realize its extent and limits. . . . I drew up a sketch for a work which might have some such title as 'Limits

of Sensuousness and of Reason.' I conceived two divisions, one theoretical, one practical. . . .

As I explored the theoretical division in its entire range, I noticed that something essential was lacking. Like others, I had overlooked this something in my extended metaphysical researches, and yet it constitutes the key to the whole secret of metaphysics.

I asked myself: what is the relation between our images or representations [*Vorstellung*] and the objects? Suppose our images are nothing but the manner in which our subject is affected by the objects, it is easily understood that they should correspond [*gemäss seien*] to the objects. Thus the fact that our sensuous images have a definite and valid reference to external objects is comprehensible. . . . On the other hand, if the objects were themselves produced by our images, in the same manner as the divine thoughts are conceived as being archetypes of the real things, then again the conformity between images and objects could be understood. But—leaving moral ends out of account—our intellect neither produces an object through its images nor does the object produce its own reproduction in the intellect. Hence the pure concepts of intellect cannot be abstracted from the data of senses. They have their sources in the nature of the soul. But neither are they there produced by the objects nor do they themselves produce the objects as would a divine mind.

In the Dissertation [no. 22] I was content to explain the nature of these intellectual representations in a purely negative manner as not being modifications of the soul produced by the objects. I had said that the sensuous images represent things as they appear and the intellectual concepts represent things as they are. But how then are these things ·given to us if not by the manner in which they affect us? On the other hand, if such intellectual representations are entirely due to our inner activity, whence then comes the agreement they are supposed to have with objects which are not their products, if this agreement is not assisted by experience? In mathematics this is quite all right because our objects are merely quantities and we can generate quantities by taking a unit a number of times. But when it comes to qualities, how my intellect should form quite by itself conceptions with which the things faithfully agree—this is a question which shows that we are still in utter obscurity as regards our own mental faculties.

Without going here into particulars, I can say that I have achieved the main point of my intentions and that I am now able to write a *Critique of Pure Reason.*[6]

Kant cannot accept the Humean theory of concepts because he is convinced the pure concepts cannot be abstracted from impressions. Neither can he accept the Leibnizian theory because he is convinced that the theory seeks to portray not the human but the divine mind. He feels compelled to maintain the genetic independence between pure concepts and sense objects. To account for the conformity between these genetically independent entities has become "the key to the whole secret of metaphysics." Given Kant's premises on the genetic relation between concepts and objects, the problem of the transcendental schematism is not only a sound but an inevitable problem. But his solution of this problem also requires some explanation because, as we saw, he has offered two kinds of schemata for the solution of one problem.

Why does Kant produce two sets of transcendental schemata for the mediation between pure concepts and appearances?

Let me propose the hypothesis that the two sets of transcendental schemata reflect two views Kant entertained on the nature of pure concepts *before schematization.* We have seen that Kant regarded the pure concepts of understanding as the concepts of the highest generality. Although he never wavered on this characterization of the unschematized categories, he appears to have had two different views on their functions. I will call these two views formal function theory and material function theory. In formal function theory, pure concepts are assumed to be mere formal concepts which can, before schematization, play only formal and not material functions. In the material function theory, pure concepts are assumed to be material concepts which can play material functions even before schematization.*

Kant expresses the formal function theory when he insists that the pure concepts can perform only logical or formal functions. (A 239 = B 298; A 245) Although pure concepts are generic, Kant appears to think, they are not material concepts, under which objects can be subsumed. That is to say, pure concepts are a special class of class-concepts which cannot function as material concepts. Such a special class of generic concepts indeed appears to be an anomaly, but Kant seems to have concluded that the pure concepts are so general and so empty of content as to retain only their formal features. That is, they are just formal concepts.

*In addition to the formal and the material function theories, Kant also entertained the double function theory, namely, that the pure concepts can at once have both the formal and the material functions. (Cf. A 79 = B 105) As we have seen in Chapter 2, this double function theory is the central premise for the Metaphysical Deduction. Kant may have reached this hybrid position either as a compromise between the formal and the material function theories or in his transition from the latter to the former. This point will become much more intelligible when we come to Chapters 7 and 8. We will not consider the implication of the double function theory for the problem of transcendental schematism in this chapter, because the double function theory presents for schematism the same kind of problems as the material function theory.

Kant expresses the material function theory when he says that the pure concepts are the concepts of an object in general. By this he means that they are the ultimate material concepts through which any object can be thought. He says, "The categories . . . think objects in general, without regard to the special mode (the sensibility) in which they may be given." (A 254 = B 309) He apparently believes that the pure concepts can play material functions. When he conceives the pure concepts as the most universal material concepts, he says that they have "transcendental meanings." (A 248 = B 305) By this expression, he appears to mean that the connotations of the categories are not bound by a special mode of sensibility. To put it another way, their connotations transcend any particular world and are valid in all possible worlds.

The pure concepts are regarded as material concepts in the material function theory and as formal concepts in the formal function theory.

We have seen that the question of transcendental schematism is the question of how the pure concepts can function as material concepts for the cognition of the phenomenal world. This question should present two different problems depending on whether the pure concepts are ab initio conceived as material concepts or not. If they are not, they have first to be converted into material concepts. The transcendental concept-schemata are precisely the material concepts that are produced by this conversion. If they are already material concepts, they have only to be applied to the objects homogeneous with them. This application is the production of the transcendental image-scehmata.

Earlier in this chapter we noted the ambiguity in the scope of the problem of transcendental schematism. We were not then certain whether Kant assumes the heterogeneity of the pure concepts from empirical intuitions only or from both pure and empirical intuitions. Consequently we could not determine whether Kant's problem lay in the application of pure concepts to the one or to both. This ambiguity simply reveals that Kant has tried to formulate the problem of the transcendental schematism on two different sets of premises. On the formal function theory of the categories, the pure concepts present a problem in their application to pure as well as empirical intuitions because they are only formal concepts under which no objects can be subsumed. On the material function theory, the pure concepts present a problem in their application to empirical intuitions only, because they are material concepts that are heterogeneous only from empirical intuitions. Thus his two different conceptions of the categories have compelled him to formulate one problem in two different versions. These two formulations of the problem have called forth two theories of the transcendental schemata: transcendental image-schematism and transcendental concept-schematism.

Let us distinguish the two versions of the problem of transcendental schematism by designating them as the I and the C versions. The I (image-schematism) version of the problem presupposes the material function theory of the categories and the C (concept-schematism) version presupposes the formal function theory. The C version of the problem requires one extra step in its solution, the conversion of formal concepts into material concepts. Since the extra step in question involves an unusual notion of conceptual transformation, let us first determine what Kant understood this to mean.

He seems to have considered conceptual transformation as a process of giving pure concepts intensions that connote the properties and relations of sense objects. For example, the pure concept of substance before schematization is the logical concept of a subject in a proposition and has no intension to connote any properties or relations in the phenomenal world. The schematization gives this formal concept the intension of permanence, which connotes a temporal property. With this intension of permanence built into itself, the formal concept becomes a material concept under which the real subjects of the phenomenal world can be subsumed. Let us take one more example. The pure concept of causation before schematization is a formal concept of the logical relation between ground and consequence and has no intension to connote any phenomenal properties or relations. The schematization gives this formal concept the intension of necessary succession, which connotes a temporal relation. Thus the formal concept becomes the material concept under which the real relation of events can be subsumed. Pure concepts are only formal before concept-schematization because they have no intensions or connotations. Transcendental concept-schematization fits them out with some intensions or connotations and enables them to function as material concepts.

The extra step of conceptual transformation is unnecessary with the material function theory of the categories. Whereas the formal function theory conceives the pure concepts as absolutely devoid of any connotations, the material function theory conceives them as having absolutely universal connotations. There is thus no need to give them any concept-schemata.

In the last chapter we pointed out that Kant characterizes the transcendental concept-schemata as the time-determinants (or determinations). We have said that 'time-determinants' mean the concepts or universals which determine the nature of time. Now we can see how transcendental concept-schematization transforms pure concepts into time-determinants. Since this is the process of giving the pure concepts the intensions that connote the properties and relations of the temporal world, it is quite natural for the transcendental schemata to function as universals or rules that determine the nature of the temporal world (or time in the broad sense).

The mediation between pure concepts and appearances will take the following different processes in the two versions of transcendental schematism:

I VERSION	C VERSION
Pure (Material) Concepts	Pure (Formal) Concepts
subsumed under	*converted into*
Pure (Formal) Intuitions	Time-Determinants
given through	*subsumed under*
Empirical Intuitions	Pure (Formal) Intuitions
	given through
	Empirical Intuitions

In the last chapter we also distinguished between the narrow and broad senses of 'time-determinant'—i.e. as the determinant of the pure intuition of time and as the determinant of the entire inner sense. When Kant speaks within the framework of the C version, he seldom distinguishes between the last two steps, that is, the application of the time-determinants to pure intuitions and then to empirical intuitions through pure intuitions. (Cf. A 145 = B 184 f.) Thus the C version usually takes the simpler form, which can be called the C' version:

C' VERSION

Pure (Formal) Concepts
converted into
Time-Determinants
subsumed under
Inner Sense

The fusion of the last two steps in the C version into one gives the "time-determinant" its broad meaning; the transcendental concept-schemata function as the determinants of the entire phenomenal world.

The two theories regarding the function of transcendental schemata are reflected in Kant's two different ways of characterizing the nature of the schematism. He asserts the function of transcendental schematism sometimes to be the restriction of the categories to the phenomenal world and sometimes to be the realization of the categories. Sometimes he makes both assertions in one sentence: "But it is also evident that although the schemata of sensibility first realize the categories, they at the same time restrict them, that is, limit to conditions which lie outside the understanding, and are due to sensibility." (A 146 = B 185 f.) Kant assumes that restriction and realization are two features of one and the same function. But it can be shown that they are in fact two different functions, which can be carried out by transcendental schemata in two different contexts.

With the formal function theory of the categories, there can be no need to restrict their use to any particular world. Since they are supposed to be only formal concepts, they cannot be used for the cognition of any objects. The only need here is to realize (real reason) them or rather to transform them into material concepts. Even this transformation creates no serious danger or possibility of extending the use of the categories beyond the phenomenal world, because the transcendental concept-schematization endows the categories only with the intensions that exclusively refer to the properties and relations of the phenomenal world.

With the material function theory of the categories, there can be no need to realize them because they are already material concepts. The real need is to restrict their use to the phenomenal world. Since they are conceived as absolutely universal material concepts, they can be applied to any objects. The need for restriction does not reflect any defect in the categories but only the limitation of our sensibility. The application of the categories beyond the phenomenal world is illegitimate only because our sensible intuition can secure no objects for them except in the phenomenal world.

By the time the student of Kant has read the Schematism, he begins to learn to distinguish between the schematized and the unschematized categories. But this usual twofold distinction is not adequate to cope with the complex theoretical situation that may be called the double version theory of transcendental schematism. The double version theory requires a threefold distinction: the formal categories, the transcendent categories, and the phenomenal categories. By the formal categories, I mean the pure concepts which are conceived only as formal concepts and whose functions are formal only. The formal categories can be assumed to be embodied in the Table of Judgments if the table lists only the formal functions of judgment. By the transcendent categories, I mean the pure concepts that are conceived as absolutely universal material concepts and that are not bound by any special mode of sensibility. They are called transcendent because they are applicable to every possible world and because they can transcend any specified domain of objects. By the phenomenal categories, I mean the material concepts that are produced by schematizing the formal categories. Kant himself stresses the phenomenal feature of the schematized categories: "The schema is, properly, only the phenomenon, or sensible concept, of an object in agreement with the category. (Numerus *est quantitas phenomenon,* sensatio *realitas phenomenon,* constants et perdurabile rerum *substantia phenomenon,* aeternitas *necessitas phenomenon, etc.)"* (A 146 = B 186) The schematized categories are called the phenomenal categories because they are suitable only for the cognition of the phenomenal world.

In Part II of this book I shall try to show how fruitful is this threefold distinction of the categories. In the meantime let me present a simple case in which the threefold distinction turns out to be eminently useful. This case is the Table of Categories. It is often asked whether the Table of Categories lists the schematized or the unschematized categories. This question presupposes, however, that there is only one set of schematized categories and one set of the unschematized categories. But this presupposition is too simple. There are in fact two sets of the unschematized categories and only one set of the schematized categories. The phenomenal categories are schematized; the formal and the transcendent categories are unschematized. There are also two sets of material categories and only one set of formal categories. The transcendent and the phenomenal categories are both material concepts.

If one admits only the twofold distinction between the schematized and the unschematized categories instead of our threefold distinction, one is bound to identify the unschematized categories with the formal categories. Then the categories in the Table can be regarded neither as schematized nor as unschematized. Let me show why this is the case.

All the schematized categories have spatio-temporal connotations, but the categories in the Table do not have such connotations. For example, the concepts of extensive and intensive magnitudes contain intensions that connote the properties and relations of the spatio-temporal continuum. In contrast to this, the concepts of unity, plurality, and totality and the concepts of reality, negation, and limitation in the Table of Categories have no exclusively phenomenal connotations. These concepts can be applied to any domain of objects. For another example, the schematized categories of substance and causation are the concepts of the permanent substratum and of necessary succession. Since the concepts of permanence and succession are uniquely temporal, these categories are applicable only to the phenomenal world. In contrast to this, the counterparts of these schematized categories in the Table are called "inherence and subsistence *(substantia et accidens)*" and "causality and dependence *(cause and effect)*." These categories are not bound to the phenomenal world because they have no spatio-temporal connotations. They can be applied to any domain of objects; they are transcendent categories. So the categories in the Table cannot be identified with the schematized categories.

But neither can the categories in the Table be identified with the unschematized categories, if 'the unschematized categories' means the formal ones. The concept of inherence and subsistence is not merely the logical concept of subject and predicate; the concept of causality and dependence is not merely the logical concept of ground and consequence. The categories in the Table are too rich to be merely formal concepts. Thus they turn out to be neither the schematized nor the unschematized categories if one assumes a simple twofold distinction between one set of the schematized and another set of the unschematized categories. So the threefold distinction is essential.

With the threefold distinction of the categories, we can state more clearly the difference between the two versions of transcendental schematism. The I version (or image-schematism) uses only one set of categories, the transcendent set; the C version (or concept-schematism) uses two sets of categories, the formal and the phenomenal sets. The C version converts the formal into the phenomenal set, while the I version does not require this sort of conceptual transformation at all.

Let me make a few points to guard against possible misunderstanding about this double version theory of transcendental schematism. I do not maintain that Kant was clearly aware of the distinction between the I and the C versions. The double version theory is proposed only because it appears to produce the most intelligible interpretation of the available text; it requires no justification other than our simple need to make the most of the *Critique*.

Kant does not introduce the distinction between the two versions of the transcendental schematism simply because he never recognized that he did in fact conceive the schematism in two versions. What is even more troublesome than his failure of distinction, however, is his tendency to fuse the two versions into one. The most obvious example of this tendency is his proclamation that a transcendental schema is at once a rule (universal) and an image (particular). It is impossible in terms of his own logic for one thing to be a universal and a particular at the same time. This self-contradictory characterization of the schema simply reflects Kant's tangled reasoning.

The fusion of the two versions can produce a few hybrid versions because the two versions involve two sequences of steps, each of which presents the opportunity for crossing the two versions. In Part II of this book, we shall see some prominent examples of Kant's own hybrid versions of the transcendental schematism.

Now that we have delineated Kant's problem and his solution, we should be prepared to test his doctrine of mediation —that is, to test how effectively or validly the two types of transcendental schemata perform their function of mediation. We will discuss this topic later, since the doctrine of mediation is meant to resolve the problem of applying the pure concepts to appearances, and the application of concepts clearly belongs to the province of judgment, which is the subject of Part II.

We have been talking about the transformation or conversion of formal into material concepts, as though the process in question were natural and obvious. But it is neither. The process in question is, we have maintained, impossible: Formal concepts cannot be converted into material concepts.

But this idea of conversion should not be casually dismissed. It appears to reflect a pregnant notion, but one which is hidden in a dark corner of Kant's mind: the notion that all material concepts have to be formed. But we cannot fully elucidate the prodigious significance this notion has in the interpretation of the Transcendental Analytic until we have completed the exhaustive analysis presented in Part II of this volume. In the meantime we may note that the double version theory of transcendental schematism may turn out to have a most pervasive consequence in comprehending Kant's doctrine of judgment.

Part II

Transcendental Judgments

Chapter 5

The Conception of A Priori Judgments

The function of transcendental schemata is to produce a priori judgments. As a preliminary to the investigation of this function, we will delineate Kant's conception of a priori judgments.

How does Kant understand the nature of a priori judgments?

Kant opens the Introduction to the *Critique* with the distinction between a priori and a posteriori knowledge. He proceeds to give one negative and two positive criteria for a priori judgments. The positive criteria are said to be their necessity and universality and the negative criterion their independence from all experience. (A 1 f. and B 2 ff.) The negative criterion can be derived from the positive criteria—on the premise that experience can never give necessity and universality—but the positive ones cannot be derived from the negative ones. We shall therefore concentrate on the two positive criteria.

Kant says that necessity and universality are coordinate criteria and are equivalent to each other. (B 4) This assertion reflects his assumption that every a priori judgment takes the form of a universal proposition that is necessarily true, or rather the form of a universally quantified propositional function that cannot be falsified. This assumption implies that a priori judgments can take neither the form of singular propositions nor that of particular propositions, since universality cannot be predicated of them.

In fact most a priori judgments do take the form of universal propositions. Mathematical judgments, which are in Kant's view a priori judgments par excellence, are usually propositional functions bound by the universal quantifier. For example, the geometrical axiom, "The straight line between two points is the shortest distance," is a universally quantified propositional function, although the axiom is stated in the form of singular proposition. A more accurate expression of the axiom would read, "For every pair of two points, there is only one straight line and that straight line is shorter than any other line connecting the two points." This amplified expression of the axiom clearly shows its universal form.

Although most a priori judgments take the form of a universal proposition, it is difficult to maintain that every a priori judgment takes that form. Let us take the assertion "Space is infinite." Undoubtedly Kant would regard this assertion as an a priori judgment; but it is not a universal proposition. The judgment in question must be a singular proposition because there is said to be only one space. There are also some a priori judgments which take the form of particular propositions. These are such mathematical judgments as "Some triangles are right-angled," "Some natural numbers are even numbers," or "Some natural numbers are greater than 5 + 7." Since universality cannot be predicated of some a priori judgments, it cannot be claimed as a universal criterion of a priori judgments.

Kant is not completely oblivious to those a priori judgments which do not take the form of universal propositions. There are occasions when he recognizes singular a priori judgments. For example, he regards arithmetical assertions such as "7 + 5 = 12" as a priori singular propositions. (A 164 = B 205) It is quite interesting to note that Kant nevertheless refuses to give arithmetical judgments the title of *axioms* on the ground that they are not universal but singular propositions. (A 165 = B 205) For the same reason he can find no a priori principles for arithmetic, the science of *quantitas*. (A 164 f. = B 204 f.) He states all his a priori principles of understanding in the form of universal propositions except for the Postulates of Empirical Thought, which are admitted to be not really a priori synthetic judgments but only "explanations" of modal concepts. All these points reflect Kant's belief that every significant a prior judgment is expressed in the form of a universally quantified propositional function.

Some may try to uphold universality as a universal criterion of a priori knowledge on the ground that singular and particular propositions can be translated into universal propositions. For example, the singular proposition "Space is infinite" can be translated into the universal proposition "(x) (if x is space, then x is infinite)." Since "$(\exists x)\ \varphi x$" is equivalent to "$\sim(x)\sim\varphi x$," the particular proposition "Some natural numbers are even numbers," can be translated into the negative universal proposition: "It is not the case that no natural numbers are even numbers." If every a priori judgment can be translated into the form of universal proposition, universality can be redeemed as a universal criterion of a priori knowledge.

But the proposed redemption would have a heavy price. In the translation of an a priori singular proposition into a universal one, the universal quantifier would become a vacuous sign and the universality of the new a priori proposition would become a useless criterion of its apriority. That is, the universality that is created by the translation would not help us at all in recognizing the judgment as a priori. To put it another way, we can know that "(x) (if x is space, then x is infinite)" is an a priori truth only if we know that "Space is infinite" is an a priori truth. A similar difficulty appears in the translation of particular a priori propositions into negative universal propositions. We can be sure of the unrestricted universality of these negative universal propositions only by knowing that the original particular propositions are a priori true. Thus the universality created by the fiat of translation can have no value in recognition and identification.

Although universality cannot be retained as a universal criterion of all a priori judgments, necessity may be still retained as such. Necessity can be predicated of any a priori judgment regardless of the form. Universality, to the contrary, can at best be considered as a criterion of that segment of a priori knowledge that is expressed in the form of universal propositions, but this only reflects the accidental circumstance that some a priori judgments take the form of universal propositions. We cannot know that a universal proposition has unrestricted universality without knowing that the proposition has the necessity of a priori truth; we can recognize the unrestricted universality of an a priori judgment only as a manifestation of its absolutely necessary truth. If so, universality is not an effective criterion even when it is accepted as a criterion of one species of a priori knowledge. Hence it would be better to reject Kant's claim that necessity and universality are two equivalent criteria of a priori knowledge and conclude that necessity is the only positive universal criterion of a priori judgments.

We have now to determine whether necessity is the defining or distinguishing property of a priori judgments. Depending on this decision, the same criterion of necessity may reflect two different concepts of a priori judgments.

Kant appears to take necessity as the defining property of a priori judgments when he says, "All analytical judgments depend wholly on the law of contradiction, and are in their nature *a priori* cognitions, whether the concepts that supply them with matter be empirical or not." *(Prolegomena* §2, b) When he takes necessity as the defining property of a priori judgments, he is maintaining in effect that the definition of an a priori judgment cannot be affected by any other feature of that judgment. Especially, it cannot be affected by the nature of its constituents, e.g. whether the constituent concepts are a priori or a posteriori. The apriority of an a priori judgment thus resides solely in its necessity.

If necessity is taken as the sole defining property of a priori judgments, the definition of a priori judgment is purely *logical*. But Kant does not always keep to this purely logical definition.

He reveals a different conception of a priori judgment in the following passage:

> Now we find, what is especially noteworthy, that even into our experiences there enter modes of knowledge which must have their origin *a priori,* and which perhaps serve only to give coherence to our sense-representations. For if we eliminate from our experience everything which belongs to the senses, there still remain certain original concepts and certain judgments derived from them, which must have arisen completely *a priori,* independently of experience, inasmuch as they enable us to say, in regard to the objects which appear to the senses, more than mere experience would teach—giving to assertions true universality and strict necessity, such as mere empirical knowledge cannot supply. (A 2)

Kant is here giving a genetic definition of a priori judgment: 'a priori judgment' means the judgment which has "arisen completely *a priori."* Such judgments are called a priori because they are derived not from the a posteriori but from the a priori sources. This genetic definition can be translated into a structural definition. Since a judgment is a concatenation of concepts for making an assertion about an object, a judgment which has risen solely from a priori sources must consist of only a priori concepts and refer only to the objects of a priori intuitions. We can express the same point in terms of subsumption: A priori judgment is the subsumption of a priori intuitions under a priori concepts.

In this genetic or structural definition, necessity need not even be mentioned, since it is no longer a defining property of a priori judgments. In terms of the Aristotelian distinction of *essence* and *property ("Essence* is the defining characteristics and the *property* flows from *essence"),* necessity is not the essence of a priori judgment but its property. The necessary truth of an a priori judgment is a consequence of its a priori origin or structure ("giving to assertions true universality and strict necessity"). This view is consonant with Kant's unshakable conviction that judgments always derive their contingency from their a posteriori sources and their necessity from their a priori sources.

The genetic definition of a priori judgment clearly reflects Kant's axiomatic view of a priori knowledge. By the latter is meant the view that a mathematical axiom is the supreme model of all a priori judgments. It is Kant's well-known theory that mathematical axioms have necessary truth because they contain no a posteriori elements of contingency, but rather consist solely of a priori elements of certainty. According to this theory, all mathematical judgments can be defined by their structural elements and their necessity can be explained by their structure. In this axiomatic view of a priori knowledge, all a priori judgments are either the primitive judgments whose necessity can be certified by their a priori structure or the derivative judgments that can be deduced from the primitive ones.

Kant's axiomatic view of the a priori principles of understanding is revealed in his assertion that "Transcendental logic ... has lying before it a manifold of *a priori* sensibility, presented by transcendental aesthetic, as material for the concepts of pure understanding." (A 76 f. = B 102) Here he is characterizing transcendental logic as the logic of the primitive a priori judgments that arise from the application of the pure concepts of understanding to pure intuitions. In the axiomatic view it is the first important step to establish that there are pure intuitions and pure concepts. Kant assumes that his Transcendental Aesthetic proves the existence of pure intuitions and that his Metaphysical Deduction establishes the a priori origin of the categories. (Cf. B 159) This assumption is essential for maintaining the genetic definition of a priori judgments and substantiating the axiomatic view of a priori truths.

Let us not overlook one important difference between

mathematical axioms and a priori principles of understanding, even when both of them are conceived as axioms: While the a priori concepts that constitute mathematical axioms are derived from pure intuitions, those that constitute a priori principles of understanding have their origin in pure understanding. But this difference has no material significance in the axiomatic view. It does not matter whether the constitutive elements of a priori judgments are derived from pure intuitions or pure understanding: The only essential point is that all those elements should be of a priori origin.

In the axiomatic view, the necessity of a priori judgments can be called axiomatic necessity, that is, the necessity of a proposition which is self-evident solely by virtue of the structure or elements of that proposition alone. According to Kant's theory of mathematics, the necessity of mathematical axioms can be demonstrated in precisely this way. Axiomatic necessity can be called the inner (or inherent) necessity of axioms because it depends on nothing outside the axioms. Kant expresses this when he asserts that a priori judgments, which "possess the character of inner necessity, must in themselves, independently of experience, be clear and distinct." (A 2) The truth of an a priori proposition is guaranteed by its inner (or inherent) necessity, just as the truth of Spinoza's adequate idea is assured by its own intrinsic properties.[1]

Besides the axiomatic view, Kant appears to have entertained one more conception of a priori judgments. In the second edition of the *Critique* Kant deletes the passage (A 2) from which we have extracted his axiomatic view. In rewriting that passage he introduces a new distinction: "*A priori* modes of knowledge are entitled pure when there is no admixture of anything empirical. Thus, for instance, the proposition, 'every alteration has its cause,' while an *a priori* proposition, is not a pure proposition, because alteration is a concept which can be derived only from experience." (B 3) He thus recognizes two kinds of a priori judgment. Whereas he gives no examples of a priori judgment in the deleted passage of the first edition, he gives two kinds of examples in the rewritten version: mathematical propositions and the causal principle. (A 4) Mathematical propositions are probably meant to be the examples of pure a priori judgment and the causal principle to be that of impure a priori judgment.

Of these two kinds of a priori judgment, only the pure one can come under the genetic definition of a priori judgment. From the genetic point of view, the impure a priori judgment has as much right to be labeled a posteriori as a priori because it consists of both the a priori and the a posteriori elements. But if Kant wants to call both the pure and the impure judgments a priori, he has to abandon his original genetic definition. Of course, he can so revise his genetic definition as to cover the impure a priori judgments. In the Introduction to the second edition, indeed he does adopt a revised genetic definition: A judgment is a priori if it contains an a priori concept although some of its elements may be a posteriori. (B 5)

Nevertheless the revised genetic definition of a priori judgments has one serious defect. According to this definition, most empirical judgments should be regarded as a priori because most of them contain some a priori concepts. Consider the judgment "The snowstorm was the cause of this accident." This plainly empirical judgment would have to be called a priori because it contains the a priori concept of causation. But this procedure would obliterate the distinction between a priori and a posteriori (empirical) judgments. In fact this obliteration takes place in the *Prolegomena,* where judgments of experience are distinguished from judgments of perception. Kant gives judgments of experience all the characteristics of a priori judgments, i.e. universality and necessity. (Cf. *Prolegomena* §§ 19, 20) This is acceptable under the revised genetic definition, for then every judgment of experience is an a priori judgment because it contains an a priori concept.

Most judgments of experience are not only obviously empirical but also singular judgments. Since universality cannot be predicated on the singular judgments of experience, Kant reformulates the meaning of 'universality' in such a way that it can be predicated on all judgments of experience regardless of their forms. The 'universality' of a judgment now means the possibility that the judgment can be an object of a universal agreement. The meaning of this modal term has therefore been shifted from the modality of a propositional truth to that of a propositional agreement. Kant indicates that the universality of judgments of experience is rooted in their necessity, that is, their necessary truth makes it possible for them to attain universal agreements. *(Prolegomena* §§ 18, 19, 20) Thus necessity again turns out to be the ultimate criterion of a priori judgments in the revised genetic definition of a priori knowledge.

But if Kant were asked why the impure a priori judgments or judgments of experience have necessity, he could no longer give the genetic explanation because they contain a posteriori elements of contingency as well as a priori elements of certainty. Since he can no longer maintain the axiomatic view of necessity within the enlarged genetic definition of a priori judgment, he needs to find a new way to explain the necessity of a priori knowledge. Immediately after enlarging the definition of a priori judgment in the second edition, Kant makes the following observation:

> Now it is easy to show that there actually are in human knowledge judgments which are necessary and in the strictest sense universal, and which are therefore pure *a priori* judgments. If an example from the sciences be desired, we have only to look to any of the propositions of mathematics; if we seek an example from the understanding in its quite ordinary employment, the proposition, 'every alteration must have a cause,' will serve our purpose. In the latter case, indeed, the very concept of

a cause so manifestly contains the concept of a necessity of connection with an effect and of the strict universality of the rule, that the concept would be altogether lost if we attempt to derive it, as Hume has done, from a repeated association of that which happens with that which precedes, and from a custom of connecting representations, a custom originating in this repeated association, and constituting therefore a merely subjective necessity. Even without appealing to such examples, it is possible to show that pure *a priori* principles are indispensable for the possibility of experience, and so to prove their existence *a priori*. (B 4 f.)

Kant does not feel obliged to account for the necessity of mathematical judgments, probably because their necessity can still be explained within the framework of the axiomatic view. But he feels the obligation to explain the necessity of the causal principle, which cannot have axiomatic necessity. For this, he tries out two different methods. The first of these is the attempt to explain the necessity of the causal principle in terms of the a priori origin of the causal concept. But this method is the legacy of the axiomatic view which can give no adequate account of the necessity of those a priori judgments that contain empirical elements. Since Kant feels the inadequacy of the first method, he appears to try out the second method, that is, the attempt to explain the necessity of a priori judgments by showing their necessity for the possibility of experience.

But this second method involves an equivocation. The necessity of the a priori principles for the possibility of experience, however, does not have the same meaning as the modal necessity of propositions. The latter means the necessary truth of propositions, while the former refers to their functional necessity, i.e. their indispensability for certain purposes. In a few cases Kant is careful enough to use two different terms to maintain the distinction between the two kinds of necessity: *Notwendichkeit* for the modal necessity and *Unentbehrlichkeit* for the functional necessity. (B 5) But in most cases he uses *Notwendichkeit* for both the modal and the functional necessity. (Cf. A 93 f. = B 126) Thus 'necessity' becomes an equivocal term whose abuse creates much confusion. For example, from the premise that the pure concepts of understanding are necessary (functional necessity) for experience, Kant's readers are often led to conclude that pure concepts produce necessary (modal necessity) propositions for experience. This erroneous inference is supported by the subreption of 'modal necessity' for 'functional necessity.' That aesthetical categories are necessary for aesthetic experience does not guarantee that those categories will produce necessary propositions for aesthetic experience.

Since Kant nevertheless wants to argue for the necessary truth of the causal principle, it is requisite for him to use modal necessity as well as functional necessity in his second method. His assertion that a priori principles are indispensable for the possibility of experience should be taken as a shortened version of the assertion that the *necessary truths* of a priori principles are indispensable for the possibility of experience. The necessity of a priori judgments that can be proved by their functions cannot be axiomatic necessity, for the necessity in question must be only instrumental or functional. Whereas axiomatic necessity is internal to the proposition, the functional or instrumental necessity is external to it. The latter can be also called postulational necessity. Whereas axiomatic necessity is inherent in the structure of a proposition, postulational necessity is established by its function.

Along with the axiomatic view, Kant has thus entertained the postulational or functional view of a priori judgment— the view that primitive a priori judgments are postulates for the possibility of experience. While the genetic view rests on the genetic or structural definition of a priori judgment, the postulational view rests on the functional or instrumental definition of the same judgment.

Kant should have felt uneasy about the postulational view. For postulates are not absolutely indispensable; a set of postulates can be always replaced by another set. Being firmly convinced of the uniqueness of his a priori principles and their absolute indispensability, he would not admit that they could be replaced by another set of postulates. But this is a groundless conviction because it is logically impossible to prove the uniqueness of any postulate.

We have tried to articulate Kant's two conceptions of a priori judgments.* We shall now try to see how Kant implements these two conceptions.

The axiomatic view of a priori judgments emerges prominently in the Transcendental Deduction of the first edition. In the A Deduction Kant divides the process of cognition into three stages: the synthesis of apprehension, the synthesis of imagination, and the synthesis of apperception. (A 98 ff.) In each of these three stages he distinguishes the a priori from the a posteriori aspect: There are transcendental (a priori) syntheses of apprehension, imagination, and apperception in parallel with the corresponding empirical (a posteriori) syntheses. Kant has been criticized for this duplication of the three cognitive faculties because this appears only to complicate his arguments in the Transcendental Deduction. But he

---

*I have adopted the two expressions 'the axiomatic view' and 'the postulational view' from C. I. Lewis.[2] Similar to the distinction between these two views is Lewis White Beck's distinction between two senses of 'the analytic proposition'—or rather what he designates as 'analytic$_1$' and 'analytic$_2$': "(1) by inspection of the sentence itself, if it is logically or linguistically true; and (2) by investigation of its role in an organized body of experience we can acknowledge."[3] While this is similar to the distinction made by Lewis, there is some technical difference between the two sets of distinctions. I should also point out that Beck makes his distinction more or less independently and that he does not attribute it to Kant.

seems to have one important purpose in that duplication—namely, to account for our knowledge of objects.

Kant's 'experience' in its technical sense means the knowledge of objects, or the objective knowledge of phenomena. To account for the possibility of experience is to explain how we come to have objective knowledge of appearances. Although our experience consists of combinations (syntheses) of representations, Kant says, not every combination of representations establishes an objective connection of phenomena. He thus has to find a way to distinguish objective from subjective combinations. He observes that this distinction cannot be made by comparing representations with objects, because objects are formed by the objective combination of representations. (A 104)

Kant now presents necessity as the only criterion for the distinction in question, that is, the objective combination of representations is necessary while their subjective combination is "haphazard and arbitrary." (A 104) Since necessity is the only mark of objective combinations, to account for the possibility of experience is to account for the possibility of the necessary combinations of representations, and this is to explain the necessity of objective representations.

Now Kant says, "All necessity, without exception, is grounded in a transcendental condition." (A 106) Here again he is affirming his conviction that necessity is provided never by a posteriori but always by a priori sources. He has thus laid the ground for making use of his distinction between the a priori and the a posteriori elements in the threefold synthesis. He can now give the genetic account of the necessity of objective representations:

> There are three subjective sources of knowledge upon which rests the possibility of experience in general and of knowledge of its objects—*sense, imagination,* and *apperception.* Each of these can be viewed as empirical,

namely, in its application to given appearances. But all of them are likewise *a priori* elements or foundations, which make this empirical employment itself possible. (A 115)

Kant is here claiming the a priori elements as the foundation of necessity, which makes possible the objective combination of empirical representations. The empirical elements of the three faculties alone can produce only haphazard and accidental representations and never necessary ones; only their transcendental elements can provide the necessary nexus for the objective combination of empirical elements. Since Kant is here using 'transcendental' in the same genetic sense as 'a priori' ('the transcendental origin' means the same as 'the a priori origin'), he is presenting a genetic account for the necessity of objective combinations.

Kant further elaborates on the same genetic account from the standpoint of transcendental apperception in the following passage:

This synthetic unity [of the pure apperception] presupposes or includes a synthesis, and if the former is to be *a priori* necessary, the synthesis must also be *a priori*. The transcendental unity of apperception thus relates to the pure synthesis of imagination, as an *a priori* condition of the possibility of all combination of the manifold in one knowledge. But only the *productive* synthesis of the imagination can take place *a priori;* the reproductive rests upon empirical conditions. Thus the principle of the necessary unity of pure (productive) synthesis of imagination, prior to apperception, is the ground of the possibility of all knowledge, especially of experience. (A 118)

Kant is here trying to determine the necessary conditions for the unity of transcendental apperception. Since the latter is the necessary unity of representations in our consciousness, its necessary conditions are none other than the conditions requisite for the possibility of experience.

Kant says that transcendental apperception can have a necessary unity only if it "relates to the pure synthesis of imagination." This assertion presupposes the three stages of cognition that Kant has distinguished in the Subjective Deduction. (A 98 ff.) Sense is the faculty that apprehends or receives representations; imagination is the faculty that combines these representations; apperception is the faculty that recognizes the combined representations in concepts. Apperception, whose recognition is the final stage of experience, operates on the materials that have been received and molded by sense and imagination. Kant now contends that our conscious representations in apperception can have a necessary unity (objectivity) only if the synthesis of imagination is a priori, that is, only if the materials provided by imagination are of a priori origin. The necessary unity of apperception cannot be established on the basis of reproductive imagination, that is, on the empirical elements provided by reproductive imagination. The necessary unity of apperception can only be grounded in the a priori elements of cognition.

Since the productive imagination presents only pure intuitions and since transcendental apperception has only pure concepts, the operation of the latter on the former should be the recognition of pure intuitions in pure concepts. Since this operation involves only a priori elements, Kant maintains, it should produce the necessary unity of apperception. If we use the technical term 'subsumption,' we can say that the subsumption of pure intuitions under pure concepts produces the necessary unity of apperception.

The recognition of pure intuitions in pure concepts or the subsumption of pure intuitions under pure concepts should produce judgments which contain no a posteriori elements at all. This is the production of a priori judgment which fits the genetic definition and which must have axiomatic necessity.

So the necessity which forms the necessary unity of transcendental apperception is the axiomatic necessity of pure a priori judgments. This is why the A Deduction can be regarded as an implementation of the axiomatic view of a priori knowledge.

Let us see how the axiomatic necessity of transcendental apperception can provide the necessity in the combination of empirical intuitions. This is the complicated doctrine of *affinity*. (Cf. A 113; 122) According to this doctrine, the production of empirical knowledge (the objective combination of empirical representations) takes two steps. The pure concepts are applied first to pure intuitions and then to empirical intuitions insofar as the latter are given through the former. Expressed in terms of subsumption, pure intuitions are first subsumed under pure concepts and then empirical intuitions are subsumed under the same concepts insofar as empirical intuitions are given through pure intuitions. Pure intuitions serve as mediators in the application of pure concepts to empirical intuitions. This is what Kant called the mediational function of transcendental imagination. We can see that this function is provided by the transcendental image-schemata. Thus the doctrine of transcendental image-schemata or rather the I version of the schematism embodies the axiomatic conception of a priori judgments.

Let us have one example of the axiomatic view in the Axioms of Intuition. (A 162 ff. = B 202 ff.) In this a priori principle, Kant tries to prove that all empirical intuitions are extensive magnitudes. His proof requires two steps: He tries to establish first that all pure intuitions are extensive magnitudes; and then that empirical intuitions are also extensive magnitudes, insofar as the latter are given through the former. These two steps can be restated in terms of subsumption: All empirical intuitions can be subsumed under the concept of extensive magnitude because they are always given through the pure intuitions of space and time, which can be subsumed under the concept of extensive magnitude. The first of these two steps is none other than the production of transcendental image-schemata. We have seen in Chapter 3 that Kant designates space as the schema of magnitude. (Cf. A 142 = B 182) To be more exact, as we have seen, he should have said that space and time are the image-schemata of the concept of extensive magnitude. As transcendental image-schemata, space and time are the particulars representing the concept of extensive magnitude. That is to say, space and time are subsumed under the concept of extensive magnitude, or the concept of extensive magnitude is applied to space and time. This first step prepares the ground for the second: the application of the concept of extensive magnitude to empirical intuitions or the subsumption of the latter under the former. Thus the transcendental imagination and its image-schemata perform the function of mediation in the application of the categories to appearances.

The axiomatic view requires the double application of the categories: the direct application to pure intuitions and the indirect application to empirical intuitions. The direct application produces the pure a priori judgment (e.g. "All pure intuitions are extensive magnitudes") which has axiomatic necessity because it involves no a posteriori elements. The indirect application produces the impure a priori judgment (e.g. "All empirical intuitions are extensive magnitudes") which can have no axiomatic necessity because it introduces a posteriori elements. Although the impure a priori judgment can have no axiomatic necessity in its own right, it can have the necessity which is derived from the axiomatic necessity of the pure a priori judgment. Thus empirical intuitions come to be combined into a necessary nexus, which is established by the combination of pure intuitions.

The a priori judgments produced by the first application of categories may be called the primitive a priori judgments; those produced by their second application may be called the derivative a priori judgments. The former have original, and the latter derivative, necessity.

It is in the *Prolegomena* that Kant most clearly implements his postulational or functional view of a priori knowledge. There he distinguishes judgments of experience from judgments of perception. *(Prolegomena* § 18) While the judgment of perception is a mere subjective (accidental) association of sense impressions, the judgment of experience is an objectively valid (necessary) combination of those impressions. The judgment of perception is arbitrary and subjective because it is "only logical connection of perceptions in a thinking subject," but the judgment of experience is necessary and objective because it is the combination of perceptions in a pure concept. *(Prolegomena* § 18) The difference between the two types of judgment lies in the nature of the combinators. The categories are the combinators for judgments of experience; the "logical connections" are the combinators for judgments of perception.

The distinction between these two types of judgment has been subject to various criticisms. The main target of these criticisms has been the assertion that judgments of perception require no categories—a claim criticized because it seems to contradict one of Kant's major tenets, namely, that the categories are the ultimate forms of all thought. Insofar as judgments of perception are judgments, Kant's critics argue, they must involve the categories that are said to be the forms of judgment. They point out that Kant's own examples of the judgment of perception do involve the forms of judgment and that the "logical connections" of these judgments cannot be anything but the forms of judgment.[4] Concurring in the implausibility of the distinction between the two types of judgment, Paton says that the distinction "may be dismissed as an afterthought and not a very happy one."[5]

The foregoing is one of the typical misunderstandings that Kant invites through his careless use of technical terms. Criticism could have been forestalled if he had distinguished between the formal and material categories. The formal categories are the forms of judgment that are required by any judgment. By 'logical connections' Kant means nothing more than the forms of judgment. We have often seen that he characterizes the formal categories as logical functions. In the *Prolegomena* in fact he is clearly using 'logical connection' as an equivalent expression for 'logical function,' for he believes that the formal categories play the logical role of connective function. There can be nothing objectionable in Kant's distinction between the two types of judgment if it is taken to mean that judgments of experience require material as well as formal categories while judgments of perception involve only the latter.

The distinction between formal and material categories does not clear up all the ambiguity because there are two sets of material categories, as we pointed out in the preceding chapter: transcendent and phenomenal categories. The Table of Categories given in the *Prolegomena* is indistinguishable from the Table of Categories in the Metaphysical Deduction and has all the appearances of being a table of transcendent categories except in one respect. This exception is the listing of *measure, magnitude,* and *whole* in parentheses after the three pure concepts of quantity. *(Prolegomena* § 21)

These parenthetically listed concepts appear to have some resemblance to the phenomenal (schematized) categories. Our suspicion is reinforced when we look at the example Kant gives for judgments of perception: "The room is warm," "Sugar is sweet," "Wormwood is bitter," and "When the sun shines on the stone, it grows warm." *(Prolegomena* § 20) These judgments involve not only some forms of judgment but also some transcendent categories such as the concepts of unity and reality. So it would seem that the transcendent categories do not separate judgments of experience from judgments of perception. Our suspicion is finally confirmed by Kant's own acknowledgment that the phenomenal categories of intensive and extensive magnitudes rather than the six transcendent categories of quality and quantity are required for the transformation of judgments of perception into judgments of experience. *(Prolegomena* § 24)

When Kant talks of the production of judgments of experience, he never refers to the necessity of mediation between the categories and empirical intuitions. He apparently assumes that the categories are as readily applicable to empirical intuitions as to pure intuitions. Since the distinction between pure and empirical intuitions is never required in his doctrine of judgments of experience, the entire inner sense should be regarded as the object for the categorial subsumption. Thus the postulational view embodies the C version of the schematism, or rather the transcendental concept-schematism. If there is any mediatory function in the C version, it should be the mediation of the transcendental concept-schemata between the formal categories and the objects of inner sense. In the *Prolegomena,* Kant understands this mediation as the transformation of judgments of perception into judgments of experience. The connective functions of the formal categories ("logical connections"), which can provide only subjective connections, are transformed into the connective functions of the phenomenal categories, which can establish objective connections.

Since judgments of experience do not derive axiomatic necessity from pure a priori judgments, their alleged necessity (objectivity) cannot be explained in the axiomatic framework. Kant tries to give a postulational account of their necessity in the following passage:

> We must consequently analyze experience in general in order to see what is contained in this product of the senses and of the understanding, and how the judgment of experience itself is possible. The foundation is the intuition of which I become conscious, that is, perception *(perceptio),* which pertains merely to the senses. But in the next place, there is judging (which belongs only to the understanding). But this judging may be twofold:

first, I may compare perceptions and connect them in a consciousness of my particular state; or secondly, I may connect them in consciousness in general. The former is merely a judgment of perception, and hence is of subjective validity only; it is merely a connection of perceptions in my mental state, without reference to the object. . . .

Quite another judgment therefore is required before perception can become experience. The given intuition must be subsumed under a concept which determines the form of judging in general relatively to the intuition, connects empirical consciousness of intuition in consciousness in general, and thereby procures universal validity for empirical judgments. A concept of this nature is a pure *a priori* concept of the understanding. . . .

If all our synthetical judgments are analyzed so far as they are objectively valid, it will be found that they never consist of mere intuitions connected only . . . by comparison into a judgment; but that they would be impossible were not a pure concept of the understanding superadded to the concepts abstracted from intuition. *(Prolegomena* § 20)

Kant is here using an analytical method of justification. He starts out with an established set of judgments of experience and then proceeds to analyze them to find out what is the source of their necessity and universality.

We may better understand Kant's analytical method by comparing it with his synthetical method. In the Introduction to the *Prolegomena,* he says that the *Prolegomena* is "based on an *analytical* method, while the *Critique* itself had to be executed in the *synthetical* style." By *Critique,* he is of course referring to its first edition. Kant's statement is highly misleading because the *Critique* contains both methods. As we will see in the next three chapters, Kant's frequent failure to keep the two methods separate produces incoherence and inelegance in his expositions.

It is in the Transcendental Deduction of the first edition nevertheless that Kant chiefly relies on a synthetical method of justification: He does not presuppose but tries to prove the objective validity of experience. He begins his proof with the construction of pure a priori judgments and tries to give a genetic demonstration of their axiomatic necessity. He concludes his proof by showing how empirical judgments can have necessity derived from the axiomatic necessity of a priori judgments.

The direction of argument in the synthetic method is the reverse of what it is in the analytic method. The analytic method resembles the method of searching a set of postulates for assumed conclusions, while the synthetic method resembles the method of deducing theorems from a set of axioms. The synthetic method can be called axiomatic, while the analytic method can be called postulational. While the synthetic method moves forward from the self-evident axioms to the deducible theorems, the analytic method moves backward from the assumed conclusions to their presupposed conditions. The one is the progressive method while the other is the regressive method. One is the method of deduction and the other the method of abduction.

The analytical method of the *Prolegomena* reflects Kant's postulational view of a priori knowledge. Let us take the case of succession. Kant holds that the subsumption of appearances under the category of causation is the requisite condition for distinguishing the objective from the subjective succession of appearances. *(Prolegomena* § 20) That is to say, the causal principle is the necessary postulate for determining the objective succession of appearances. When Kant takes the postulational view of a priori knowledge, he maintains that his a priori principles specify only what categories are necessary for what types of experience (judgments of experience). *(Pro-*

legomena §§ 24, 25, 26) He means to express the same point in saying that a priori principles are "simply rules for the objective employment" of the categories. (A 161 = B 200)

When Kant takes the axiomatic view of a priori knowledge, he asserts that a priori principles are not only true in themselves but "the source of all truth." (A 237 = B 296) That is to say, all empirical propositions derive their truth from the necessary truth of a priori principles. This merely restates that the necessity of the connection of empirical representations is derived from the necessity of the connection of pure intuitions. In this axiomatic vein of thought, Kant holds that "all empirical laws are only special determinations of the pure laws of understanding." (A 127) In the axiomatic systems, it is the axioms that constitute the source of all truths which the derived theorems can have. Kant's axiomatic doctrine of a priori truth reflects the nature of truth in axiomatic systems.

When Kant takes the postulational view of a priori knowledge, he maintains that a priori propositions such as mathematical propositions are not by themselves knowledge. (B 147) He further maintains that only experience can impart truth to a priori propositions. (A 157 = B 196 f.) In postulational systems, postulates are neither true nor false. They are merely assumed to account for the propositions which are independently accepted as true. Kant's postulational doctrine of a priori truth reflects the nature of truth in postulational systems. In his postulational view, Kant holds, the ultimate locus of truth is experience, or rather the system of all judgments of experience.

Let us stress one fundamental difference between the two views of a priori knowledge. While the axiomatic method tries to prove the validity of experience, the postulational method does not. The latter simply presupposes the validity of our experience. The analytical method neither intends nor tries to prove the truths of empirical judgments which constitute the system of our experience.

Because of this fundamental difference between the two views of a priori knowledge and the two methods of its justification, Kant's favorite expression, "the categories (or the a priori principles) are necessary conditions for the possibility of experience," conceals an obnoxious ambiguity. The categories, or a priori principles, can be called the necessary conditions of experience in either of the two roles they can play, that is, as a set of axioms or as a set of postulates for the genesis of experience. The necessary conditions will provide an entirely different kind of necessity depending on whether they have the axiomatic or the postulational function. When Stephan Körner and many others take delight in their efforts to refute the transcendental deduction, they generally take it for granted that the transcendental argument takes only the postulational pattern.[6] This is a misunderstanding which Kant himself invited by his own failure to distinguish between his two methods of transcendental argument.

In the next chapter we shall see how the two views of a priori knowledge operate in the production and demonstration of a priori principles of understanding. Toward the end of the last chapter, I pointed out Kant's tendency to fuse the two versions of the transcendental schematism. One of the consequences of this fusion is to produce some hybrid forms of a priori knowledge, containing both the axiomatic and the postulational elements. Therefore, we will encounter three types of a priori judgment.

Chapter 6

The Production of A Priori Judgments

Kant produces eight a priori principles from his eight transcendental concept-schemata. In this chapter we will see how these transcendental judgments embody Kant's two conceptions of a priori knowledge.

THE AXIOMS OF INTUITION (A 162 ff. = B 202 ff.)

> [In A]* Principle of the pure understanding: All appearances are, in their intuition, extensive magnitudes.
>
> [In B] Their principle is: All intuitions are extensive magnitudes.

This a priori principle is built on the concept of extensive magnitude. Extensive magnitude is defined by Kant as the representation of a whole which is produced by an extensive synthesis, the successive addition of homogeneous parts. (A 162 = B 203) The notion of extensive synthesis is central to Kant's proof of the Axioms of Intuition. His proof consists of two steps: (1) his demonstration that all pure intuitions are extensive magnitudes; and (2) his conclusion that all empirical intuitions are bound to be extensive magnitudes insofar as pure intuitions are the forms of all intuitions or appearances.

The first step of Kant's proof is based on the nature of space and time and the concept of extensive magnitude. Since space and time can be apprehended by extensive synthesis, he argues, all pure intuitions must be extensive magnitudes. (A 162 f. and

*Here, as in the citations (and elsewhere throughout this volume), A refers to the first edition of the *Critique of Pure Reason,* and B to the second edition.

B 202 f.) The second step of his proof is based on the relation between pure and empirical intuitions. Since pure intuitions are only the formal features of appearances or empirical intuitions, Kant argues, the latter must possess the extensive magnitudes of the former.

The second of these two steps in Kant's proof can be accepted with no reservation because it is tautological. But the first step cannot be accepted because it involves the dubious notion of extensive synthesis. In Chapter 3 we have explained why Kant could not maintain his doctrine of extensive synthesis, the doctrine that an extensive magnitude is a whole produced by a successive addition of homogeneous parts. We have also noted that an extensive magnitude can be subject to the operation of successive division as well as to the operation of successive addition. Neither of these two operations can have primacy over the other. The primacy of successive addition over successive division can be maintained in fact only on the condition that an extensive magnitude can be produced by putting together extensionless parts. The primacy of parts over their whole in extensive magnitudes can be maintained only on the condition that all extensions consist of ultimate quanta. Both of these two conditions are incompatible with Kant's theory of space and time. Thus the first step of Kant's proof should be rejected along with his notion of extensive synthesis.

Let us now see whether or not the Axioms of Intuition can be freed from the erroneous notion of extensive synthesis. In Chapter 3 we have pointed out that the correct definition of extensive magnitude is the magnitude of the extensive (extended) properties. To prove that space and time are extensive magnitudes, Kant has to show first that space and time are extended, an assertion implied in his doctrine of space and time. He has to show next that the extensive properties of space and time are continuously variable because only variable properties can have quantitative determinations. He may claim that this assertion is also deducible from the a priori knowledge of space and time. Thus the assertion that space and time are extensive magnitudes can be sustained by a correct definition of extensive magnitude and his a priori doctrine of pure intuitions.

The foregoing reformulation of the proof of the Axioms of Intuition has one additional merit—that of avoiding the conflict between the Axioms of Intuitions and the Transcendental Aesthetic. In the Aesthetic Kant has maintained that the whole is prior to its parts in the representation of space and time. (A 25 = B 40; A 32 = B 48) He propounds an exactly opposite doctrine in the Axioms of Intuition: The parts are prior to their whole in the apprehension of space and time. There is no need to invite the conflict between *totum syntheticum* and *totum analyticum*. As we noted a little earlier, there is no basis on which to justify the primacy of the parts over the whole or of the whole over the parts in the apprehension of extensive magnitudes. In Chapter 3 we have pointed out that the concepts of whole and part are not even essential to the representation of extensive magnitude. If they are to be used in the extensive synthesis at all, therefore, they should be used only on an equal footing.

Kant's proof of the Axioms of Intuition is axiomatic or progressive. Pure intuitions of space and time are first subsumed under the pure concept of extensive magnitude, and then empirical intuitions or appearances are subsumed under the same concept through the mediation of pure intuitions. The first of these two subsumptions creates the transcendental image-schemata for the concept of extensive magnitude: Space and time become pure images representing the concept of extensive magnitude. These transcendental image-schemata mediate the application of the pure concept to empirical intuitions. The first of the two steps in Kant's proof is supposed to have axiomatic necessity because it involves no empirical elements of contingency. The second of the two steps is supposed to have a derivative necessity, which flows from the axiomatic necessity of the first.

We have seen that the validity of the first step can be supported only by the doctrine of a priori intuitions. We shall not concern ourselves here with criticizing Kant's doctrine of pure intuitions, because it is no longer taken seriously. We may simply note that the rejection of this doctrine should invalidate Kant's entire proof for the Axioms of Intuition.

Let us note one significant feature of the axiomatic view of a priori knowledge: The axiomatic necessity of pure a priori judgments is rooted in the a priori knowledge of pure intuitions. In the last chapter we have seen that pure a priori judgments can have axiomatic necessity because they consist only of a priori elements and contain no a posteriori elements. As it stands, this account of axiomatic necessity requires some improvement. We need ask why a priori elements introduce certainty (and a posteriori elements contingency) into judgments. Kant never raises this question; he seems to assume that the answer is obvious—that the mind should have an a priori knowledge of its a priori concepts and a priori intuitions. (Cf. A 614 = B 642) This assumption is a legacy of continental rationalism.

The entire tradition of innate ideas rests on the rationalistic tenet that the mind must have a clear and distinct knowledge of its own possessions. It was always taken for granted that innate ideas must be clear and distinct and that clear and distinct ideas must be innate to the mind. The equivalence of innate ideas and clear and distinct ideas was neither questioned nor explained because of the rationalistic faith in reason's self-knowledge. Kant himself reflects this faith in the Transcendental Aesthetic, where pure reason is called on to display its a priori knowledge of its pure intuitions, and in the Metaphysical Deduction, where pure reason is again required to make an a priori tabulation of all its pure concepts.

Let us then assume that pure reason has an a priori knowledge of its a priori elements. Since the pure a priori judgment is the subsumption of pure intuition under a pure concept, one can claim a priori justification for this subsumption. Let us take the example of subsuming the pure intuitions of space and time under the concept of extensive magnitude. We have already seen that space and time can be rightly subsumed under the concept of extensive magnitude because space and time have precisely those variable extensive properties commensurate with the concept. We can have an a priori justification of this subsumption in the a priori knowledge of the properties of pure intuitions. This a priori justification is none other than the axiomatic necessity of pure a priori judgments. Thus axiomatic necessity is ultimately rooted in the a priori knowledge of a priori intuitions.

The relation of axiomatic necessity and a priori knowledge of pure intuitions directly touches on the relation between mathematical knowledge and a priori principles of pure understanding. Kant often stresses the generic difference between a priori principles of understanding and mathematical propositions. While the latter proceeds from intuitions to concepts, the former proceeds from concepts to intuitions. (A 160 = B 199) The former are intuitive and the latter discursive. Kant reveals some ambivalence, however, when he tries to determine the genetic relation of these two branches of a priori knowledge. He holds mathematical knowledge sometimes to be subject to the a priori principles of understanding and sometimes to be independent of these principles. For example, he expresses the latter view in the following passage:

> The principles of the Transcendental Aesthetic . . . are matters which do not come within the range of our present inquiry [of the *a priori* knowledge of understanding]. For similar reasons mathematical principles form no part of this system. They are derived solely from intuition, not from the pure concept of understanding. (A 149 = B 188)

Mathematical knowledge is independent of pure understanding because the pure concepts of understanding are not required in the genesis of mathematical truths.

Kant does not always stick to this doctrine of the autonomy of mathematics:

> But there are pure *a priori* principles that we may not properly ascribe to the pure understanding, which is the faculty of concepts. For though they are mediated by the understanding, they are not derived from pure concepts but from pure intuitions. We find such principles in mathematics. The question, however, of their application to experience, that is, of their objective validity, nay, even the deduction of the possibility of such synthetic *a priori* knowledge, must always carry us back to the pure understanding.
>
> While, therefore, I leave aside the principles of mathematics, I shall none the less include those [more fundamental] principles upon which the possibility and *a priori* objective validity of mathematics are grounded. These latter must be regarded as the foundation of all mathematical principles. (A 159 f. = B 188 f.)

Now Kant holds that the a priori principles of understanding is the foundation of mathematical knowledge.

Of these two views on the relation between the intuitive knowledge of mathematics and the discursive knowledge of understanding, the principle of the Axioms of Intuition is meant to propound the dependence of mathematical knowledge on the principles of understanding. One of the functions of this a priori principle is to explain how the axioms of mathematics are generated and why those axioms have truths of axiomatic necessity. Kant makes this point right after concluding his proof of his first a priori principle. (A 163 = B 204) In the second edition of the *Critique* he calls his first principle of understanding the principle of axioms: "THE AXIOMS OF

INTUITION—Their principle is: All intuitions are extensive magnitudes." (B 202) He clearly means to say that this is the principle governing the generation of all mathematical axioms. Since axioms constitute the foundation of all mathematics, the Axioms of Intuition turns out to be the single principle that governs the genesis of all mathematical truths.

Thus Kant's ultimate aim in the Axioms of Intuition appears to be the construction of an axiomatic proof of the a priori principle that governs the production of all axioms. If so, he is attempting to realize an impossible aim. Since all axiomatic proofs are rooted in the a priori knowledge of pure intuitions, it is impossible to construct an axiomatic proof for the Axioms of Intuition without presupposing the a priori knowledge of space and time. Since the axioms of mathematics must be included in this a priori knowledge, as it turns out, these axioms are used in constructing an axiomatic proof of the very a priori principle that is supposed to govern the production of themselves. The result is a vicious circle.

The most important point we must bear in mind about axiomatic proofs is that they cannot be constructed without presupposing a priori or axiomatic knowledge of pure intuitions.

THE ANTICIPATIONS OF PERCEPTION (A 166 ff. = B 207 ff.)

[In A] The principle which anticipates all perceptions, as such, is as follows: In all appearances sensations, and the *real* which corresponds to it in the object *(realitas phenomenon),* has an *intensive magnitude,* that is, a degree.

[In B] In all appearances, the real that is an object of sensation has intensive magnitude, that is, a degree.

This a priori principle is built on the concept of intensive magnitude. The two formulations of the principle in A and B differ in one point: While the A formulation asserts the intensive magnitude of both sensation and the real, the B formulation asserts the intensive magnitude only of the real. But this difference does not show up in the two proofs of the two editions. In both versions the intensive magnitude of sensation is first meant to be established as the premise that proves the intensive magnitude of the real. (A 168 = B 210; B 208)

In Chapter 3 we have seen that Kant's definition (or conception) of intensive magnitude has exactly the same defects as his definition of extensive magnitude. We have also seen that Kant abandons the priority of the whole (unity) over its parts (multiplicity) in the definition of intensive magnitude when he comes to redefine it in the second edition. We have also noted that the correct definition of intensive magnitude is the magnitude of intensive (nonextended) properties. Kant himself comes close to accepting this definition in a *Prolegomena* footnote, where he says, "The quantity of quality is degree." *(Prolegomena* §26, note 7) Fortunately, his proof of the Anticipations of Perception does not seem to be affected by the nature of this definition.

Kant's proof consists of two steps: his attempt to prove the intensive magnitude of sensation and then his attempt to deduce from this the intensive magnitude of the real. In order to establish the first of these two steps, Kant has to prove that every sensation is nonextended and that its property is always continuously variable. The first of these two points can be established by the definition of sensation as the matter of intuitions. Within his doctrine of intuitions, Kant can claim that matter of intuitions cannot be extended because all extended properties belong to the forms of intuitions. This is precisely what he does in his assertion: "Perception is empirical consciousness, that is, a consciousness in which sensation is to be found. Appearances, as objects of perception, are not pure, merely formal, intuitions, like space and time. . . . Appearances contain in addition to intuition the matter for some object in general." (B 207) He makes the same point in saying that "neither the intuition of space nor that of time is to be met with in [sensation]." (B 208) Within Kant's doctrine of intuitions, it is tautological to assert that sensation is nonextended or intensive.

What cannot be tautological even within Kant's doctrine of perception is his claim that the properties of sensation are capable of quantitative determination. Kant has to prove that the sense properties are continuously variable. He says, "Every sensation, however, is capable of diminution, so that it can decrease and gradually vanish." (A 168 = B 210) This is not a proof but an outright claim, for which Kant does not present even a semblance of proof. That sense properties are capable of quantitative determination can never be given an a priori proof because it is an empirical assertion.

In the second step of his proof, Kant claims that the intensive magnitude of sensation corresponds to the intensive magnitude of the real, which is the cause of sensation. (A 168 = B 210; B 208) By the real, Kant means the physical matter which is supposed to be the cause or correlate of sensation. That the real is capable of quantitative determination is also an empirical assertion that can be validated not by a priori argument but by a posteriori fact. That the real is the cause of sensation is another empirical assertion that can never be supported by a priori argument. Thus the second step of Kant's proof perpetuates the mistake of the first step. His ultimate aim in the Anticipations of Perception is to combine Leibniz' doctrine of matter with that of Descartes and to maintain that the essence of matter is not only its extension but also its nonextended properties. (A 174 f. = B 216) However salutary his theory of matter may be, it cannot be proven in an axiomatic argument.

Since the Anticipations of Perception is just a string of empirical assertions, it can fit into neither the axiomatic nor the postulational view of a priori knowledge. Kant himself reveals his uneasiness about the apriority of this principle of understanding, when he confesses amazement at an a priori principle which can anticipate the empirical features of experience. (A 175 = B 217)

In the *Prolegomena* Kant gives a postulational proof for the Anticipations of Perception as he does for all the other a priori principles. There he argues that the category of intensive magnitude is necessary for making objective judgments of sense qualities and their corresponding realities (physical matter). *(Prolegomena* §§19, 24) In the same vein of postulational argument, he claims that the Anticipations of Perception together with the Axioms of Intuition renders possible the application of mathematics to both the formal and the material features of experience or nature. *(Prolegomena* §24)

From these assertions we can carve out two postulational arguments in support of Kant's second a priori principle: (1) It is a necessary condition for making objective judgments of sense qualities and their correlates; and (2) it is a necessary condition for the application of mathematics to the contents of intuitions. The second of these two arguments is easy to dispose of. It apparently rests on the premise that mathematics is the science of quantity or magnitude. On this premise, it is tautological to say that sense qualities and their correlates must be capable of quantitative determination if they are to become the objects of mathematical calculations.

The first of the two postulational arguments is far more difficult to maintain than the second. Kant is convinced that all sense qualities are private feelings. Most of the judgments which he gives as examples of judgment of perception are judgments of sense qualities. *(Prolegomena* §19) They are judgments like "The room is warm, sugar sweet, and wormwood bitter." (See also A 28 f.) Granting that these are reports of subjective feelings, it is still difficult to maintain that the quantitative determination of these feelings should result in objective judgments. There are two important reasons for regarding this as an implausible claim. First of all, we have not yet developed the necessary instruments for measuring our feelings or sensations. A postulational argument should always begin with an established fact and search for its necessary conditions, but the quantitative determination of our sensations may be a future possibility rather than a present fact. Secondly, if the sense qualities are private and subjective in their very nature, they cannot become public and objective by the process of quantitative measurement. Quantitative measurement is no magic process that can convert subjective data into objective data. Kant must have been aware of this point because he says about the judgments of sense qualities in a footnote:

> I freely grant that these examples do not represent such judgments of perception as ever could become judgments of experience, even though a concept of the understanding were superadded, because they refer merely to feeling, which everybody knows to be merely subjective and which of course can never be attributed to the object, and consequently never become objective. *(Prolegomena* § 19, note 1)

Probably because Kant came to be convinced that even quantitative measurement cannot yield objective determinations of sense qualities, he decided to reformulate the Anticipations of Perception in the second edition. As we have noted, the B formulation of this a priori principle does not refer to the intensive magnitude of sense qualities but only to that of the real (physical matter). If that was his reason for reformulating the Anticipations of Perception, Kant should not have used the quantitative determination of sense qualities as an essential step in his proof of the principle.

The assertion that the quantitative determination is a necessary condition for making objective judgments of the real is also difficult to maintain. This assertion implies either one of the following two conditions: (1) Without quantitative determination, every judgment of the real is a judgment of perception; or (2) without quantitative determination, no judgment, whether subjective of objective, can be made about the real. If the first condition is assumed, the assertion that quantitative determination is a necessary condition for establishing objective judgments of the real would run into exactly the same difficulties as does the assertion that quantitative determination is a necessary condition for making objective judgments of sense qualities. Assuming the second condition would require us to close our eyes to a host of objective judgments which are made about the real without quantitative determination.

No one would doubt the value of quantitative instruments and language in facilitating our judgments and communications. But it is an altogether different matter to claim that quantitative determination is a necessary condition for having objective judgments on the material feature of our experience. Thus one of the two postulational arguments in support of the Anticipations of Perception is impossible to maintain, while the other is tautologous.

THE FIRST ANALOGY *(Principle of Permanence of Substance)*
(A 132 ff. = B 224 ff.)

> [In A] All appearances contain the permanent (substance) as the object itself, and the transitory as its mere determination, that is, as a way in which the object exists.
> [In B] In all change of appearances substance is permanent; its quantum in nature is neither increased nor diminished.

The First Analogy is built on the concept of the permanent substance or substratum. The difference between the two formulations of the First Analogy reflects Kant's ambivalence concerning the conception of substance. He is torn between the conception of substance as prime matter (as in the A formulation) and as physical matter (as in the B formulation). We will not concern ourselves with the difference between these two conceptions of substance except when it materially affects Kant's proofs of the First Analogy.

Most of the arguments Kant advances in proof of the First Analogy are postulational and regressive in form. Let us first examine all of the postulational arguments. The first is that the permanence of substance is necessary for the objective determination of succession and coexistence. (A 182 = B 225) This argument claims that the First Analogy is the common foundation for the Second and Third Analogies. Later when we come to them we shall have a chance to inquire whether or not these two Analogies are dependent on the First Analogy. For the moment let me point out that Kant presents no convincing argument for his claim. Let me also point out that all temporal relations should be just the properties and relations of the substance if this claim is true. That time is an intrasubstantial property and relation is Spinoza's doctrine, which violently clashes with Kant's doctrine of pure intuitions. Kant's doctrine of pure intuitions entails that time and space as forms of intuitions are prior to or independent of the contents of intuitions. The independence of time cannot be maintained if all the objective time relations become possible only within the context of one permanent substance.

The second of Kant's postulational arguments is that permanent substance is necessary for temporal magnitude "which can be entitled duration." (A 183 = B 226) This argument should not be construed to claim that permanent substance is necessary for the possibility of temporal magnitude as such. This claim is much stronger than the one Kant actually makes and furthermore is incompatible with Axioms of Intuition which is meant to establish among other things the possibility of temporal magnitude, or rather the extensive magnitude of time. Kant only claims the permanent substance is necessary for duration. He can offer no sound proof for this claim, if 'the permanent substance' is taken in its strict sense, that is, the substance which remains the same throughout all time. By this expression, however, he may mean only the enduring substance which need not be permanent (changeless). Then his claim would be tautologous because duration is none other than the duration of an enduring substance.

The third of Kant's postulational arguments is that the permanent substance is necessary for the unity of time:

> If some of these substances could come into being and others cease to be, the one condition of the empirical unity of time would be removed. The appearances would then relate to two different times, and existence would flow in two parallel streams—which is absurd. There is only one time in which all different times must be located, not as coexistent but in succession to one another. (A 188 f. = B 231 f.)

Kant can maintain this argument only if he accepts a doctrine of time like the doctrines of Leibniz and Spinoza. His doctrine of pure intuitions requires that the unity of time be independent of the unity of the content of the phenomenal world. It is rather the unity of time and space that provides the unity of the contents of space and time. Precisely the opposite of this Kantian doctrine of space and time is asserted by the argument under review, for it claims that the unity of time depends on the unity of the contents of time. Thus this argument can be accepted only at the cost of repudiating the Transcendental Aesthetic.

In the second edition of the *Critique* Kant adds one more argument in proof of the First Analogy. (B 225) It begins with the premise that time is permanent. Since time is not perceivable, he argues, the permanence of substance is necessary for perceiving the permanence of time. This argument takes the familiar pattern of the postulational proof because it attempts to establish the existence of the permanent substance on the basis of its functional necessity. But it cannot be regarded as completely postulational because of its initial premise which is based on a priori knowledge of pure intuition. Above, in our examination of the Axioms of Intuition, we noted that a priori knowledge of pure intuitions always provides the initial step in the axiomatic proof. This initial step is none other than the transcendental image-schema, or the subsumption of pure intuition under a pure concept. The proposition "Time is permanent," is a judgment which can be made by subsuming time under the concept of permanence and is equivalent to the assertion that time is the pure image (schema) of permanence. For this reason, as we saw in Chapter 3, Heidegger thought that Kant had given an image-schema for the concept of substance.

Kant's new argument in the second edition for the First Analogy does not follow the axiomatic pattern, although it does begin with an axiomatic premise. If it were to adhere to the axiomatic pattern, it should go on to claim that the content of time must be permanent because time itself is permanent. Although it begins with an axiomatic premise, however, it ends with a postulational conclusion; it is a fusion of the axiomatic and the postulational patterns. We can call it a hybrid proof or a mixed argument.

Let us see how well this hybrid proof for the First Analogy fares. The assertion that time is permanent is not easy to comprehend. As Heidegger says, time is a "pure *now*-sequence."[1] Since every "now" passes away every moment, it is equally legitimate to say that time is perpetually perishing. Because of this transitoriness of time, the eternal or the unchangeable has usually been conceived as transcending time. It may be just an abuse of language to say either that time is permanent or that time is passing away. The properties of permanence or transitoriness may be properly predicated not of time but only of what is in it.

There is one special reason that should make Kant hesitate to proclaim outright that time is permanent: The assertion gives the pure intuition of time the essential characteristic of substance and runs counter to his doctrine of pure intuitions. One of the grave objections Kant has against the theory of absolute space and absolute time is that such a theory commits the mistake of treating two nonentities *(Undinge)* as substantial beings: "They have to admit two eternal and infinite self-subsistent non-entities." (A 39 = B 56) It is probably the fear of committing this mistake that has held him back from claiming pure time as the image-schema of the concept of substance. To regard pure time as the schema of the concept of substance is to treat time not simply as one permanent thing among others but as the exemplary instance of all permanent things. A sense of this, however vague, must have prevented Kant from going to this Heideggerian extreme. Since he is unwilling to accept the substantiality of time, he cannot properly claim its permanence.

We now come to the assertion that the permanent substance is necessary for perceiving the permanence of time. As Paton points out, this assertion can be maintained only on the condition that the permanence of substance is itself perceivable.[2] If the permanence of substance is not perceivable, the presence of substance would be of no use in our perception of the permanence of time. Hence it is important to determine whether or not Kant's doctrine of the phenomenal world allows him to hold the perceivability of the permanence of substance.

When Kant talks of substance and its permanence, he assumes that the world of appearances consists of two strata, the substratum and the superstratum. Since the perpetually changing superstratum is of no use in our perception of the permanence of time, he argues, the substratum must be permanent. (B 225) Even if the substratum is permanent, however, its permanence cannot be perceived, simply because the substratum itself is not open to perception. The demarcation between the substratum and the superstratum is drawn by the yardstick of perceivability: The superstratum of the phenomenal world is that stratum which is open to perception; its substratum is that stratum which is closed to perception. By definition, the substratum cannot be perceived, and its permanence cannot be used for perceiving the permanence of time.

Kant would meet the same difficulty if he advanced his argument on the premise that the substance is prime matter. We have seen that he conceives substance chiefly as prime matter in the first edition. (A 184 = B 227; A 186 = B 229) He admits that nothing can be said of the substratum as prime matter except that it is the subject of accidents. Substance conceived as prime matter can never be perceived because whatever is perceivable about it is one of its accidents. Probably because of the imperceivability of prime matter, Kant seems to have replaced his conception of substance as prime matter with that of substance as physical matter in the second edition of the *Critique*. Since no one would question the perceivability of physical matter, he may have thought, his new conception of substance would fit much better into his new proof of the First Analogy.

There is an important difference between the perceivability of matter and the perceivability of its permanence. Physical matter may be perceived, but its permanence cannot. The latter point is well attested to by the fact that the law of the conservation of matter has been only a postulate of the physical sciences. The imperceivability of the permanence of substance is therefore not affected whether substance is conceived as prime matter or physical matter.

Thus Kant's hybrid argument for the First Analogy does not fare any better than his postulational arguments. In fact, the hybrid argument fails to attain the efficacy of either the axiomatic or the postulational method. It starts out with an alleged axiomatic knowledge ("Time is permanent") and tries to prove it with a postulational argument. The hybrid argument is an ill-conceived mongrel, which is as malformed as the expression "the postulationally established axiom."

THE SECOND ANALOGY (A 189 ff. = B 232 ff.)

[In A] *Principle of Production:* Everything that happens, that is, begins to be, presupposes something upon which it follows according to a rule.

[In B] *Principle of Succession in Time, in Accordance with the Law of Causality:* All alterations take place in conformity with the law of the connection of cause and effect.

The Second Analogy is built on the concept of necessary succession. It has been well established that Kant has entertained both the traditional conception of causation and the Humean phenomenalistic conception. By 'necessary succession' Kant refers variously to both of these. The ambivalence in his conception of causation is linked with his ambivalence in the conception of the entire phenomenal world. Throughout his lengthy proof of the Second Analogy, he vacillates between his conception of the phenomenal world as a congeries of sense representations and his conception of it as a locus of substantial entities.

The difference between these two conceptions of the world and between the two ways of conceiving the nature of causal chains is what underlies the different formulations of the Second Analogy in the two editions of the *Critique.* The causal principle in the first edition is meant to be a rule governing the *events* of the phenomenal world. These events do *happen* but need not be substantial existences. In the second edition, Kant replaces "everything that happens" with "all alterations." For Kant 'alteration' is the technical word that designates the change of substance. So the causal principle in the second edition is meant to be the law governing the activities of substantial entities. We will not concern ourselves any further with these differences except when they materially affect the efficacy of Kant's arguments in proof of the Second Analogy.

Paton says that Kant offers six proofs for the validity of the causal principle.[3] Five of these six proofs are postulational, while only one is axiomatic. Kant's main contention, which runs through all his postulational arguments, is that the causal category or principle is necessary for the determination of objective successions. His arguments implementing this thesis become exceedingly involved, chiefly because he cannot bring himself to choose between two different contexts of argumentation: the world of mere impressions and the world of substantial objects.

When Kant argues in the context of the phenomenalistic world, he begins with the premise that an object of perception is only a congeries of perceptions. Since the objects of perception can have no existence independent of perceptions, he argues, the distinction between objective and subjective successions cannot be made by comparing perceptions with the independently existing objects of perception. (A 191 = B 236) He holds that the distinction can be made only by the nature of successions, that is, objective successions are irreversible while subjective successions are reversible. Since irreversible successions are necessary ones, he concludes, the concept of necessary succession is necessary for the determination of objective successions.

The main difficulty in assessing this argument lies in correctly understanding the nature of the links that Kant claims exist between objective and irreversible succession and between irreversible and necessary succession. Sometimes he gives the impression that the two links are the links of synonymity, that is, 'objective succession' means 'irreversible succession,' and 'irreversible succession' means 'necessary succession.' In that event, 'objective succession' would be synonymous with 'necessary succession' (causal sequence) and the idea of the irreversible succession has been introduced only to establish their equivalence. Kant presupposes this equivalence in his repeated claim that the necessity of objective successions is rooted in the necessity of causal nexus. (Cf. A 191 = B 236; A 196 = B 241; A 202 = B 247) Once this equivalence is established, however, it becomes tautologous to say that the concept of causation is necessary for the determination of objective succession.

Since Kant would not be happy to see his causal principle turn into a tautological proposition, he should have maintained that at least one of the two links in question is synthetic. But it is highly unlikely he would have said that the link between 'irreversible succession' and 'necessary succession' is anything more than verbal because he often claims their equivalence. In that event, the link between 'objective succession' and 'irreversible succession' must be regarded as synthetic. If so, Kant's argument boils down to the assertion that the objectivity of objective successions can be identified only by their irreversibility. This is a dubious assertion. If it were true, a baseball referee could make his decision only by consulting the criteria of reversibility and irreversibility, that is, whether the arrival of the ball and the runner is reversible or irreversible. The criteria of reversibility and irreversibility are often unavailable and, in any case, dispensable in determining the objectivity of sequential orders. Even when the criteria are available, they are often useless. Thus Kant's postulational argument becomes untenable once it is taken as something more than a tautologous assertion.

When Kant advances his arguments in the context of the substantial world, he assumes that the order of existence is distinguishable from the order of perceptions and holds that the latter order is causally determined by the former. He makes this point, for instance, in his assertion that "we must derive the *subjective succession* of apprehension from the *objective succession* of appearances." (A 193 = B 238) Because of this causal relation, he argues, the category of causation is necessary for the inference from the order of perception to the order of objective succession. If this is Kant's intent, his proof would stand on an empirical assertion. For the causal relation between the order of objective succession and the order of apprehension (perception) can be only empirically determined. If so, the Second Analogy would forfeit the title of "an a priori principle."

Whether Kant's postulational arguments are taken in the context of the phenomenalistic world or the substantial world, they have one serious drawback in common. All postulational arguments should begin with our common experience because they are meant to reveal the necessary conditions of it. The common drawback of Kant's arguments is precisely their failure to be anchored in our ordinary experience. Contrary to Kant's arguments, we usually determine objective succession without invoking the causal principle. Even in science, the independent determination of objective succession is a prerequisite for the elaborate search of a causal nexus. Thus Kant's arguments run counter to our experiences in science and ordinary life.

That Kant has failed in all his postulational arguments for the Second Analogy is, however, fortunate for transcendental philosophy. If he had succeeded, he would have presented conclusive proof of the causal theory of time, that is, the theory that temporal order is established by causal order. If the objective temporal order can be determined only by the knowledge of the causal order, there would be no way to reject the causal theory of time. Grünbaum, a most eloquent modern proponent of the causal theory of time, in fact claims that this theory occupied an important place in the mind of Kant.[4] It is quite certain that he has in mind the Second Analogy in making this claim.

But Kant cannot accept the causal theory of time without abandoning his own doctrine of pure intuitions because the causal theory of time is a special version of the relative theory of time. One of the central features in his doctrine of time as a priori intuition is the claim that temporal relations are prior to or independent of the relations of the contents of time. Within this theory of time, it is impossible to maintain that the objective temporal order is equivalent to the causal order or that the latter is indispensable for coming to recognize the former. Thus this well-known postulational proof for the Second Analogy can be accepted only at the cost of repudiating Kant's main contention in the Transcendental Aesthetic.

We now come to Kant's axiomatic argument for the Second Analogy. Since the argument is brief and sketchy, let us quote it in its entirety:

> If, then, it is a necessary law of our sensibility, and therefore a *formal condition* of all *perceptions,* that the preceding time necessarily determines the succeeding (since I cannot advance to the succeeding time save through the preceding), it is also an indispensable law of *empirical representation* of the time series that the appearances of the past time determine all existences in the succeeding time, and that these latter, as events, can take place only in so far as the appearances of past time determine their existence in time, that is, determine them according to a rule. (A 199 = B 244)

This proof consists of two steps: the application of the pure concept of causation to time; and then its application to empirical intuitions through time. That "the preceding time necessarily determines the succeeding [time]" means that any two adjacent moments of time stand in a causal relation. Pure time can be subsumed under the concept of cause and effect; time is the pure image of the concept of causation.

If time is the pure image or schema of the concept of causation, every moment of time must have the power to act as a causal agent ("the preceding time necessarily determines the succeeding"). But this is to attribute one of the essential features of a substantial being to time. Hence the assertion that pure time presents the exemplary instances of causal relations conflicts with Kant's doctrine of time as the form of intuitions.

By the assertion that "the preceding time necessarily determines the succeeding," Kant may simply mean the obvious fact that the flow of time is irreversible. He may further equate this irreversibility with the causal relation between the adjacent moments of time, since he has assumed the interchangeability of 'the irreversible succession' with 'the causal succession.' If so, Kant is maintaining that the flow of time is irreversible because every moment of time acts as a causal agent upon the succeeding moment. This assertion also amounts to attributing the causal power to every moment of time, or rather to claiming every moment of time as a substantial being. Thus this interpretation also turns out to be objectionable in the light of Kant's doctrine of pure intuitions.

The second step in Kant's axiomatic proof for the Second Analogy is to infer from the causal relation of pure intuitions to the causal relations of empirical intuitions. He is rather indecisive on the validity of this type of inference. For example, he once approves and once disapproves the inference from the continuity of time to the continuity of alteration in time. (A 171 = B 213; A 209 = B 254)

His ambivalence is understandable because this type of inference can take either the form of an analytic inference or that of a synthetic one. For example, the inference from the continuity of pure intuitions to that of empirical intuitions would be analytic, if the continuity of the latter is conceived to be ontologically indistinguishable from that of the former (that is, if empirical intuitions are assumed to be continuous not in their own right but only by virtue of being the contents of the continuous formal intuitions). The same inference would be synthetic, if the continuity of empirical intuitions is conceived to be ontologically distinguishable from that of pure intuitions (that is, if empirical intuitions are assumed to be continuous in their own right rather than by virtue of being the contents of the continuous formal intuitions).

The inference from the nature of pure intuitions to that of empirical intuitions can have axiomatic certainty only when it takes the form of an analytic inference; it must have all the contingency of empirical inferences when it takes the form of a synthetic inference. Kant's axiomatic proof of the Axioms of Intuition is acceptable as an a priori argument because it is an analytic inference from the extensive magnitude of pure intuitions to that of empirical intuitions. Kant feels uncertain about the alleged axiomatic inference from the continuity of time to that of alteration in time, because he is uncertain whether the continuity of empirical intuition is ontologically distinguishable or indistinguishable from that of pure intuition.

In fact, this uncertainty reflects the difficulty in distinguishing the intrinsic properties of empirical intuitions from their extrinsic properties, that is, those properties that empirical intuitions have, not in their own right but only by virtue of being the contents of formal intuitions. This difficulty in turn reflects the difficulty of determining what properties pure and empirical intuitions have as intrinsic and extrinsic properties, respectively. For the sake of convenience, let us refer to this difficulty as the problem of the sense-property demarcation.

Without presupposing the demarcation of sense properties, it is impossible to determine whether any proposed inference from the nature of pure intuitions to that of empirical intuitions is analytic or synthetic. Unfortunately, however, Kant does not even think of undertaking this demarcation, although his distinction between pure and empirical intuitions can never be really complete without such a move. In place of a clear demarcation, Kant simply relies on the familiar and yet vague and flexible distinction between form and content (or matter) —the distinction between formal and material intuitions— whenever he feels the need to presuppose the demarcation in question. In fact, by taking advantage of this vague and flex-ible distinction, he tries to pass off some contingent (synthetic) inferences for indubitable (a priori) arguments.

Let us return to the proposed a priori inference from the causal relation of pure intuition to that of empirical intuition. This inference can be also conceived as analytic or synthetic, depending on whether the causality of empirical intuition is assumed to be its extrinsic or intrinsic property. If empirical intuition is assumed to have causal relation not on its own right but only by virtue of being the content of formal intuition, which has causal efficacy as its intrinsic property, then the in-ference in question would be absolutely certain. This certainty is obtained by transferring the original locus of causal relation from empirical to pure intuitions; but this is incompatible with Kant's doctrine of formal intuitions. If empirical intuition is assumed to have causal relation on its own right rather than by virtue of being the content of formal intuition, the infer-ence would be as contingent as any empirical inference. Thus Kant's axiomatic argument for the Second Analogy likewise fails to hold up.

THE THIRD ANALOGY (A 211 ff. = B 256 ff.)

[In A] *Principle of Community:* All substances, so far as they coexist, stand in thoroughgoing com-munity, that is, in mutual interaction.

[In B] *Principle of Coexistence, in Accordance with the Law of Reciprocity or Community:* All sub-stances, in so far as they can be perceived to coexist in space, are in thoroughgoing reciprocity.

This a priori principle is built on the concept of mutual causation. Kant defines mutual causation as reversible suc-cession. (A 211 = B 258) He seems to have forgotten, how-ever, that he has identified reversible succession with subjective succession. If the category of community means the concept of mutual causation, he must identify it with the concept of reversible necessary succession rather than reversible succession.

Kant gives only a postulational proof for the Third Analogy. Distinguishing between a spatial community *(communio spatii)* and a dynamical community *(communio* or *commercium),* he argues that the latter concept is a necessary condition for the perception of the former. The B formulation of the Third Analogy far more clearly manifests the postulational character of this proof ("in so far as they can be perceived to coexist in space") than its A formulation. This proof has many of the same defects we have detected in the postulational arguments for the Second Analogy. We will not go over those but only point out one complication introduced by Kant's careless schematization of the pure concept of community. In the Second Analogy he has argued that the reversibility of reversible successions reveals the lack of necessary nexus. Now he wants to claim that the same reversibility reflects the nexus of reciprocal causation. These two incompatible claims have come to be anchored on the concept of reversibility because the notion of reversible succession has been used as equivalent once to the concept of subjective succession and once to the concept of reciprocal causation.

In our examination of the First Analogy, we have noted that one of Kant's argument there claims that the First Analogy is the common ground supporting the Second and the Third. We have also seen that this claim rests on the premise that the temporal relations of succession and simultaneity (coexistence) are possible only as the intrarelations of one single substance. If this is true, the unity of nature as a single substance can never be separated from proving the validity of the Second and Third Analogies. But, as we have seen, Kant never appeals to the substantial unity of nature in his proofs of these two Analogies. Thus the Second and the Third Analogies do stand as independent a priori principles and hence cannot be used in providing a postulational proof of the First Analogy.

THE POSTULATES OF EMPIRICAL THOUGHT IN GENERAL (A 218 ff. = B 265 ff.)

[*The First Postulate*] That which agrees with the formal conditions of experience, that is, with the conditions of intuition and of concepts, is *possible.*

[*The Second Postulate*] That which is bound up with the material conditions of experience, that is, with sensation, is *actual.*

[*The Third Postulate*] That which in its connection with the actual is determined in accordance with universal conditions of experience, is (that is, exists as) *necessary.*

Kant says that these three Postulates are not a priori principles but simply explanations of the modal concepts. (A 219 = B 266) Hence they require no proofs. But we must examine whether they are correct or incorrect explanations or definitions. Within the transcendental doctrine of experience, Kant's definitions of possibility and actuality are indeed acceptable. The possible must conform to the formal conditions of both sense and thought; the actual must fulfill the material condition of experience. What is strange is his definition of the necessary, which he defines as that which fulfills the conditions of being possible and actual at the same time. Surely this is an unusual conception of the necessary.

This definition may appear to serve the elegant architectonic function of combining the first two concepts of the modal triad into its last concept, but it in fact involves an awkward redundancy. Since whatever is actual is usually regarded also as possible (whatever conforms to the material conditions of experience must also conform to its formal conditions), it is superfluous to add the *possible* to the *actual* in order to produce the *necessary*. The *necessary* that is formed by this superfluous combination would be no different from the *actual*. So the third modality itself turns out to be a gratuitous concept. This is an embarrassing modal situation.

It is probably to avoid this embarrassment that Kant converts *modal necessity* into *causal necessity* in the course of his exposition of the modal categories. (A 227 = B 279) In Chapter 3 we have seen that this surreptitious conversion makes the Third Postulate a mere adjunct to the Second Analogy. Architectonic integrity cannot permit such an inelegant surreptitious operation.

Kant's explication of the First Postulate also contains an objectionable transformation of the modal concept. In the course of his exposition, he identifies possibility with objective reality. (A 221 = B 268) To say that a concept is objectively real is to say that the class denoted by the concept is not empty, or rather that it is not an empty concept. 'Objectively real' is really synonymous with 'actual' rather than with 'possible.' Kant denies the possibility of the fictitious concepts on the ground that they are not objectively real. (A 222 = B 269) But this denial is misguided. Let us take the fictitious concept of a winged horse. This is an empty concept and has no objective reality because there are no winged horses. But the concept of the winged horse is possible because the concept can be formed in accordance with the formal conditions of sense and thought.

We now come to Kant's startling contention that the three domains of modality are conterminous with one another (A 230 ff. = B 282 ff.) We need not worry about the boundary line for the domain of the necessary because it can be determined by the boundary lines of the possible and the actual. The central question is whether the domain of the possible is larger than, or the same as, the domain of the actual. Kant presents the following argument against conceiving the domain of the possible to be larger than the domain of the actual:

Moreover, the poverty of the customary inferences through which we throw open a great realm of possibility, of which all that is actual [the objects of experience] is only a small part, is patently obvious. Everything actual is possible; from this proposition there naturally follows, in accordance with the logical rules of conversion, the merely particular proposition, that some possible is actual; and this would seem to mean that much is possible which is not actual. It does indeed seem as if we were justified in extending the number of possible things beyond that of the actual, on the ground that something must be added to the possible to constitute the actual. But this [alleged] process of adding to the possible I refuse to allow. For that which would have to be added to the possible, over and above the possible, would be impossible. (A 231 = B 284 f.)

No one would try to add the impossible to the possible because to do so is impossible. What should be added to the possible to make it actual is the material condition of experience. Kant's rhetorical claim that only the impossible is left to be used in the actualization of the possible rests on the hidden premise that whatever lies outside the domain of the possible is the impossible. But his rhetoric misfires because it is based on an incorrect premise. Since the material conditions of experience do not enter into the definition of the possible, they can be legitimately added to the possible. The material conditions of experience belong neither to the domain of the possible nor to that of the impossible. Kant's argument would be valid only on the condition that every feature of experience is exhaustively claimed by the domains of the possible and the impossible. In that event, the two categories of the possible and the impossible would be enough to perform all the modal functions, and there would be no room for the categories of actuality and necessity.

There are two extraneous reasons, either of which may have prompted Kant to maintain the coextensivity of the possible with the actual. One of these reasons may have been his identification of the possible with the objectively real. This erroneous identification should entail the coextensivity of the possible with the actual because the objectively real is equivalent to the actual. The other extraneous reason is his identification of modal necessity with causal necessity. Since Kant is convinced of the universal causal necessity, he seems to have thought that only the necessary can be actual and possible. From this he may have concluded that the three modal domains are coextensive with one another. It is indeed true that only the necessary is possible and becomes actual in a world tightly governed by the universal causal law. But the possible that is defined in the context of the material laws of nature is real possibility. This should be distinguished from the formal possibility that is defined in the context of only the formal conditions of experience. The possibility of the First Postulate is not the real but the formal possibility. The confusion of these two types of possibility is as objectionable as the confusion of the possible with the objectively real.

We have pointed out quite a few anomalous features in Kant's doctrine of modalities. Now I suspect that many of them are due to his attempt to reform the traditional usage of the modal concepts. In Chapter 1, we have seen that Kant rejects the traditional modal concepts on the ground that modal concepts can have nothing to do with the content of knowledge. There we have also noted that he wants to replace the traditional (alethic) modes with his epistemic modes. Whereas the former have been given the illegitimate function of characterizing the content of knowledge, he believes, the latter will be given the only legitimate modal function—that of characterizing the modes of knowledge. While the alethic modes are meant to reflect the internal structures of propositions (their content), the epistemic modes are meant to characterize their external relations to their knowers (their modes of being known).

In spite of his decision to reform the entire modal logic, Kant never succeeds in making a clean break with traditional modal concepts. He often speaks of both the old and the new modal concepts in the same breath. Even worse than this is his tendency to propound his new modal ideas in the old language, which invites his readers to interpret them in the context of the alethic modalities, rather than in that of the epistemic modalities, and even justifies such an interpretation. These expository defects show up prominently, for example, in his contention that the domains of the three modalities are conterminous to one another.

In reading through Kant's exposition of this contention, one can never be certain whether he is talking of the alethic or the epistemic modes. Some of his remarks can be read only in the context of the former; others can be read only in the context of the latter; and most of his remarks can be read in either context. But when, instead of examining all its constituent arguments, we confront his contention in its general outline, we can see that it should be accepted in the context of the epistemic modes. Kant's contention is obviously implausible, if it is read in the other context, for we all intuitively feel that some possibles need not be actual or necessary. But the same contention gains surprisingly in plausibility as soon as it is placed in the context of the epistemic modes. There can be nothing objectionable in claiming that every empirical proposition can be known on three different levels (possible, actual, and necessary), that is, all three epistemic modes can be predicated of every object of knowledge. Then the three modal domains must be conterminous to one another and each of them must contain every true empirical proposition.

We have already noted the oddity in Kant's definition of necessity. This oddity may also disappear once the definition is transferred from the context of the alethic modes to that of the epistemic modes. Although the definition of necessity as the joint product of possibility and actuality does indeed sound strange in the language of the alethic modes, the definition of necessity as the conformity to both the formal and the material conditions of experience can be regarded as quite sensible in the language of the epistemic modes. This definition of necessity has a remarkable affinity with the functional necessity of the postulational method, because the conformity in question is the necessary condition for the possibility of experience. This necessity is quite different from the necessity of the axiomatic method. The axiomatic necessity really belongs to the domain of the alethic modalities, because it is a necessity inherent in the proposition as we have pointed out in the last chapter. In contrast to this, functional necessity belongs to the domain of epistemic modalities, because both of them characterize the external functions of propositions rather than their internal structures.

Kant cannot repudiate the traditional or the alethic modalities as long as he retains the axiomatic view of a priori knowledge. Neither can he retain the traditional modal concepts once he abandons the axiomatic view in favor of the postulational one. His conversion of the alethic to the epistemic modalities is integrally connected to his transition from the axiomatic to the postulational view of a priori knowledge.

This concludes our investigation of Kant's a priori principles and his proofs of those principles. In the following chapter we will review his doctrine of a priori judgments in the light of this investigation.

Chapter 7

The Foundation of A Priori Judgments

Now that we have seen the implementation of Kant's two conceptions of a priori judgments in the production and demonstration of his a priori principles, we should take up the task of assessing his doctrine of a priori knowledge. First, however, we must gain a little more extensive comprehension of the fundamental ideas that sustain this doctrine. We have seen that two versions of the transcendental schematism underlie the two conceptions of a priori judgments and that those two versions are in turn based on two different notions concerning the functions of the categories. From our present vantage point of having surveyed the execution of Kant's two conceptions of a priori judgments, we must try to understand how this cluster of related ideas has been woven into the transcendental nest for the hatching of Kant's doctrine of a priori knowledge. For this exploration, we shall retrace our steps and reinvestigate problems of the pure concepts of understanding.

Why and how did Kant come to hold two different
notions concerning the functions of the
pure concepts of understanding?

To gain a broad perspective on this problem, let us go back to Kant's *Inaugural Dissertation* of 1770, which presents among other things his pre-Critical view of the function of the categories. There he distinguishes between sensory knowledge and intellectual knowledge. *(Dissertation* §§ 5, 6) The former is knowledge of the sensible world or of things as they appear (phenomena); the latter is the knowledge of the intelligible world or of things as they are (noumena). *(Disserta-*

tion § 4) Sensory knowledge requires the use of both sense and intellect, but intellectual knowledge requires the use only of intellect. Although the faculty of intellect is employed in gaining both sensory and intellectual knowledge, it performs different functions in two different domains of knowledge. Kant says of these two functions of intellect:

> As for the intellectual . . . it is, above all, to be clearly remarked that the use of the intellect, that is, of the superior faculty of the mind, is double. By the first use, the very concepts of objects or of relations are *given,* and this is the *real use;* by the second use, concepts, whencesoever given, are only *subordinated* to one another, the lower to the higher (the common marks), and compared with one another according to the principle of contradiction; and this is called the *logical use. (Dissertation* § 5)

The two functions of intellect are called its real and its logical uses. The real use of intellect is the employment of its real or material concepts. It is to these concepts that Kant refers in "the very concepts of objects or of relations." He says that these concepts have their origin in the intellect and not in the senses: The concepts involved in the real use of intellect "are given through the very nature of intellect, not abstracted from any use of the senses, and do not contain any form of sensitive cognition as such." *(Dissertation* § 6) These intellectual concepts are sometimes called the concepts of understanding and sometimes the primary concepts of things and relations. *(Dissertation* §§ 9, 23) In the *Dissertation* he has not yet adopted the characteristic expression of later works (i.e. 'a priori'). Very occasionally he uses the expression 'connate': The concepts of understanding are said to be connate to the intellectual faculty. *(Dissertation* § 8)

Kant believes that these intellectual concepts of things and relations are not required in the logical use of intellect. In Chapter 3 we have pointed out that Kant understood the ultimate function of logic (the logic of classes) to be that of classification. It is to this function that Kant refers in the "subordination" of the lower to the higher. He believes that the intellect can discharge this function by using the single logical principle of contradiction. Besides this logical principle, some real (material) concepts are also necessary for understanding the sensible world. These real concepts are however derived from the senses:

> In things sensual and in phenomena, that which precedes the logical use of intellect is called appearance [apparentia], and the reflective cognition which arises from the intellectual comparison of a number of appearances is called experience [experientia]. Thus the only path from appearance to experience is by reflection according to the logical use of intellect. The common concepts of experience are called empirical, and its objects phenomena; the laws of experience, and of all sensitive knowledge in general, are called laws of phenomena. Thus empirical concepts do not become intellectual in the real sense by being brought to a greater universality, and so pass out of the class of sensitive knowledge. However high they ascend by way of abstraction, they always remain sensitive. (Dissertation § 5)

Appearance becomes experience through the intellectual operation of comparison, the operation of classification. It is through this operation that empirical concepts are abstracted from senses. These are the real (material) concepts which are derived from senses and used in the understanding of the sensible world. Kant does not yet claim the need of logical or formal concepts for the logical use of intellect. Its logical use is conceived as a simple operation, which can stand solely on the logical principle of contradiction.

Kant enters his Critical period when he rejects the possibility of knowing the intelligible world. Even in the *Dissertation* he was not terribly sanguine about the knowledge of noumena. There he held that we can have only a symbolic knowledge of noumena because we have no intuition of the intelligible things. *(Dissertation* § 10) He also held that we can have a genuine knowledge only of phenomena because only sensible objects are really present in our perceptions. *(Dissertation* § 11) Since in his Critical period he claims the intuition of objects as an essential condition for their cognition, he must deny the possibility of knowing the intelligible objects which cannot be given in sensible intuitions.

Even with this restriction of the domain of knowledge to the sensible world, he does not abandon his doctrine of intellectual concepts. For he now begins to see the need of these concepts in the cognition of phenomena, both for the logical use of intellect and for its real use in knowing the phenomenal world.

In the *Critique of Pure Reason,* Kant no longer conceives the logical use of intellect in such a simple fashion as he did in the *Dissertation.* There he thought that the principle of contradiction was all that was needed for the logical use of intellect; he now holds that the logical use of intellect requires a set of logical or formal concepts as well. Since these logical concepts cannot be derived from the senses any more than logical truths can be abstracted from the sensible world, Kant claims that they must have an intellectual or a priori origin.

In the *Critique* Kant also elaborates his earlier, simple view of knowing the phenomenal world. In the *Dissertation* he assumed that the logical use of intellect was all that was required of the intellect in gaining sensory knowledge. He now sees that the cognition of the sensible world requires the real use of intellect as well as its logical use. In the *Dissertation,* to be sure, he had already admitted the role of real concepts in knowing sensible objects. But he had assumed that these concepts were derived from the senses. He now believes that empirical concepts cannot be derived without using a special set of real concepts, that is, the most general concepts of an object. Without these concepts, he now holds, the mind cannot even recognize and compare sensible objects in order to abstract empirical concepts. Since these real concepts must be prior to the derivation of all empirical concepts, Kant holds, they must have an intellectual or a priori origin.

In his Critical period Kant thus recognized two sets of a priori concepts, one of formal concepts and one of material concepts. In Chapter 4 we encountered these two sets of primitive concepts on their functional level and marked their difference with the two labels "the material function theory" and "the formal function theory" of the categories.* There we have argued that the pure concepts of the understanding in their primitive state are assumed to be material concepts in the material function theory and to be formal concepts in the formal function theory. We have also seen that these two different views of pure concepts present two different problems in application, which result in two different versions of the transcendental schematism.

I have sketched the transformation in Kant's doctrine of a priori concepts as a preliminary setting for our original question: Why and how did Kant come to hold two different notions concerning the functions of the pure concepts of understanding? Since Kant has left little explanation for this change in doctrine, we have to reconstruct the motives and reasoning which must have induced him to hold these categorial doctrines.

---

*Kant means to remind us of the material function of pure concepts of understanding by calling them categories. This follows the well-established Aristotelian tradition of calling ultimate material concepts categories. If he were to adhere strictly to this tradition, he should deny the name 'categories' to formal concepts. But terminological accuracy was not always one of Kant's virtues.

In the initial stage of his Critical period, he had not yet in all likelihood hit upon the doctrine of logical or formal concepts. Certainly, in the *Dissertation* we can find no evidence to indicate that he had entertained anything vaguely resembling such a doctrine. There he appears to assume that all concepts are real or material. There he recognizes the possibility of classifying concepts according to their origins (intellectual or sensory), but not the possibility of classifying them according to their functions (formal or material). When he decided to shift the employment of intellectual concepts from the intelligible to the sensible world, he appears to have taken for granted that those concepts would remain material concepts in whatever domain they might be used.

The belief that all intellectual concepts are material constitutes the fundamental continuity in Kant's transition from the *Dissertation* to the initial phase of his Critical period. During this transitional period, as his *Reflexionen* reveals, he spared no effort to form a complete list of intellectual concepts.[1] In the *Dissertation* he had never thought of forming such a list. There he did list a few intellectual concepts. This was not intended to be a complete list of intellectual concepts but only to give some examples: "Concepts of this sort are: possibility, existence, necessity, substance, cause, etc., with their opposites or correlates." *(Dissertation § 8)* Compare this random list of samples with some of the complete lists of pure concepts Kant tried to form during the initial phase of his Critical period: "The concepts of existence (reality), possibility, necessity, ground, unity and plurality, parts, all, none, composite and simple, space, time, change, motion, substance and accident, power and action, and everything that belongs to ontology proper."[2] This new list can be regarded as an expansion of the old one; however the expansion appears to have been guided not only by Kant's desire to be complete but also by the shift in the categorial function from the noumenal to the phenomenal world.

Thus the transition from the pre-Critical period to the initial phase of the Critical period can be characterized as an attempt to make a simple shift in the use of intellectual concepts from the intelligible to the sensible world: The shift in question does not involve the functional transformation of the formal into the material categories.

The need for this functional transformation arose only when Kant decided to conceive the pure concepts of understanding to be merely formal rather than material concepts in their primitive state. Evidently he made this decision in the course of composing the *Critique,* because it contains both views of the categories. Hence this decision can be profitably used to demarcate the Critical period into two phases, early and late. These may be called the First and the Second Phase of the Critical period. The First Phase is characterized by the material view of reason and the Second Phase by its formal view. By 'the material view of reason' is meant the doctrine that the pure reason is ab initio equipped with a set of a priori material concepts; by 'the formal view of reason' is meant the doctrine that the pure reason is ab initio equipped with a set of no a priori material but only of a priori formal concepts.

The material view of pure reason is anchored in the material function theory of its primitive concepts, while its formal view is linked to their formal function theory.

The material view of reason constitutes the continuity between Kant's pre-Critical period of the *Dissertation* to the First Phase of his Critical period, while their demarcation is established by the shift of the categories from the noumenal to the phenomenal employment. The phenomenal use of the categories constitutes the continuity between the First and Second Phase of his Critical period, while their demarcation is established by his shift from the material to the formal view of reason.

From all these considerations emerges the following intriguing question:

*Why did Kant shift from the material to
the formal view of pure reason?*

Kant appears to have adopted the formal view of reason
simply because he realized the untenability of its material
view. In order to see the implausibility of the latter view, we
have to place it in the context of the historical debate on the
genesis of ideas—i.e. the dispute between Locke and Leibniz
on the origin of ideas. Since the Locke-Leibniz debate was
rooted in one of the central questions governing the philosophical currents of the seventeenth and the eighteenth centuries,
it was addressed not merely to one but to a host of issues. Of
these issues, the most relevant one to our present discussion
concerns how the mind comes into possession of the material
concepts adequate for knowing the world. Before Kant, this
question of material concepts and their adequacy to their objects had been answered in two radically different ways.

Hume had faithfully adhered to Locke's doctrine of tabula
rasa and had tried to account for the correspondence of our
ideas to sensible objects by means of his copy theory of ideas:
If all our ideas are copies of sense impressions, there is no need
to explain why they conform to the objects of the senses. The
only challenge to this theory could come from the discovery of
ideas that cannot be derived from sense impressions. The discovery of such ideas would be doubly challenging. In the first
place, their existence would amount to an immediate refutation of the copy theory. In the second place, their employment
could not be accounted for within the copy theory. Ideas not
derived from sense impressions would correspond to the objects of the senses only by a miracle. For these reasons, Hume's
operational account of the genesis of the idea of causation is
meant not only to explain that genesis without damaging the
copy theory, but also to justify its use therein. Thus the copy
theory is not only a theory of genesis but also a theory of
justification.

Leibniz could not avail himself of the simple virtues of the copy theory in explaining the genesis of innate ideas and in justifying their employment. He holds that these ideas are not copies of sense impressions but the innate possessions of the rational mind. But this cannot be the final account of the genesis of innate ideas because the appeal to the nature of finite beings cannot be left as the ultimate one within his metaphysical system. Since every finite being is held to be created by God, innate ideas must have been implanted in the rational mind by the Creator. Let us call this account of innate ideas the innate theory in contrast to the copy theory.

As opposed to the copy theory, the innate theory has the serious drawback of placing the genetic account in the mythological domain. The theory that the Creator implants innate ideas in the rational soul sounds as mythological as any myth of creation. Moreover, this theory cannot stand, without an additional premise, as a full account of the applicability of those innate ideas to the world. The required additional premise is that God creates things to which innate ideas correspond, or that He inserts no innate ideas into the human mind which fail to correspond to such things. This would be a Leibnizian version of the postulate of divine veracity. Thus the innate theory is deficient because it can neither explain the genesis of innate ideas nor justify their application without introducing mythological premises.

As Bertrand Russell maintains, there may be really two versions in Leibniz' philosophy—an esoteric version for the initiate and an exoteric version for the vulgar.[3] If so, the innate theory with all its mythological trappings belongs to the exoteric version. The esoteric counterpart of the innate theory appears to be the theory of intellectual intuition: the notion that the rational mind intellectually intuits innate ideas in the divine mind. In support of this theory, we can cite the following passage from Leibniz:

Among other differences which exist between ordinary souls and minds *(esprits),* some of which differences I have already noted, there is also this: that souls in general are living mirrors or images of the universe of created things, but that minds are also images of the Deity or Author of nature Himself, capable of knowing the system of the universe.[4]

By 'ordinary souls' Leibniz means sensory souls; by 'mirrors' and 'images' he means the pictures that are obtained in their intuitions. So he may be pointing out the difference between intuitions belonging to sensory souls and those of intellectual souls ("minds"). That is, the former type of soul has sensible intuition of created things and the latter has intellectual intuition of the Creator. It is thus intellectual intuition that enables the intellectual souls to have a fellowship with God.[5]

If the theory of innate ideas is interpreted as being grounded in the doctrine of intellectual intuition, it shows a remarkable isomorphism with the theory of sensory ideas. Innate ideas are derived through intellectual intuition; sensory ideas are derived through sensible intuition. The application of innate ideas can be justified by intellectual intuition and the application of sensory ideas by sensible intuition. When the doctrine of innate ideas is formulated in the context of intellectual intuition, 'intellectual ideas' is a much more proper term than 'innate ideas.' In fact, Kant uses 'intellectual ideas' rather than 'innate ideas' in the *Dissertation*.

Time and again in the *Critique* Kant denies the possibility of intellectual intuition for human beings. Even in the *Dissertation* he had not accepted this doctrine. *(Dissertation* § 10) It is probably the disavowal of intellectual intuition that led him to deny the possibility of knowing the intelligible world. Without it, indeed, it is impossible to explain how the mind comes into possession of intellectual ideas and how the mind knows that such ideas are adequate for knowing the intelligible world.

When Kant shifted the use of intellectual ideas from the intelligible to the sensible world, he may have thought that the function of those ideas in the domain of senses need not pre-suppose the doctrine of intellectual intuition. He could then repudiate the doctrine of intellectual intuition without jeopardizing the doctrine of intellectual ideas so long as their use is limited to the sensible world. If this is the case, he must have soon realized that his was a naïve assumption.

The doctrine of intellectual intuition is also required to explain the mind's possession of intellectual concepts, even if they are applicable only to the phenomenal world. Since they are supposedly a set of real concepts that connote the ultimate properties and relations of phenomenal objects, to have these concepts would be tantamount to having insight into the ultimate structure of the phenomenal world. But this insight could only be an intellectual one. This cannot be explained by the doctrine of sensory intuition, but only by that of intellectual intuition. But Kant could not bring himself to embrace this doctrine in order to get out of his theoretical difficulty.

In order to overcome this difficulty, I suspect, Kant formulated the theory of object-formation. By this I mean his well-known doctrine that the objects of the phenomenal world are formed by the combination of the sensory manifold and that the categories, as the most general concepts of an object, provide the patterns for this combinatory operation. This is none other than Kant's doctrine of synthesis. If the doctrine is true, it can account for the necessary conformity of phenomenal objects with intellectual concepts. Kant tried to substantiate his object-formation theory by means of the transcendental image-schematism. As we have seen, however, he could not implement his doctrine of the image-schematism beyond the Axioms of Intuition. Thus the doctrine of object-formation had to be abandoned, and his arduous attempt to save the material view of reason came to naught. This concludes the First Phase of his Critical period.

Kant appears to have adopted the formal view of reason on his repudiation of its material view. If intellectual concepts are not real concepts but only logical ones, the possession of them cannot amount to the possession of intellectual insight into the fundamental nature of the phenomenal world. Unlike real concepts, logical concepts are not concepts of objects and their properties and relations. A set of logical concepts can by themselves tell nothing about the nature of objects. For this reason, if a priori concepts are merely formal, their presence in the mind prior to experience requires no explanation. Just this is the decisive advantage of identifying a priori concepts with formal concepts.

Whereas every real concept must be linked to some kind of intuition, logical concepts can transcend every possible intuition. Kant may have thought that, since logical concepts are prior to or independent of all possible intuitions, they can form the matrix for the truths of logic which can never be refuted by the evidences of intuitions. Thus he seems to have reached the Second Phase of his Critical period, in which he adopted the position that the human intellect can perform only formal or analytical functions with its a priori concepts alone.

By adopting this position Kant had to face the problem of explaining how formal reason develops into material reason. First of all, he had to explain how the mind comes to acquire a set of material categories. For this task he adopted the theory of concept-transformation, which assumes that the material categories are obtained by the transformation of formal into material concepts. This is his doctrine of the transcendental concept-schematism.

*What position did Kant eventually take
on the Locke-Leibniz dispute?*

If Kant's a priori concepts are regarded as real concepts, it is impossible to find a substantial difference between his theory of a priori concepts and Leibniz' theory of innate ideas. At best, we can detect about three points of difference between them. First, Kant is using a different term ('a priori concepts') from the one Leibniz used ('innate ideas'). Second, Kant recognizes only a few intellectual concepts, while Leibniz recognizes a great many of them. Third, Kant tries to establish a systematic unity among intellectual concepts, while Leibniz makes no such attempt. None of these differences, however, is significant enough to keep Kant out of the Leibnizian camp. In fact, Kant's material view of reason is the culmination of Leibniz' doctrine of innate ideas.*

But Kant's formal view of reason cannot be accommodated in the Leibnizian camp. For his formal view of reason is indistinguishable from Locke's doctrine of tabula rasa, as far as the problem of material concepts is concerned. This is indeed radical enough to set Kant apart from the Leibnizians.

Some may be tempted to soften Kant's break with the Leibnizians on the ground that his a priori concepts, though initially formal, are potentially material concepts. Leibniz admits that innate ideas are at first only potentially present in the mind. Since Locke's tabula rasa can be taken as a metaphor of potential presence of innate ideas in the mind, Leibniz takes pains in distinguishing two types of potentiality:

> Accordingly I have taken as illustration a block of veined marble, rather than a block of perfectly uniform marble or than empty tablets, that is to say, what is called by philosophers *tabula rasa*. If the soul were like these empty tablets, truths would be in us as the figure of Hercules is in a block of marble, when the block of marble is indifferently capable of receiving this figure or any other. But if there were in the stone veins, which should mark out the figure of Hercules rather than other figures, the stone would be more determined towards this figure, and Hercules would somehow be, as it were, innate in it, al-

---

*This point will be more fully explained in the remainder of this chapter and in the following one.

though labour would be needed to uncover the veins and to clear them by polishing and thus removing what prevents them from being fully seen. It it thus that ideas and truths are innate in us.[6]

Although a piece of marble is a potential statue, Leibniz wants to make it clear, its potentiality can be conceived in two different ways—as predetermined or indeterminate. A piece of veined marble has a determinate potentiality, while a piece of veinless marble has an indeterminate potentiality. A piece of blank marble would be exactly like a *tabula rasa*. Leibniz is conceding that his theory of ideas would be indistinguishable from Locke's theory if innate ideas are potentially present in the mind in the same manner as statues are potentially present in veinless marble.

Our problem is to decide which marble, veined or veinless, is a more suitable metaphor for capturing Kant's formal view of the pure reason. This decision can be made only by correctly interpreting the doctrine of the transcendental concept-schematism, which is meant by Kant to substantiate his formal view of reason. We can make a strong case for the metaphor of veined marble, if the doctrine of concept-schematism is taken to be a doctrine of conceptual development, namely, the development of formal into material concepts. For example, the doctrine may then be taken to assert that the formal concept of the logical subject develops into the material concept of the phenomenal substance. Under this interpretation of the transcendental concept-schematism, Kant's formal concepts may be regarded as potential material concepts or, conversely, his a priori material categories may be regarded as potentially present in pure reason in its formal state.

There are times when Kant himself appears to understand the transcendental concept-schematism as a process of development. For example, when he says that the schematism realizes *(realisieren)* the categories, he may very well be using 'realization' as a synonym of 'development.' (Cf. A 146 = B 185 f.) But there are a few weighty reasons against accepting this interpretation of the doctrine of the transcendental concept-schematism. We must now examine them.

If Kant's formal concepts are indeed potential material ones, we should expect that each would develop into a material concept. That is, there should be a neat one-to-one correspondence between the set of a priori formal concepts that are said to precede the transcendental concept-schematization and the set of a priori material concepts that are produced by that operation. But we cannot find such a neat one-to-one correspondence between Kant's formal and his phenomenal categories because his transcendental concept-schematism begins with twelve formal categories and produces eight phenomenal categories. Therefore we cannot regard the transcendental concept-schematism as the development of the potential into the actual material categories.

This argument may be criticized as merely presenting prima facie evidence against the concept-development theory of the transcendental schematism. But it can be reinforced by a technically more substantial one. If Kant's formal concepts are potentially material, they would cease to be formal when they are fully developed into material concepts. This should be so because no potential entities can any longer retain their potentialities when they are fully actualized. But the transcendental concept-schematism is supposed to leave intact the analytical functions of the formal concepts even after their development into material concepts. Thus the concept-development theory of the transcendental schematism violates the fundamental principle governing the process of actualization.

Perhaps because Kant knew that the concept-schematism cannot be regarded as a process of actualization, he called it a process of conversion *(Verwandlung)* rather than development. (Cf. A 321 = B 378) Even his assertion that the schematism "realizes" the categories can be accommodated within the concept-conversion theory of the schematism, if his assertion is taken to mean that the schematism transforms *logical* concepts into *real* ones. If this theory of concept-transformation is a correct interpretation of the concept-schematism, it can still be claimed that Kant's material categories are in a sense virtually present in pure reason in its formal state. That is to say, the concept-transformation theory of the transcendental schematism also supports the metaphor of veined marble and clearly establishes continuity between Kant's formal view of reason and Leibniz's doctrine of innate ideas.

But we have already indicated the implausibility of the concept-transformation theory. In Chapter 4 we suggested that Kant must have understood this transformation as the process of specifying the most general generic concepts into more specific ones. If the concept-schematism is such a process of specification, it may very well be regarded as a process of conversion or development. But we have also pointed out that this notion of specification stems from Kant's erroneous conception of logical concepts as the most general generic concepts. We have argued that the difference between logical and real concepts is a difference not in degree of generality but in kind. Since formal concepts are not generic ones, they cannot become objects for the logical operation of specification. Therefore the concept-conversion theory of the schematism is implausible.

In fact, all the arguments we have employed against the concept-development theory of the schematism are equally effective against the concept-conversion theory. In particular, the argument based on the continuation of the formal concepts' analytical functions even after their alleged conversion into material concepts can also conclusively dispose of the concept-conversion theory of the schematism. If the concept-schematism is really the process of transforming formal into material concepts, no formal concepts would be left after their alleged transformation into material concepts. Contrary to this expectation, the concept-schematism is understood to leave intact the analytical functions of the formal concepts even after their alleged conversion.

Neither the concept-conversion nor the concept-development theory is acceptable as a meaningful interpretation of Kant's doctrine of the transcendental concept-schematism, principally because neither of them can account for the fact that pure reason does retain formal concepts—in their analytical functions—even after having obtained material categories. An adequate explanation of this fact thus stands as the most compelling challenge for any significant interpretation of Kant's doctrine in question. The concept-formation theory appears to be the only interpretation of the concept-schematism that can meet this challenge.

By the concept-formation theory of the schematism, I mean the theory that the concept-schematism is the process of forming material concepts by using formal concepts. If formal concepts are merely used in the formation of material concepts, they can be retained for their original analytical functions even after the formation of material concepts. The concept-formation theory thus appears to be the fruitful idea that Kant was groping for under the name of 'concept-schematism.' He comes quite close to firmly grasping this idea in the following passage:

> We demand in every concept, first, the logical form of a concept (thought) in general, and secondly, the possibility of giving it an object to which it may be applied. In the absence of such object, it has no meaning and is completely lacking in content, though it may still contain *the logical function* which is required *for making a concept* out of any data that may be presented. [Italics added] (A 239 = B 298)

The context in which this remark is made gives the impression that Kant intends it to be not a special observation only about a priori concepts but a general observation about all concepts. But this remark cannot be valid for full-fledged generic concepts, because these concepts cannot be said to be lacking in meaning and content in the absence of objects. Whether there are horses or not, the concept of horse must carry the meaning of 'horse.' Thus Kant's observation is applicable only to his a priori concepts. He means to maintain that a priori concepts contain only logical functions for making concepts out of objects of intuitions. This assertion is quite close to the claim that a priori concepts are no more than logical concepts used in the formation of material concepts from the objects of intuitions.

Whereas the concept-development and the concept-transformation theories substantiate Leibniz' metaphor of veined marble, the concept-formation theory supports his metaphor of veinless marble. If the latter theory is the correct interpretation of Kant's transcendental schematism, his theory of material concepts is a decisive break with Leibniz' and a substantial link with Locke's.

In all fairness it must be admitted that most of the remarks Kant makes in characterizing the nature of the transcendental concept-schematism are meant to propound the concept-conversion or the concept-development theory. But we cannot take those remarks at their face value, for two compelling reasons. First, as we have already implied, those remarks make little sense if they are taken exclusively in their apparent forms; that is to say, the notion of converting or developing formal into material concepts is technically an absurd one. Second, Kant's own performances in the production of the transcendental concept-schemata resemble far more the operation of concept-formation than that of concept-conversion or concept-development. We can elucidate this point by reviewing some of the results of our investigation in Chapter 3.

As we pointed out there, Kant maintains that the three pure concepts of quantity are used in generating extensive magnitudes and that the three pure concepts of quality are used in generating intensive magnitudes. It would be far more correct to say, however, that the pure concepts of quantity are used in generating the concept of extensive magnitude and that the pure concepts of quality are used in generating the concept of intensive magnitude. Of course, the pure concepts of quantity and quality cannot by themselves generate the concepts of extensive and intensive magnitudes. The former can be used in forming the latter in confrontation with the objects which have extensive and intensive properties. Thus we can maintain the thesis that the concepts of intensive and extensive magnitude are two of the a priori material concepts that have been generated by using a priori formal concepts in the domain of sensible objects.

Kant's performances in the schematization of the relational categories on the other hand may appear to give stronger support to the concept-conversion or the concept-development theory of the schematism. It may be argued that the logical concept of a subject is converted or developed into the real concept of a substance and that the logical concept of ground and consequence is converted or developed into the real concept of cause and effect. However, to repeat, the conversions or developments in question have all the absurdities of converting or developing formal into material concepts. Moreover, if the conversion were really feasible, the real concept of causation would be assimilated into the logical concept of implication. There are occasions, to be sure, when even Kant vaguely hints at the notion of forming relational categories. In the following passage we may catch one of these rare moments:

Secondly, in order to exhibit *alteration* as the intuition corresponding to the concept of *causality,* we must take as our example motion, that is, alteration in space. Only in this way can we obtain the intuition of alterations, the possibility of which can never be comprehended through any pure understanding. For alteration is combination of contradictorily opposed determinations in the existence of one and the same thing. Now how it is possible that from a given state of a thing an opposite state should follow, not only cannot be conceived by reason without an example, but is actually incomprehensible to reason without intuition. . . . Lastly, the possibility of the category of *community* cannot be comprehended through mere reason alone. . . . We can, however, render the possibility of community—of substances as appearances —perfectly comprehensible, if we represent them to ourselves in space, that is, in outer intuition. (B 292 f.)

This passage appears in a special note called General Note on the System of the Principles which Kant attached to the end of Chapter 2 of the Analytic of Principles in the second edition. His overt aim for writing this note was to stress the importance of intuition, especially outer intuition, in exhibiting the objective reality of the categories. A casual reading of the passage may not catch anything more than an elaboration of this overt claim, but a closer inspection reveals the hidden thesis: Pure reason cannot even understand the meanings of the phenomenal categories without the aid of intuitions.

Kant maintains that pure reason cannot understand the meaning of alteration. This assertion implies that pure reason cannot understand the meaning of the phenomenal category of causation because alteration is an integral feature of this category. To be sure, Kant makes no use of the notion of alteration in producing the concept-schema of *causation*. Instead he uses the notion of *succession* in forming the concept of necessary succession as the schema for *causation*. But the notion of succession can be obtained only in the phenomenal field. Pure reason cannot comprehend the meaning of *succession* without the aid of intuitions, any more than it can by itself comprehend the meaning of *alteration*. If so, pure understanding cannot by itself comprehend the meaning of the phenomenal category of causation. Since it would indeed sound strange to say that pure understanding possesses a category whose meaning is incomprehensible, it is much more sensible to say that pure understanding cannot possess that category prior to its exposure to the domain of intuitions.

Kant does indeed assert that intuition plays only the function of exhibiting the meanings of the phenomenal categories. This assertion could be taken at its face value only on the premise that pure understanding has the categories and yet does not know their meanings before their meanings are exhibited. Since this premise entails the absurd consequence of having a concept whose meaning is incomprehensible, the only way to make sense out of Kant's assertion is to interpret his notion of 'exhibiting the meaning' in an unusual way, that is, to assume that 'to exhibit the meaning of a category' means to provide an exemplary instance for the ostensive formation of the meaning of a category. If this is so, the domain of intuitions is essential not merely for exhibiting but also for forming the meanings of the categories.

The phenomenal categories could still be called a priori concepts, if the transcendental concept-schematism is taken to be a process of concept-development or concept-conversion. For the process of conceptual conversion or development would establish a genetic continuity between formal and phenomenal categories. Under the concept-formation theory of the schematism, however, it is impossible to establish such a continuity and to justify calling the phenomenal categories a priori concepts. Still, within the framework of transcendental philosophy, there may be one last reason for calling the phenomenal categories a priori concepts: They are formed in the domain of a priori intuitions.

But even this reason turns out to be flimsy, for two good reasons. First, the doctrine of a priori intuitions is itself a dubious doctrine which can be maintained only by ignoring post-Kantian developments in geometry and physics. This objection may be regarded as unfair because it is external rather than internal, that is, it is not based on Kant's own doctrine of pure intuitions. But the merit of any criticism could not be affected by its internality or externality, so long as it is based on reasonable ground. And yet I have no desire to press this external objection any further. Instead let me present the second point which can be pressed on Kant's own ground.

The second objection is that almost none of the phenomenal categories can be formed in the domain of a priori intuitions. A priori intuitions can provide a proper domain for the formation of the phenomenal categories only if the former can present exemplary instances for the latter. Of the eight phenomenal categories, a priori intuitions can offer exemplary instances only for the concept of extensive magnitude. A priori intuitions of space and time can offer no exemplary instances for the concept of intensive magnitude; only a posteriori intuitions can do that. Pure intuitions can do no better for the relational categories. If space and time could present exemplary instances for the relational categories, as has been pointed out in Chapter 6, space and time would be two substantial entities rather than mere formal intuitions. The phenomenal category of possibility can find no exemplary instances in pure intuitions because it encompasses in itself all mathematical and relational categories. The phenomenal category of actuality cannot fare any better than that of intensive magnitude because both categories are concerned with the material features of intuitions. The phenomenal category of necessity will have the combined drawbacks of the categories *possibility* and *actuality* because *necessity* is made by the combination of possibility and actuality.

It is interesting to point out what may appear to be only a coincidence: The category for which space and time can provide exemplary instances coincides with the category for which Kant has given a transcendental image-schema. We have seen that he provides the image-schema for no other categories but the category of extensive magnitude. We have now found that space and time can provide exemplary instances for no other category. This is actually no coincidence at all, because transcendental image-schemata are precisely the exemplary instances that pure intuitions can provide for the categories.

Since all the phenomenal categories except one can be formed only in the domain of both pure and empirical intuitions, they are indistinguishable from empirical concepts. And even the single exception could not be tolerated once the implausible doctrine of a priori intuitions is repudiated. The phenomenal categories may be regarded as more primitive or more general than any other empirical concepts, but the distinction between a priori and a posteriori concepts can no longer be allowed to stand as the line of demarcation between the phenomenal categories and the empirical concepts. Thus the concept-formation theory of schematism implies that there are not two but only one kind of real or material concepts. If so, these concepts can allow only the distinctions of degree such as those based on the order of generation or the scope of generality.*

We have already pointed out the great affinity which Kant's theory of concept-formation has with Locke's theory of ideas, namely the thesis that the mind begins as a tabula rasa or a piece of veinless marble as far as real or material concepts are concerned. But we should not overlook one decisive difference between the two. Kant's "veinless marble" is not as com-

---

*George A. Schrader has argued for a limited version of the concept-formation theory, but his version is markedly different from mine in the following respects: (1) he does not recognize the formal view of the categories; (2) he assumes the categories to be primitive material concepts; (3) he further assumes a generic distinction between them and empirical concepts; and finally (4) he confines his formation theory to the domain of empirical concepts. For details, see his "Kant's Theory of Concepts," in Robert Paul Wolff, ed., *Kant* (Anchor Books, Garden City, Doubleday, 1967).

pletely empty as Locke's "blank tablet," because the former has a set of a priori formal concepts while the latter does not. Let us now try to explain how Kant's doctrine of formal concepts constitutes a decisive difference between his theory of mind and the orthodox empiricist theory of mind—i.e. the copy theory.

If all ideas are truly copies of impressions, they cannot be said to have been formed by the mind, as Kant's theory claims. Kant's formation theory still entails the spontaneity of intellect, while Hume's copy theory entails its receptivity. In addition to this difference in the nature of intellectual activities, there is an equally important difference in their products. Kant's concepts are universals (or rules); Hume's ideas are particulars. If ideas are truly copies of impressions, they can never attain the universality of concepts but must always retain the particularity of impressions. Kant, in contrast, always insists on the universality of concepts.

The universality of material concepts can be explained by the use of formal concepts in the formation of material ones. For this we recall Kant's conception of logic. In Chapter 2 we pointed out that the only logic he knew was the logic of classes. Because of this limited view of logic, we there surmised, he must have understood the ultimate function of logic to be the formation of classes and the specification of their relations. Since a priori formal concepts are the fundamental notions concerning classes and their relations, he appears to have thought, they can be used for the formation of material concepts—which are understood to be either the concepts of classes or of their relations. Thus the concept-formation theory of schematism can very well fit into Kant's conception of logic. It is this concept-formation theory that Kant might have used to account for the universality of all material concepts. The a priori formal concepts are used not only to form all material concepts but also to account for their universality.

That Kant can give a proper account of this universality

constitutes a decisive advantage of his formation theory over Hume's copy theory. Since Hume cannot adequately explain the universality of ideas, he cannot sustain even some of his fundamental distinctions. For example, let us take the distinction between relations of ideas and matters of fact. While the former are the domain of certainty, Hume claims, the latter are the domain of probability. But if ideas are truly copies of impressions, they cannot produce propositions of certainty any better than matters of fact. In its strict form, Hume's copy theory cannot accommodate the doctrine of abstract ideas or the notion of definitions, which provides the source of certainty attributed to the relations of ideas. Since the ideas must retain all the particularity and contingency of impressions, they can never be rescued from the domain of probability. Thus the copy theory cannot allow the distinction between relations of ideas and matters of fact to equate with the distinction between the domain of certainty and that of probability. If one faithfully adheres to the copy theory, one would be ultimately forced to accept Mill's doctrine of logical principles, namely, that even the truths of logic are derived from, and can be justified only by, experience.

Under the concept-formation theory, Kant's material concepts can be called neither a priori nor a posteriori concepts. They cannot be called a priori concepts because they cannot be derived from a priori sources alone; they cannot be called a posteriori concepts because they are not replicas of sense objects. They can be called both a priori concepts and a posteriori concepts. They can be called a priori concepts because they are the products of the spontaneous intellect; they can be called a posteriori concepts because they are formed in the domain of sense objects. The distinction between a priori and a posteriori concepts, which must have been indispensable in the First Phase of Kant's Critical period, has thus become obsolete in its Second Phase.

Kant's theory of concept-formation conclusively resolves

the Locke-Leibniz dispute on the genesis of ideas by simply undercutting its premise. The unquestioned premise for their disputations was the assumption that ideas must be generated either from intellect or from senses. This premise can be brushed aside by Kant's thesis that neither intellect nor senses can be an independent matrix for the genesis of material concepts. It is his profound insight to see that real concepts can be formed by intellect only in the domain of senses. Therefore every material concept is a joint product of understanding and sensibility.

We have tried to unravel all the tangled strands of thought that have guided Kant's transition from his pre-Critical to his Critical period and from the First Phase of the latter to its Second Phase. The central concern of those tangled thoughts is the problem of accounting for the conformity of our concepts with objects. Kant shifted the employment of intellectual concepts from the noumenal to the phenomenal world because he realized the impossibility of accounting for the conformity between concepts and object in the noumenal world without the doctrine of intellectual intuition. This was his transition from the pre-Critical to the Critical period. To account for the conformity between concepts and objects in the phenomenal world, Kant tried out the theory of object-formation and then that of concept-formation. The former is the product of the material view of reason and the latter is the product of its formal view. The former marks the First Phase of his Critical period and the latter its Second Phase.

We have tried to spell out the differences between Kant's two views of reason and categories as a preliminary to showing how these two views provide the foundations for his two conceptions of a priori judgments. We must now clearly establish the links these two views have with the two versions of the transcendental schematism which are Kant's two models for the production of a priori judgments.

How do the two views of the categories determine the functions of the transcendental schematism in its two versions?

We have called the two versions of the transcendental schematism the I (image-schematism) and the C (concept-schematism) versions. These two versions can be represented in the following diagram:

I VERSION	C VERSION
Transcendent Categories	Formal Categories
↑	↓
subsumed under	*used to form*
↑	↓
Pure (Formal) Intuitions	Phenomenal Categories
↑	↑
given through	*subsumed under*
↑	↑
Empirical Intuitions	Inner Sense

The I version is the model for producing the axiomatic a priori judgments; the C version is the model for producing the postulational a priori judgments. The first version underlies the progressive or synthetic method of proof; the second underlies the regressive or analytic method of proof.

In addition to these points of difference, which we have already noticed, we must point out one more significant difference. In the above diagram I have tried to indicate this difference by the direction of the arrows, which are meant to show the direction of conformity. In the I version, empirical intuitions conform to the forms of intuitions which are imposed by pure intuitions, and pure intuitions conform to the forms of thought which are imposed by the transcendent categories. Empirical intuitions can be said to conform to the transcendent categories through the mediation of pure intuitions. In the C version, the formal categories conform to the inner sense when they are used to form the phenomenal categories in conformity with the objects of inner sense.* Furthermore, the sense objects

*Even if the transcendental concept-schematism is taken to be a theory of concept-conversion or concept-development rather than

conform to the phenomenal categories when the former are subsumed under the latter. The phenomenal categories can be said to mediate between the formal categories and the objects of intuition.

We can restate this matter of conformity or conformation in terms of concession. In the I version, the transcendent categories make no concession to pure intuitions, which in turn make no concession to empirical intuitions. In the C version, the formal categories make the concession of being used in the formation of the phenomenal categories, and the objects of inner sense make the concession of being subsumed under the phenomenal categories.

The nature of conformation or conformity is unidirectional in the I version and bidirectional in the C version.

In this directional character of conformation we can locate perhaps the most significant link in Kant's doctrine of judgment, or even of his entire epistemology. In order to elucidate its significance, we have to place it in the context of the 1772 letter to Marcus Herz. There he wrote that "the key to the whole secret of metaphysics" was to discover the way to explain the agreement between our thoughts and objects:

> I asked myself: what is the relation between our images or representations [*Vorstellung*] and the objects? Suppose our images are nothing but the manner in which our subject is affected by the objects, it is easily understood that they should correspond [*gemäss seien*] to the objects. Thus the fact that our sensuous images have a definite and valid reference to external objects is comprehensible. . . . On the other hand, if the objects were themselves produced by our images, in the same manner as the divine thoughts are conceived as being archetypes

---

of concept-formation, this would not affect the direction of conformity in the C version.

of the real things, then again the conformity between images and objects could be understood. But—leaving moral ends out of account—our intellect neither produces an object through its images nor does the object produce its own reproduction in the intellect. Hence the pure concepts of intellect cannot be abstracted from the data of the senses. They have their sources in the nature of the soul. But neither are they there produced by the objects nor do they themselves produce the objects as would a divine mind.

In the *Dissertation* [no. 22] I was content to explain the nature of these intellectual representations in a purely negative manner as not being modifications of the soul produced by the objects. I had said that the sensuous images represent things as they appear and the intellectual concepts represent things as they are. But how then are these things given to us if not by the manner in which they affect us? On the other hand, if such intellectual representations are entirely due to our inner activity, whence then comes the agreement they are supposed to have with objects which are not their products, if this agreement is not assisted by experience? In mathematics this is quite all right because our objects are merely quantities and we can generate quantities by taking a unit a number of times. But when it comes to qualities, how my intellect should form quite by itself conceptions with which the things faithfully agree—this is a question which shows that we are still in utter obscurity as regards our own mental faculties.[7]

Kant is confronted with two alternatives: either concepts produce objects or objects produce concepts. The latter is obviously the Humean model: all concepts (ideas) are copies (reproductions) of impressions. The former can be shown to be the Leibnizian model. Although the human intellect is not a creative intellect in the absolute sense, Leibniz holds, it is much like the divine creative intellect:

> As regards the rational soul or *mind (l'esprit),* there is in it something [innate ideas] more than in the monads or even in mere *(simple)* souls. It is not only a mirror of the universe of created things, but also an image of the Deity. The mind has not merely a perception of the works of God, but it is even capable of producing something which resembles them, although in miniature. For, to say nothing of the wonders of dreams, in which we invent without trouble (but also without willing it) things which, in our waking hours, we should have to think long in order to hit upon, our soul is architectonic also in its voluntary activities and, in discovering the scientific principles in accordance with which God has ordered things *(pondere, mensura, numero, etc.),* it imitates, in its own province and in the little world in which it is allowed to act, what God does in the great world.[8]

Although there is nothing startling in claiming the creative functions of the rational soul in dreams and actions, it is quite unusual to maintain that the human soul is creative ("capable of producing something which resembles [the works of God]" and "architectonic") in the discovery of scientific principles. In order to explain this point, we have to introduce the fundamental principles of Leibniz' ontology and epistemology.

Leibniz holds that every object is made of simples or primitive entities. Because of this ontological principle, he maintains that to understand an object is to grasp its real definition, i.e. the definition that shows clearly and distinctly the combination of all the simples in the object.[9] That is, we can understand an object by breaking it down into all its constituent primitives and finding out how it has been originally constructed.* So our process of discovery retraces the process of the divine creation. For this reason, Leibniz claims that the human intellect resembles the architectonic character of the divine intellect. In this figurative sense, the human intellect produces (constructs or creates) the objects of its cognition. We can therefore claim that the thesis that concepts produce objects is the Leibnizian model.†

Kant never questioned the validity of the Humean model in the realm of sensations: "Thus the fact that our sensuous images have a definite and valid reference to external objects is comprehensible." But he could not accept the same model in the domain of intellectual concepts because it was incompatible with the spontaneity of intellect. Thus he was forced to adopt the Leibnizian model in accounting for the human intellectual activities. We have seen that he tried to implement the Leibnizian model in the I version of transcendental schematism and that he had to adopt the theory of object-formation in explaining the conformity of intellectual concepts with objects. We have also seen that he ran into obstacles in implementing this program.

In the letter to Herz, Kant expresses his dissatisfaction with the Leibnizian model. He is willing to accept it in the domain of morals apparently because he believes that the human intellect is completely autonomous in the moral sphere. He must have realized the significant difference between the theoretical and the practical intellect, namely, that the former can-

*Leibniz inherits this logic of the simples and complex from Descartes, who first propounded it in his Rules V and VI.

†The Leibnizian model is the model of *synthesis*. Even the term 'synthesis' was originally a favorite of Leibniz, although it is nowadays usually understood to have a Kantian origin. As indicated by the title of one of his short treatises, "On Universal Synthesis and Analysis, or the Art of Discovery and Judgment," Leibniz conceived synthesis as the reverse process of analysis and regarded it as the central feature of a cognitive process. His doctrine of synthesis and analysis underlies his program of *characteristica universalis*.

not be as free in producing or forming its objects as the latter. Even in the domain of theoretical intellect, he is prepared to accept the Leibnizian model for mathematical cognitions: "In mathematics this is quite all right because our objects are merely quantities and we can generate quantities by taking a unit a number of times." Here he is clearly describing his doctrine of extensive synthesis, which underlies the Axioms of Intuition. We have seen that the Axioms of Intuition was the only a priori principle which he succeeded in establishing through the I version of the transcendental schematism.

Now Kant sees that the Leibnizian model cannot work in the domain of physics because, unlike mathematical objects, empirical objects cannot be produced by the human intellect. Since the Leibnizian model runs aground on the reef of empirical objects, he appears to have decided to abandon the object-formation theory (the I version of schematism) and to adopt the concept-formation theory (the C version of schematism).

The C version of the transcendental schematism and its concept-formation theory constitute the truly Kantian model. In the letter to Herz, Kant looks with suspicion upon even the mere presence of a priori material concepts in the human mind, which he had taken for granted in the *Dissertation*. So when he adopts the C version, he rejects his previous doctrine of the transcendent categories and instead adopts his new doctrine of the formal categories. He now holds that the formal categories are used in the formation of the phenomenal categories, which will conform to the empirical objects. Whereas the I (image-schematism) version dictates the formation of objects, the C (concept-schematism) version recommends the formation of concepts. The former is a theory of object-formation; the latter is a theory of concept-formation. One presupposes the independent existence of concepts; the other presupposes the independent existence of objects.

The C version also demands, however, the conformity of

objects to concepts. It is assumed in the Humean model that all impressions can be known by immediate insight. That is, there is no need to bring objects under concepts for cognition. But it is a fundamental premise of the C version that no objects can be known in immediacy. Objects must conform to concepts; they must be subsumed under concepts. The particularity of objects can be experienced only through the universality of concepts.

The Kantian model recommends a reciprocal adjustment between concepts and objects, while the Leibnizian and Humean models dictate a unilateral subordination of either one to the other. It is precisely this reciprocal spirit of contrapuntal maneuver between concepts and objects that is echoed in Kant's famous dictum: "Thoughts without content are empty, intuitions without concepts are blind. It is, therefore, just as necessary to make our concepts sensible, that is, to add the object to them in intuition, as to make our intuitions intelligible, that is, to bring them under concepts." (A 51 = B 75) We can with equal right make either of two assertions: that the Leibnizian and the Humean models have been assimilated into the Kantian model or that the Kantian model has superseded the Leibnizian and Humean models. Whichever way we put it, the Kantian revolution has been implemented by the concept-formation theory of transcendental schematism, which has supervened over the Locke-Leibniz disputations on the genesis of ideas.

If the letter of February 21, 1772, to Marcus Herz truly reveals Kant's decision to reject both the Leibnizian and Humean models, it is perhaps the only extant document which records Kant's transition from the I to the C version of the transcendental schematism, or rather from the First to the Second Phase of his Critical period.* This transition is per-

*This transition appears to offer the best explanation for the extraordinary delay in the publication of the *Critique*. In the Herz letter, Kant promised to publish his magnum opus "within some three months."

haps the most momentous event in Kant's philosophical career, for it is precisely this event that brings to fruition, after a long period of incubation, those prodigious insights that are worthy of bearing his name.

But the world had to wait nine more years to see its publication. Shortly after writing the Herz letter, Kant may have come up with the postulational program and then tried to accommodate it within the framework of his previous axiomatic program. It may have been this difficult task of accommodation that took nine years. The Metaphysical Deduction may be taken as fairly reliable evidence in support of this view. As we have seen in Chapter 2, Kemp Smith suspects that the Deduction was probably the cause of the delay. But this suspicion can have different implications, depending on what significance is given to the Deduction. Since Kemp Smith assumes that the function of the Deduction lies solely in the systematic derivation of the categories, he believes that the categorial derivation alone perhaps held up the publication of the *Critique*. In Chapter 4, however, we have shown that the Metaphysical Deduction presupposes the double function theory of the categories, which Kant is likely to have provisionally adopted in his transition from the material view to the formal view of pure reason. If so, the problem of the categorial derivation should be taken only as a surface manifestation of his prodigious struggle in making the transition from the First to the Second Phase of his Critical period.

Chapter 8

The Twin Programs for the Analytic

By this time I hope I have explained adequately how Kant came to formulate the two views of a priori knowledge that we have designated the axiomatic and postulational views. I have tried to show how these two views must have been connected with his two genetic doctrines of material concepts, and why only one of these is truly Kantian while the other is still Leibnizian in spirit. I have also tried to show how his two views of a priori knowledge are grounded in the two versions of transcendental schematism. I have argued that only the C version is authentically a Kantian model while the I version is substantially a Leibnizian model. This general claim that Kant has formed two systematically intertwined clusters of epistemological doctrines will be called the "twin program theory."

It is the chief contention of this theory that Kant had two programs intended to account for the genesis of a priori knowledge. It is indeed one of the misfortunes of transcendental philosophy that Kant never fully recognized he had conceived two programs rather than one. His failure to separate them constitutes one of the main sources for the unwieldy complexity and systemic ambiguity in his construction of transcendental logic. Now it is necessary to show how Kant's twin programs governed the organization of the Transcendental Analytic.

Let us begin with the most baffling feature in the organization of the Transcendental Analytic: the relation between its two main divisions, which are called the Analytic of Concepts and the Analytic of Principles. These titles may give the impression that the two subdivisions implement the division of

Kant's labor into two phases, the first subdivision treating the problem of concepts and the second subdivision the problem of judgments. The problem of concepts would consist of questions concerning a priori concepts (their origin, their nature, their number, their interconnections, etc.), while the problem of judgments would consist of questions concerning a priori judgments (their production, their justification, their limitations, etc.). But this sort of division of labor cannot be found in the Transcendental Analytic. Indeed, a closer scrutiny reveals that the two subdivisions duplicate the labor instead of dividing it.

The Analytic of Concepts consists of two chapters: Chapter I, The Clue to the Discovery of all Pure Concepts of the Understanding; and Chapter II, The Deduction of the Pure Concepts of Understanding. Chapter I contains the Metaphysical Deduction and Chapter II the Transcendental Deduction; the former treats the problem of concepts and the latter the problem of judgments. Transcendental Deduction is in danger of being misconstrued as a resolution of the problem of concepts because Kant expresses the nature of its task in the language of concepts. That is, this Deduction is said to be the justification of a priori concepts. But 'the justification of a priori concepts' is an elliptical expression for 'the justification of the necessary applicability of a priori concepts.' Since the application of the categories is nothing more or less than the production of a priori principles, the Transcendental Deduction is therefore the justification of a priori judgments. Thus the second chapter of the Analytic of Concepts, as it turns out, treats the problem of judgments.

The Analytic of Principles also consists of two main subdivisions: Chapter I, The Schematism of the Pure Concepts of Understanding; and Chapter II, The System of all Principles of Pure Understanding. The Appendix, called the Amphiboly of Concepts of Reflection, is really an appendage to the entire Transcendental Analytic rather than to the Analytic of

Principles, because it spells out the difference between the functions of the concepts of reflection and the functions of the pure concepts of understanding. Chapter III, The Ground of the Distinction between Phenomena and Noumena, can claim no unique connection to the Analytic of Principles—or to any part of the entire Transcendental Analytic. This chapter can be more fittingly attached as an appendix to the Transcendental Aesthetic or the Transcendental Dialectic than to the Transcendental Analytic. Whereas the problems of the Analytic can be resolved without appealing to the distinction between phenomena and noumena, the problems of the Aesthetic and the Dialectic cannot be so divorced. While one of the central functions of the Aesthetic is to establish in the realm of intuitions grounds for the distinction between the sensible and the intelligible world, one of the central functions of the Dialectic is to confirm the same distinction in the realm of thought. Thus neither the Phenomena and Noumena nor the Amphiboly really belongs to the second division of the Transcendental Analytic.

The division of labor between the Schematism and the Principles is not so clearly drawn as it is between the Metaphysical and Transcendental Deductions. The Schematism is not devoted solely to the treatment of the problem of concepts, nor is the Principles devoted solely to the treatment of the problem of judgments. There is rather considerable overlap.

The Schematism contains two doctrines, that of transcendental image-schematism and that of transcendental concept-schematism. The former belongs to the problem of judgments, while the latter belongs to the problem of concepts. For the former is concerned with the application of the transcendent categories; the latter is concerned with the generation of the phenomenal categories. But the weight of the Schematism is not equally divided between these two problems: It produces eight transcendental concept-schemata but only two transcendental image-schema. Hence the Schematism can be considered as a treatise concerned mainly with the problem of concepts, which only incidentally sheds some light on the problem of judgments.

The Principles is apparently addressed to the problem of judgments, but we have seen in Chapter 3 that it contains a far more substantial exposition of the individual concept-schemata than the Schematism. Thus the Principles is not devoted to only one of the two problems any more than is the Schematism. But there is no doubt that the Principles is essentially concerned with the demonstration of a priori judgments and only incidentally with the explication of the meanings of the phenomenal categories. Therefore it can be considered as a treatise essentially devoted to the problem of judgments and only incidentally dealing with the problem of concepts.

Thus the division of labor between the two subdivisions of the Analytic of Concepts is duplicated in the division of labor between the two subdivisions of the Analytic of Principles. If so, we must raise the question:

*Why does the Analytic of Principles duplicate
the performances of the Analytic of Concepts?*

There might be some who would regard this question as unnecessary, because they could not detect the duplication. In fact, a few theories have been proposed which are meant to account not for the duplication but for the division of labor between the two main divisions of the Transcendental Analytic. These theories may be called the nonduplication theories, if ours is called the duplication theory. Since our question presupposes the existence of duplication, we should test the merit of the nonduplication theories before attempting to answer the question.

One of the nonduplication theories holds that the relation

of the Analytic of Concepts to the Analytic of Principles is the relation of the general to particulars.[1] While the former, it is claimed, is meant to prove the necessity of the categories *in general* for the possibility of experience, the latter is meant to prove the necessity of each of the *particular* categories for the possibility of experience. This theory derives a certain plausibility from the fact that the Transcendental Deduction pays no attention to the individual differences of the categories while the Principles presents a separate proof for each a priori principle. This plausibility turns out to be only apparent, however, when we consider the following. If the Analytic of Concepts, in respect to the Analytic of Principles, stands in the relation of the general to particulars, the former should play the role of a preface to the latter. But Kant gives no indication that the Transcendental Deduction is only provisional or a preliminary to the Principles. Nor does he intimate that in the Principles he is picking up the argument that he has only broached in the Transcendental Deduction. To all appearances, the Transcendental Deduction is presented as if it were as conclusive an enterprise in itself as the Principles.*

The theory in question might gain more plausibility if the Analytic of Concepts contained only the Transcendental Deduction, and if the Analytic of Principles contained only the Principles. For it is far more plausible to maintain that the Transcendental Deduction stands to the Principles in the relation of the general to particulars than to maintain that the entire Analytic of Concepts stands in the same relation to the entire Analytic of Principles. The theory in question there-

---

*Toward the end of the B Deduction Kant says that the Schematism will provide a fuller account of his theory in the Transcendental Deduction. (B 167) This appears to be merely an afterthought inserted into the second edition. Even this remark says nothing, moreover, about the overall relation between the Analytic of Concepts and the Analytic of Principles.

fore deserves serious attention only if it can account for the additional features of the two main divisions of the Transcendental Analytic—that is, if it can substantiate the case that the relation of the Metaphysical Deduction to the Schematism is also a relation of the general to particulars. But the case would be indefensible.

Another of the nonduplication theories holds that the Analytic of Concepts is concerned with ordinary experience while the Analytic of Principles is concerned with scientific experience. Kemp Smith expresses this view when he says that "while the Analytic of Concepts deals almost exclusively with ordinary experience, in the Analytic of Principles the physical sciences receive their due share of consideration."[2] This theory gains considerable support from two sources: first, from the ultimate appeal to the possibility of experience in the Transcendental Deduction, if 'the possibility of experience' is meant to be an elliptical expression for 'the possibility of ordinary experience'; second, from the well-accepted belief that the Analogies are the axiomatizations of Newtonian physics.[3] But these two sources cannot sustain the weight of the theory in question.

Kant gives no indication that the experience whose possibility is examined in the Analytic of Concepts is ordinary rather than scientific. Nor does he give any intimation that his a priori principles are concerned with the possibility of scientific rather than ordinary experience. We cannot even be certain that he was fully aware of the difference between the two kinds of experience. For example, the fact that he formulates the First Analogy once in terms of prime matter and once in terms of physical matter may reveal his instinctive and yet indecisive awareness of the difference between the two kinds of experience. This is not to deny the great influence Newtonian physics had on the development of the *Critique,* but it is an altogether different matter to force upon it the post-Kantian distinction between ordinary and scientific experience.

The very absence of the distinction in the *Critique,* in fact, enables us to find an argument which precisely contradicts or even reverses the contention of this theory. The Transcendental Deduction is meant to explain the a priori laws of nature. (A 127) Kant calls the cognition of these a priori laws of nature the pure science of nature. *(Prolegomena* § 15) The Second Analogy, which is as scientific in its conceptual apparatus as any other a priori principle, is said to have the function of establishing objective as distinct from subjective successions. For this reason, Kant says that the causal principle is concerned with the "ordinary employment" of understanding rather than its scientific employment. (B 4) Since nothing could be more fundamental to scientific experience than the discovery of the a priori natural laws and since nothing could be more essential to ordinary experience than the distinction between subjective and objective successions, it is plausible to maintain that the Analytic of Concepts is concerned with scientific experience, while the Analytic of Principles is concerned with ordinary experience.

The foregoing argument is presented only to show the absurdity of the attempt to carve out the distinction between ordinary and scientific experience within transcendental philosophy. Such an attempt is absurd precisely because Kant never entertained the possibility of the split between ordinary and scientific experience within the domain of his "pure science of nature" or of his "universal physics." (Cf. *Prolegomena* § 15) His pure science of nature should never be mistaken for one of the special sciences, because the former is intended to be the common foundation of the latter. His universal physics as such a common foundation is not meant to be distinguished from common ordinary perceptual experience. Thus the unity, or rather identity, of Kant's universal physics with ordinary experience is as firmly assumed as in the case of Aristotle's physics. This is why Kant feels no need to introduce the distinction between ordinary and scientific experience.

Apart from the absurdity of relying on the distinction in question, this second theory of nonduplication also runs aground on the twin rocks of the Metaphysical Deduction and the Schematism. If the Analytic of Concepts were to stand in the relation of ordinary to scientific experience to the Analytic of Principles, then the Metaphysical Deduction would stand in the same relation to the Schematism. This would mean that the transcendent categories derived in the Metaphysical Deduction are concerned with the possibility of ordinary experience and that the phenomenal categories formed in the Schematism are concerned with the possibility of scientific experience. But this would be an absurd claim.

The two theories of nonduplication we have examined are chiefly concerned with the relationship of the Transcendental Deduction and the Principles. Being limited by this chief concern, they are unable to accommodate the Metaphysical Deduction and the Schematism. We should, however, turn to a nonduplication theory which is not preoccupied with this relationship. We can find such a theory in a familiar group of assertions made in interpretation of the transcendental schematism.

Hegel says that the transcendental faculty of judgment in the Schematism is "a perceptive understanding or an understanding perception."[4] That is to say, the faculty of judgment is the union of two faculties, understanding and intuition, which Kant presented as independent faculties before the Schematism. Hegel's assertion can be construed in two different ways. When it is construed narrowly, it can have no other significance than that of characterizing the nature of transcendental schematism. When it is construed more broadly, however, it can have the significance of explaining the organization of the *Critique* itself. Hegel may very well mean to say that intuition is presented as an independent faculty in the Transcendental Aesthetic, that understanding is presented as another independent faculty in the Analytic of Concepts, and that the Schematism brings together these two faculties as inseparable components of the faculty of judgment. This further implies that the Analytic of Principles as a whole is the union of the Transcendental Aesthetic and the Analytic of Concepts.

It should be noted, of course, that this third theory was never explicitly asserted by Hegel but only suggested by his dictum on the transcendental schematism. It should also be pointed out that the acceptance of Hegel's dictum does not necessarily entail the acceptance of any theory on the relation of the Analytic of Concepts and the Analytic of Principles. For example, Peirce accepts Hegel's dictum and yet regards Kant's doctrine of schematism as only an afterthought which can have no integral connection with any other parts of the transcendental logic.[5] Weldon echoes a view similar to Peirce's.[6]

The theory that is meant to establish a connection between the two main subdivisions of the Transcendental Analytic in terms of the doctrine of schematism comes up against an insurmountable obstacle in the very ambiguity of that doctrine. We have repeatedly stressed the fact that the Schematism contains not one but two doctrines. Both the doctrine of concept-schematism and the doctrine of image-schematism are doctrines of mediation. When Hegel calls the faculty of judgment the union of two faculties, he does not see that the third faculty in question can take on an entirely different significance, depending on whether it is to perform the function of concept-schematism or that of image-schematism. The Schematism can claim no novelty in presenting the latter function because it has been already introduced as the function of transcendental imagination and apperception in the Transcendental Deduction. As far as the function of transcendental image-schematism is concerned, the Schematism only repeats, or at best elaborates, the performance of the Transcendental Deduction. Hence this feature of the transcendental schematism is of little value to nonduplication theories in general.

The function of concept-schematism, on the other hand, is indeed a novel feature of the Schematism, but it is incompatible with the doctrine of intellect as presented in the Transcendental Deduction. As we have seen, the Transcendental Deduction stands on the material view of reason whereas the transcendental concept-schematism rests on the formal view of reason.* Whereas the Transcendental Deduction begins with a set of material concepts and tries to show their necessary application, the transcendental concept-schematism begins with a set of formal concepts and proceeds to convert them into a set of material concepts. Because of this theoretical incompatibility, the doctrine of concept-schematism can never assimilate the doctrine of understanding presupposed and developed in the Transcendental Deduction.

Since the Schematism and the Transcendental Deduction either duplicate or contradict each other, they cannot help us to establish continuity between the two sections of the Transcendental Analytic. It might be plausible to maintain that the Analytic of Principles is the fusion of the Analytic of Concepts and the Transcendental Aesthetic, if the Analytic of Concepts contained only the Metaphysical Deduction. For this Deduction treats the function of understanding in complete isolation from the function of sensibility, while the Transcendental Aesthetic treats the function of sensibility in the same manner. If the Schematism were to immediately follow the Metaphysical Deduction, the former could be regarded as the attempt to reconsider the two faculties in their joint operations. But the Transcendental Deduction comes

---

*Here I have in mind chiefly the A Deduction. As we will soon see, some passages of the B Deduction reflect the formal view of reason.

between the Metaphysical Deduction and the Schematism and presents one of Kant's theories on the cooperation of sense and intellect. Hence it is impossible to maintain that the Analytic of Principles presents the faculty of intuitive understanding by combining the intuition of the Transcendental Aesthetic and the understanding of the Analytic of Concepts.

I hope we have seen enough fair samples of the nonduplication theories. Since none of them has turned out to be tenable, we had better take the duplication theory seriously. Beyond such negative grounds, our duplication theory has two prima facie pieces of evidence in its favor. First, the Analytic of Concepts and the Analytic of Principles cover exactly the same two topics. Second, Kant himself never indicates any connection between these two sections of the Transcendental Analytic. The two sections have been constructed so independently of each other that the reading of one without the other neither presents grave obstacles in comprehension nor invites the danger of distortion. In fact, we encounter serious difficulties only when we try to view them together and establish their continuity, not only because they duplicate each other but also because they display incompatible features.

Since we should not rest our case only on prima facie evidence, we shall adduce some more positive evidence in its support. We can find it in our twin program theory. Since Kant has formed two programs for the production of a priori knowledge, we shall maintain, he must have used two programs in the organization of the Transcendental Analytic. This twin program theory will explain not only the similarity but also the incompatibility of the Analytic of Concepts and the Analytic of Principles.

The twin programs are the axiomatic and the postulational. Before proceeding to use them in explaining the organization of the Transcendental Analytic, we had better be clear about their characteristic differences. Let us therefore first enumerate the differences which we have already noted and then connect them with some further differences, which we have not yet mentioned.

The axiomatic program presupposes the material view of reason; the postulational program presupposes its formal view. The former begins ;with a set of primitive material (transcendent) categories, while the latter begins with a set of formal categories and proceeds to form the phenomenal categories. The former is executed through the I (image) version of the transcendental schematism and the latter through its C (concept) version. The I version results in the synthetic or progressive method of justification and the C version in the analytic or regressive method of justification.

The postulational program presupposes the independent existence of objects, while the axiomatic program does not. The latter demands the formation of objects; the former recommends the formation of concepts. *Synthesis* is the model of cognition in the axiomatic program, while it is *judgment* in the postulational program. Synthesis performs the function of *constructing* objects; judgment performs the function of *determining* the nature of the independently existing objects. Mathematics provides a model for the function of *construction*, and physics for the function of *determination*.

The two programs also differ in the direction of conformity between concepts and objects. Since the function of synthesis is to construct objects in accordance with concepts, the axiomatic program demands the *conformity of objects to concepts*. Since the function of judgment is to determine (or specify) the nature of the independently existent objects, the postulational program demands the *conformity of concepts to objects*. The conformity of objects to concepts entails the coherence theory of truth; the conformity of concepts to objects entails the correspondence theory of truth.

Let us now try to tabulate these points of difference between the two programs in the following chart:

AXIOMATIC PROGRAM	POSTULATIONAL PROGRAM
Material view of reason	Formal view of reason
The I version of schematism	The C version of schematism
Formation of objects	Formation of concepts
Function of synthesis	Function of judgment
Construction of objects	Determination of objects
Conformity of objects to concepts	Conformity of concepts to objects
Coherence theory of truth	Correspondence theory
Synthetic method of proof	Analytic method of proof
Procedure of mathematics	Procedure of physics

We can now use this chart to explain how Kant's twin programs govern the organization of the Transcendental Analytic. We shall begin with the Analytic of the first edition because its revision in the second edition introduces further complications—which will be taken up after we have explained the organization of the Analytic of the first edition.

The Transcendental Deduction of the first edition is an implementation of the axiomatic program. In the A Deduction Kant does not admit the independent existence of empirical objects, that is, independent of the acts of representation. (A 105) It is the act of synthesis that generates empirical objects. Therefore Kemp Smith is correct in claiming that Kant recognizes the independent existence of only the transcendental object.[7] But these references to the transcendental object do not weaken but rather strengthen our case.

Kant introduces the transcendental object to clarify the relation of our representations to the objects of representations. (Cf. A 104 ff.) He says that all representations generally refer to some objects of representations and that this reference to objects is the source of necessity or constraint for our representations. (A 104) He even goes on to say that the transcendental object is the only object to which our representations can be referred. Since by 'the transcendental object' he means the transcendent object, he maintains it to be a mere x, which cannot be called upon to confer necessity on our representations.

Kemp Smith maintains that Kant's use of 'the transcendental object' is a residual from his pre-Critical doctrines because Kant is trying to refer our representations to the noumenal object.[8] But this charge is not well founded. If Kant were to say that the objectivity of our representations can be determined by reference to the transcendental object, he would certainly be echoing his pre-Critical doctrine that the world of noumena is accessible and knowable. On the contrary, he is now holding that the transcendental object is inaccessible and unknowable. This is indeed one of the best-known Critical doctrines, invoked here to clarify the meaning of 'objectivity,' which lies behind our objective representations. Since all appearances are our representations and since all appearances are the appearances of the transcendental object, Kant argues, all our representations are the representations or appearances of the transcendental object. This direct reference of our representations to the transcendental object reflects Kant's assumption that there are no empirical or phenomenal objects that are not our representations, or rather that empirical objects are not objects of representations but only representations.

It is this thesis concerning construction of phenomenal objects that underlies Kant's assertion that nature as a whole is produced by the understanding. The material feature of nature cannot be produced but can only be given; its formal feature, however, cannot be given but can only be constructed by the understanding. Since nature as a whole is nothing more than the totality of empirical objects, the construction of the latter must entail the construction of the former.

The construction of empirical objects requires the categories. Since the categories are the concepts of an object in general, they can function as the general pattern for the construction of objects. And since the categories are the patterns for the construction of empirical objects, the objects must conform to the categories. Thus the conformity of objects to concepts constitutes the central thesis of the A Deduction. At the opening of the Transition to the Transcendental Deduction of the Categories, Kant presents the following two alternatives:

> There are only two possible ways in which synthetic representations and their objects can establish connection, obtain necessary relation to one another, and, as it were, meet one another. Either the object alone must make the representation possible, or the representation alone must make the object possible. In the former case, this relation is only empirical, and the representation is never possible *a priori*. This is true of appearances, as regards that [element] in them which belongs to sensation. In the latter case, representation in itself does not produce its object in so far as *existence* is concerned, for we are not here speaking of its causality by means of the will. None the less the representation is [the] *a priori* determinant of the object, if it be the case that only through the representation is it possible to *know* anything *as an object*. (A 92 = B 124 f.)

One alternative is to produce concepts which conform to objects; the other is to produce objects which conform to concepts. As far as the formal features of objects are concerned, Kant maintains, the function of synthesis is to produce objects which conform to the categories. It is this conformity of all empirical objects to the categories that makes the understanding the source of all a priori laws of nature. (A 127)

Since the A Deduction demands the construction of objects in conformity with concepts, its entire argument turns on the subjective sources of cognition. Kant recognizes this point when he says that the necessity of objective representations can be accounted for by reference not to objects but to the formal unity of consciousness. (A 104 f.) To ground his argument on the subjective sources of cognition, Kant introduces the three faculties of intuition, imagination, and understanding and their synthetic functions. (A 98 ff.) He further distinguishes between the a priori and the a posteriori elements in these three faculties. As we pointed out in Chapter 5, this distinction is designed to prepare the ground for the generation of axiomatic necessity of pure synthesis. This necessity is produced in the recognition of the synthesis of pure intuitions through the pure concepts of understanding. (A 118) It is this necessity of pure synthesis that establishes the objective *affinity* of the empirical representations. (A 122)

It is not necessary to repeat the argument (in Chapter 5) that the categorial function in the recognition of pure synthesis involves the I version of transcendental schematism. But let us stress the fact that the subjective sources constitute the fountainhead of objectivity. In the Preface to the first edition Kant distinguishes between the subjective and the objective aspects of the A Deduction. (A xvi) He goes on to maintain that only the objective deduction is essential to his argument and that the failure of the subjective deduction cannot affect its validity. But this cannot be accepted as a correct account of his own performances in the A Deduction.

The two aspects of the A Deduction can be distinguished from each other but cannot be separated. Since the A Deduction does not recognize the existence of objects apart from the acts of construction, the very existence of objects cannot be separated from the subjective sources of cognition. This inseparability makes it senseless to talk of the separability of the objective aspect of the A Deduction from its subjective aspect. Furthermore, Kant has himself declared that the necessity of objective representations can be derived only from the transcendental sources of the subject. (A 106) For these reasons, the objective deduction cannot take a single step without reliance on the subjective deduction.

That the A Deduction makes its ultimate appeal to transcendental subjective sources can be further elucidated by pointing out the important function that is played by transcendental apperception. Kant's final argument in the A Deduction is that the conformity of appearances to the categories is the necessary condition for consciousness. (A 123–25) On its surface, this argument becomes tautological once the relation of the categories and consciousness is clearly established.

For Kant, 'transcendental consciousness' is synonymous with 'transcendental apperception,' which is in turn synonymous with 'pure understanding.' It is tautological to say that nothing can be an object of pure understanding without conforming to its pure concepts, because pure understanding can take note of things only through its categories. It is equally tautological to say that nothing can become an object of transcendental consciousness except by conformity to the categories, because transcendental consciousness is none other than pure understanding. If nothing conforms to the categories, there can be nothing for the consciousness to be conscious of. Consciousness of nothing is no consciousness. Therefore the conformity of objects to the categories is the necessary condition for the possibility of transcendental consciousness as well as for the possibility of empirical objects or rather the entire phenomenal world.

I hope to have marshaled enough evidences in support of the view that the A Deduction is the implementation of the axiomatic program. Now we have to determine how the other half of the Analytic of Concepts fits into the axiomatic program. The Metaphysical Deduction does not fit neatly into the axiomatic program. The central idea that governs the Metaphysical Deduction is the notion of judgment; the forms of judgment are adopted as the clue for the derivation of the categories. We have said that judgment is the model of cognition in the postulational program while synthesis is the model of cognition in the axiomatic program. For this reason, it is likely that Kant developed his method of the categorial derivation in the context of the postulational program rather than in that of the axiomatic program.

The Metaphysical Deduction belongs to the A Deduction by virtue of its results, because it derives neither the formal nor the phenomenal categories, but the transcendent ones. In the opening section of the A Deduction, Kant claims that the categories are not limited by any conditions of sensibility because they are the absolutely universal concepts of an object. (A 88 = B 120) The Metaphysical Deduction produces precisely these absolutely universal concepts.

In confirmation of the view that the Metaphysical Deduction belongs to the axiomatic program only by virtue of its results, we may cite the point developed in the last chapter, namely, that Kant's double function theory of the categories is his attempt to accommodate his previous material view of reason within his later formal view of reason. It is by virtue of this double function theory that Kant tries to establish a route of derivation from his Table of Judgments to his Table of Categories. (A 79 = B 104) This fact clearly shows that this Deduction has been conceived within the conceptual framework of the postulational program and yet is used, by fiat, to yield the results which are required for the axiomatic program. It is in fact this fiat that pervades most of the arbitrary features of the Metaphysical Deduction which have been examined in Chapters 1 and 2. Of course, this fiat might have resulted from Kant's attempt to unite his two programs into one.

Let us now see how the postulational program is implemented in the Analytic of Principles. Kant's execution of this program is complicated by the fact that he still retains a substantial portion of the axiomatic program in the Analytic of Principles. In spite of this complication, as we shall see presently, the postulational program is the dominant idea governing the organization of the second division of the Transcendental Analytic.

We have seen that the doctrine of concept-schema belongs to the C version of the schematism while the doctrine of image-schema belongs to the I version. The Schematism is the continuation of the axiomatic program insofar as its doctrine of image-schematism is concerned, but it is the initiation of the postulational program insofar as its doctrine of concept-schematism is concerned. Since the Schematism produces no more than two image-schemata and no less than eight concept-schemata, it is clearly dominated by the postulational program. The two image-schemata are not even called schemata; they are called only "pure images." (Cf. A 142 = B 182) This should also indicate the waning force of the axiomatic program.*

In the *Critique* the Schematism introduces for the first time the notion that the pure concepts of understanding are only formal concepts prior to their schematization. It is also the first occasion for presenting the doctrine of the phenomenal categories. It also undertakes the first formal examination of the nature of judgment. Thus the Schematism introduces almost all the essential features of the postulational program.

The Schematism contains no formal discussion on the nature of objects. But it is impossible to comprehend the Schematism without appealing to the implicit presuppositions about their nature, because the Schematism is concerned with the application of concepts to objects. The Schematism retains the axiomatic program's doctrine of empirical objects, insofar as it is construed to contain the doctrine of image-schematism. This doctrine stands on the presupposition that empirical intuitions are in themselves amorphous and can gain the essential fea-

*It is most likely that Kant began the Schematism as a means to implementing the axiomatic program only to realize its impossibility. Sometime after realizing this, he must have conceived the postulational program and then tried to adapt the Schematism to it.

tures of an object only by conforming to the forms of intuition. It is this amorphousness of empirical intuitions that creates the need for the construction of empirical objects.

The Schematism also introduces the postulational program's doctrine of empirical objects when it is construed to present the doctrine of concept-schematism. Transcendental concept-schematism is intended to transform formal concepts into material concepts adequate for the determination of independently existent objects. For this reason, the doctrine of concept-schematism must presuppose the independent existence of empirical objects. The concept-schemata are called the transcendental time-determinants (determinations), probably because they have the function of determining the nature of independently existent objects.

Now we can better understand Kemp Smith's distress regarding Kant's doctrine of subsumption. In Chapter 4 we noted his complaint that Kant's doctrine of subsumption misrepresents the function of the categories because the categories are meant to play not the function of subsumption but that of synthesis. Kemp Smith stops short of substantiating his complaint because he fails to see the need to specify the difference between the two functions. The important difference between them is concerned with the nature of objects.

The function of synthesis presupposes no independently existent objects because its purpose is to construct them. But the function of subsumption presupposes the existence of independent objects because the subsumption of objects under concepts must always be posterior to the existence of objects. The commensurateness of concepts to objects, which justifies the function of subsumption, can become an important issue only in the context of independently existent objects. Subsumption has the function of conforming concepts to objects, while synthesis has the function of conforming objects to concepts.

Let us now see how the Principles implements the postulational program while retaining the axiomatic program. In the introductory remark to the Principles Kant says that the a priori principles can be proved not in the objective fashion but only "from the subjective sources." (A 149 = B 188) The proof from the subjective sources is the synthetic method of proof, which was relied on in the A Deduction. When Kant comes to the proof of each a priori principle, he produces a purely axiomatic proof only for the Axioms of Intuition. As we saw in Chapter 6, he retains some trace of the axiomatic method in the mixed (axiomatic–postulational) argument for the First Analogy and tries out an axiomatic proof in one short paragraph for the Second Analogy. Except for these three occasions, he employs the postulational method of proof throughout.

The notion of judgment is a dominant idea in the Principles. In the two introductory sections of the Principles, Kant discusses the highest principle of all analytic judgments and the highest principle of all synthetic judgments. To be sure, his discussions of these two highest principles still retain a substantial residue of his doctrine of synthesis. In fact it would appear that he tries to assimilate the doctrine of synthesis into that of judgment. If this is so, he never fully succeeds, for he fails to bring himself to abandoning the doctrine of object-formation. But the notion of judgment nevertheless remains as a dominant one throughout his proofs of the a priori principles because every a priori principle is treated as a proposition or a judgment.

The Principles, accordingly, implements the doctrine of determining the nature of independently existent objects, while retaining the doctrine of constructing objects in conformity with concepts. The Axioms of Intuition clearly retains the doctrine of construction; the function of extensive synthesis is the function of object-formation. Insofar as intensive magnitudes cannot be constructed, however, the Anticipations of Perception abandons the doctrine of construction. In this way, the First Analogy clearly relies on the doctrine of determination; the substantial empirical objects cannot be constructed. The Second Analogy is highly ambiguous, as we saw, in its doctrine of objects: the causal chains are viewed sometimes as embodied in the alterations of substantial entities and sometimes as embodied in the successions of sense impressions. The former view reflects the doctrine of determination; the latter reflects the doctrine of construction. The Third Analogy, finally, carries over all the ambiguity of the Second Analogy on the doctrine of objects.

In general the notion of determination is the dominant force in the organization of the Principles while the notion of construction is the recessive one. But the dominant notion is never given a decisive edge over the recessive notion. It is only in the context of Kant's indecision between these two notions of objects that we can make some sense out of his curious characterization of the difference between the mathematical and the dynamical principles. The former he calls constitutive and the latter regulative principles. This division of the a priori principles of understanding cannot cohere with the assertion that the pure concepts of understanding have constitutive functions while the pure concepts of reason have only the regulative functions.

We cannot give the same meanings to 'constitutive' and 'regulative' in the two cases. The mathematical principles are probably called constitutive because they are used for the construction of objects; the dynamical principles are probably called regulative because they cannot be so used. (Cf. A 179 = B 222) If the distinction between the two is taken in this sense, it is quite different from the functional distinction between the pure concepts of understanding and the pure concepts of reason.

I hope to have presented sufficient evidence that the Analytic of Principles implements the postulational program while retaining a substantial residue of the axiomatic program. Let us now see how these two programs react with each other in the second edition of the *Critique*.

The Transcendental Deduction in the second edition opens with the doctrine of combination, which appears to echo the object-formation theory of the A Deduction. (B 129 ff.) But Kant connects this doctrine of combination with the function of judgment rather than with that of synthesis: Representations are combined not to form an object but to arrive at an objective determination of an object. (B 142) He recognizes two types of combinations, the subjective and the objective. The latter corresponds to the objective phenomena, while the former does not. Then he presupposes the independent existence of empirical objects and the correspondence theory of truth. He adopts the postulational method for the distinction of the objective from the subjective combination of representations. At the same time, his rejection of the axiomatic method is reflected in his repudiation of the subjective deduction of the first edition.

In the B Deduction Kant also introduces the doctrine of the formal categories as an integral feature of the doctrine of judgment. (B 143) But he does not recognize the need of converting them into material categories before their application. Instead, when Kant comes to face the question of their application, he completely forgets the doctrine of the formal categories and proceeds on the assumption that the categories are transcendent: "The pure concepts of understanding are free from this limitation [of sensible intuition], and extend to objects of intuition in general, be the intuition like or unlike ours." (B 148) Thus he reintroduces the transcendental synthesis *(synthesis speciosa)* of pure imagination in Section 24 of the B Deduction. He says that the application of the categories to the transcendental synthesis of imagination is their first application and that this is the ground for their later application to empirical representations. (B 152) This is precisely the I version of the transcendental schematism and the doctrine of the objective affinity. Thus Kant repeats his main contention of the A Deduction.

Toward the end of the B Deduction, Kant brings up the question of the conformity of concepts with objects. This is the same question which he took up at the beginning of the A Deduction. He presents the same two alternatives: Either objects conform to concepts or concepts conform to objects. He concludes by opting for the conformity of objects to concepts in the case of the pure concepts of understanding, the same alternative that he adopted in the A Deduction. (B 166 f.)

With this brief survey we can see that the B Deduction accommodates some of the essential features of the postulational program in its first half and then reverts to the axiomatic program in its second half.

In the *Prolegomena* Kant appears to combine the two programs even more strangely than in the B Deduction. There he also adopts some essential features of the postulational program. He claims to rely on the postulational rather than the axiomatic method of justification, and does employ the term 'judgment' rather than 'synthesis.' But the adoption of 'judgment' is not a substantial but only a superficial maneuver, because judgment in the *Prolegomena* has precisely the same function as synthesis in the axiomatic program. Judgments of perception and judgments of experience are two ways of constructing objects by the combination of representations. Thus the *Prolegomena* does not recognize the independent existence of empirical objects and instead advocates the object-formation theory. Hence it also presupposes the coherence theory of truth. Kant tries to prove the validity of the categories on the ground that they are necessary for the coherent organization of representations in experience. In brief, he substantively sticks to the axiomatic program while adopting some superficial features of the postulational program.

Since Kant tries to present the substantive features of one program through the language of the other, he is in danger of falling between two stools, because a combination of the two programs fails to attain the full force of either. For example, let us consider Kant's argument that the categories transform the subjective combination of representations into the objective combination. This argument gains neither the full force of the progressive proof nor that of the regressive proof. It cannot attain the former because it does not appeal to the transcendental synthesis of pure intuitions; it cannot attain the latter because it does not appeal to the independent existence of empirical objects. Thus Kant's central argument in Part Two of the *Prolegomena* can never amount to anything more than a dogmatic assertion.

If we shift our attention from the Transcendental Analytic to the *Critique* as a whole, we may make a case for the claim that the postulational program gets some reinforcement in the second edition while the axiomatic program dominates in the first. As Kemp Smith points out, the synthetic method of proof is rigorously employed in the Transcendental Aesthetic of the first edition.[9] He is also correct in observing that the analytic method is used there only to confirm the result of the synthetic method.[10] The synthetic method of the A Deduction gets diluted in the B Deduction.

Kant presents his axiomatic definition of a priori knowledge in the Introduction to the first edition. (A 2) He presents his postulational definition of a priori knowledge in the Introduction to the second edition. (B 3 ff.) It is not necessary here to dwell on these points since they have been extensively covered in Chapter 5. Again, in the Introduction to the second edition, Kant formulates the main question of the *Critique* as "How are a priori synthetic judgments possible?" This may indicate his willingness to see his enterprise in the context of judgment rather than synthesis.

In the Principles of the second edition Kant stresses the independent existence of empirical objects. In his general observation on the function of the Analogies, he accentuates the distinction between perceptions (or representations) and objects of perceptions. (B 218 f.) Moreover, he accentuates the distinction between experience and perceptions in his definition of experience as the "knowledge which determines an object through perceptions." (B 218) When he comes to the Second Analogy, he attaches one special parenthetical paragraph at the beginning of his proof, where he says that every objective succession governed by the causal law is an alteration of a substance. (B 233) This stipulation resolves the ambiguity of the Second Analogy in the first edition concerning whether objective successions are *constructed* through synthesis or *determined* through judgment. Since Kant never implies that substantial entities can be constructed, he appears to have attached the parenthetical stipulation in order to resolve the ambiguity in favor of the independent existence of empirical objects.

That Kant equates the independent existence of empirical objects with their substantial nature clearly shows up in the Refutation of Idealism, which is attached to the Postulates of Empirical Thought in the second edition. (B 274 ff.) There he tries to disprove both dogmatic and problematic idealism by demonstrating the necessity of substantial entities (the permanent) for the possibility of consciousness. The prominence of the axiomatic program in the first edition must have been one of the main reasons that led many of Kant's readers to construe his doctrine as but one more version of idealism. Since the axiomatic program propounds the construction of all empirical objects instead of admitting their independent existence, it can be rightly branded as an idealistic doctrine.

In his attempt to absolve himself from the idealistic charge, Kant appeals to the necessity of the First Analogy for the possibility of self-consciousness, that is, the thesis that the permanent substance is necessary for the determination of one's existence in time. (B 375 f.) He assumes that this thesis establishes the existence of external objects as firmly as that of the self-consciousness, simply because he equates the substantial entities with external ones ("This permanent cannot, however, be something in me."). (B 275) He appears to take for granted the equivalence in question on the assumption that substantial entities cannot be constructed. That he makes this assumption can be further supported by his refusal to construct the transcendental image-schema for the category of substance. Thus in the second edition Kant stresses the independent existence of empirical objects by stressing their substantiality.

Kant attaches a general note to the Principles in the second edition, called the General Note on the System of the Principles. (B 288 ff.) It is in this general note that he reveals the most dramatic turn in his thought. As we have argued in the last chapter, this dramatic turn is his shift from the concept-transformation theory to the concept-formation theory of schematism. This note is about the closest Kant comes to espousing the radical theory that all material concepts are formed and that none of them is innate to the mind.

I hope I have adequately shown that Kant had twin programs for the organization of the Transcendental Analytic. Now that we have seen how Kant conceived the twin programs and how he tried to execute them, we must take up the task of assessing their relative merits. There are two different ways of evaluating these two programs: (1) They can be judged in the light of Kant's implementations of them, or (2) they can be judged in the light of their promises. In Chapter 6 we have seen the serious flaws in Kant's attempts to prove the a priori principles. For this reason the two programs can never receive a fair assessment if they are judged solely in the light of Kant's own performance. Therefore it would be best to evaluate them in the light of their own promises.

The axiomatic program cannot be executed for all the pure concepts of understanding. Since this program depends on the I version of the schematism, it demands that pure intuitions of space and time present exemplary instances for all the categories. We have seen that space and time can present transcendental image-schemata only for the concept of extensive magnitude. Since space and time cannot present image-schemata for the other categories, the axiomatic program cannot go beyond the Axioms of Intuitions. It must have been this failure in the execution of the axiomatic program that prompted Kant to devise the postulational program.

In the postulational program Kant repudiates or sometimes even reverses some of the fundamental features of the axiomatic program, in which he had held that the categories can be applied directly only to pure intuitions and only indirectly to empirical intuitions through the mediation of pure intuitions. In the postulational program, he repudiates this two-stage theory in the application of the categories and claims the entire inner sense as the object for their direct application. There are a few occasions where Kant takes an even more extreme position than this—specifically in the Analogies, where he claims that the categories of substance and causation can be applied to time only through the content of time because time cannot be perceived by itself. This claim is exactly the opposite of that in the axiomatic program: the categories can be applied only indirectly to the pure intuition of time through the mediation of its content. Whether he takes a moderate or extreme position, he has come to see that the substantial entities required for most of his a priori principles cannot be constructed by the transcendental synthesis of pure intuitions but must be assumed to have independent existence as the content of time.

In our examination of the Axioms of Intuition in Chapter VI we saw that the axiomatic method of proof depends on the a priori knowledge of pure intuitions. It is often debated whether Kant's exposition of the Transcendental Aesthetic is final or provisional. Kant himself is ambiguous on this question. We can now see that this ambiguity is due to the presence of the two programs: The Aesthetic must be final for the axiomatic program and provisional for the postulational program, because the a priori knowledge of pure intuitions is essential to the axiomatic program and inessential to the postulational program.

Once we notice that the axiomatic program is dependent on the a priori knowledge of pure intuitions, we can also realize that all the synthetic propositions produced by this program turn out to be analytic propositions. For example, the proposition 'all pure intuitions are extensive magnitudes' must be analytic if its truth can be proven by the axiomatic method. This proposition can be proven in the axiomatic method on the supposition that pure intuitions provide exemplary instances (image-schemata) for the concept of extensive magnitude. This supposition must however be, not a posteriori, but a priori, for if the supposition is a posteriori, the entire proof would fail to be a priori. But this supposition can be made a priori only with the a priori knowledge of pure intuitions that is expressed by the original proposition to be proved. Thus all a priori synthetic propositions that can be produced by the axiomatic program turn out to be analytic as soon as we spell out the a priori knowledge of pure intuitions which is relied on by the axiomatic method of proof. Consequently, the axiomatic necessity reveals itself to be the analytic necessity which is grounded in the a priori knowledge of pure intuitions.

All the defects of the axiomatic programs are derived from its reliance on the a priori knowledge of pure intuitions. Without this a priori knowledge, the axiomatic program cannot take even a single step. But all the a priori judgments that can be produced in reliance on this a priori knowledge can have only the analytic necessity guaranteed by the same a priori knowledge. Since the axiomatic program not only stands on the dubious foundation of the intuitive a priori knowledge but also promises no true synthetic knowledge, we can find little use for it.

The postulational program, on the other hand, is not bound to the dubious doctrine of a priori intuitions, since it is designed to justify a priori synthetic propositions not by their *origins* but by their *functions*. In truth, as we have seen in Chapter 6, some of Kant's postulational proofs for his a priori principles are incompatible with his doctrine of pure intuitions. Thus the postulational program dictates the repudiation of Kant's main contention in the Transcendental Aesthetic. Although Kant has not fared very well in executing this program, we cannot afford to dismiss it. There are many synthetic propositions whose truths we accept in an a priori manner for functional reasons. These propositions may not be exactly the same as Kant's a priori principles, but their existence alone can attest to the significance of the postulational program.

At this stage of our inquiry, we cannot justly evaluate Kant's postulational program. For, as we will see in the remainder of this volume, the postulational program is in its nature more "dialectical" than "analytical." Hence it is impossible to gain an adequate understanding of this program without comprehending the Transcendental Dialectic. Therefore we must now turn our attention to Kant's doctrine of transcendental inferences.

Part III

Transcendental Inferences

Chapter 9

The Concepts of Pure Reason

Kant distinguishes pure reason from pure understanding on the basis of their functions. The functions of pure reason are transcendent, while the functions of pure understanding are immanent. He locates the origin of their functional divergence in the difference of their concepts. The pure concepts of reason are transcendent; the pure concepts of understanding are immanent.

Kant recognizes three concepts of pure reason in the domain of cognition: the concepts of the self (the subject), of the world (the object), and of God (the universal being). He tries to find a systematic method for the derivation of these transcendent concepts as he did for the derivation of the categories. He claims to find such a method in the forms of syllogism. (A 321 = B 378) This is to employ fundamentally the same method for the derivation of the pure concepts of reason as was used for that of the pure concepts of understanding—to use formal concepts in the derivation of material ones.

We have already exposed the fallacy in Kant's claim of using formal concepts in the derivation of material ones in our examination of the Metaphysical Deduction. Fortunately Kant does not stick to his original intention and try to perform a metaphysical deduction of the pure concepts of reason. Instead of their deduction or derivation, he argues for their development or formation. He invokes the forms of syllogism to explain not their derivation but their formation. This is the decisive difference which belies the apparent similarity between his presentation of the two sets of pure concepts.

Kant's presentation of the pure concepts of reason has a

hidden affinity with his schematization of the pure concepts of reason. Just as he has argued for the formation of the material concepts of understanding from its formal concepts, he is now going to argue for the formation of the material concepts of reason from its formal concepts. Kant himself compares the two procedures:

> The form of judgments (converted into a concept of the synthesis of intuitions) yielded categories which direct all employment of understanding in experience. Similarly, we may presume that the form of syllogisms, when applied to the synthetic unity of intuitions under the direction of the categories, will contain the origin of special *a priori* concepts, which we may call pure concepts of reason, or *transcendental ideas*. (A 321 = B 378)

Kant does not claim that the forms of syllogism are converted into the pure concepts of reason: The genesis of the pure concepts of reason is not described as the process of converting or transforming formal into material concepts. Thus his derivation of the transcendent concepts is different not only from the metaphysical deduction of the immanent concepts but also from their genesis through the process of concept-schematization.

The genesis of the pure concepts of reason appears to be a more complex process than the schematization of the pure concepts of understanding. Kant says that the pure concepts of reason are produced by the application of the forms of syllogism "to the synthetic unity of intuitions under the direction of the categories." When he comes to explain this somewhat complex process, he does not use the three forms of syllogism but the three forms of synthesis for the relational categories. (A 323 = B 379) The three forms of synthesis are the categorical synthesis, the hypothetical synthesis, and the disjunctive synthesis. Kant maintains that these three forms of synthesis yield the concepts of the self, of the world, and of God when they are used under the concept of the unconditioned. (A 323 = B 379 f.)

The three forms of synthesis should not be confused with the three forms of syllogism. Since the former have nothing to do with syllogism, their use in the formation of the pure concepts of reason can establish no connection between the concepts of pure reason and syllogism. The concept of the unconditioned remains as the only element which can be used to establish some connection between them. Kant regards the concept of condition for the conditioned as the central logical concept governing the syllogistic deductions. (A 321 f. = B 378) He says that the premises of a syllogism are the conditions to assure the conditional truth of its conclusion. For example, the proposition 'Caius is mortal' can be treated either as an independent judgment of experience or as the conclusion of the syllogism that begins with the major premise 'All men are mortal.' In the former case, the proposition 'Caius is mortal' must stand all by itself without the support of any other propositions. In the latter case, the truth of the same proposition can be guaranteed by the truth of the major premise. The premise is the condition for assuring the truth of the conclusion.

The premise of a syllogism need not be an unconditional truth. Since its truth may require the warrant of a higher premise, Kant says, the complete enumeration of the conditions for some conditional truth leads to the formation of prosyllogisms. (A 323 = B 379) For example, the premise 'All men are mortal' is not an absolute truth. Its truth can be guaranteed by a further condition if it can be deduced from the higher premise 'All living things are mortal.' Prosyllogism is the regressive operation of generating an ascending series of syllogisms or an ascending series of conditions for a conditional truth. (A 331 = B 388)

While the syllogism embodies the logical notion of condition, Kant holds, the prosyllogism embodies the logical notion of the unconditioned condition or the totality of conditions. (A 323 = B 379 f.) He says that *the unconditioned* is the correct meaning of the abused term 'the absolute' because it is the opposite of the *conditioned*. (A 324 f. = B 380 ff.) He maintains that this formal concept of the unconditioned or the absolute develops into the three concepts of the unconditioned entities under the three forms of synthesis: "We have therefore to seek for an *unconditioned,* first, of the *categorical* synthesis in a *subject;* secondly, of the *hypothetical* synthesis of the members of a *series;* thirdly, of the *disjunctive* synthesis of the parts in a *system."* (A 323 = B 379) The pure concept of the self is generated by seeking the absolute in the categorical synthesis; the pure concept of the world is generated by seeking the absolute in the hypothetical synthesis; and the pure concept of God is generated by seeking the absolute in the disjunctive synthesis.

Here Kant presupposes that every synthesis is a finite or conditioned operation which needs to be complemented by further syntheses. This is a reasonable presupposition which we need not question. Neither will we question his claim that the notions of the condition and the unconditioned are the logical notions embodied in syllogism and prosyllogism. But we cannot accept his claim that the three forms of synthesis are linked with the three pure concepts of reason. All the three forms of synthesis are the methods of constructing objects of experience in the domain of intuitions. If they are used to seek the unconditioned, they should all result in one idea, the idea of the totality of the objects of experience. This is none other than the idea of the world.

The search for the absolute in the form of the categorical synthesis should result not in the concept of the self but in that of the unconditioned substance, i.e. the concept of the world as an unlimited permanent substance. The concept of the self cannot be sought in the form of the categorical synthesis, because only the objects of experience can be sought in the domain of synthesis, and the self is not an object of experience. To be sure, Kant maintains that the self can be an object of inner sense. But the self that can be distinguished from the world cannot be an object of synthesis because it is the very agent of synthesis. The self as the subject of experience can never be reached as a product of synthesis. Of course, there is no reason to expect that the form of the categorical synthesis will have any special connection with the concept of the self that the other forms of synthesis cannot have.

The concept of God cannot be obtained through the form of the disjunctive synthesis. By the disjunctive synthesis, Kant really means the conjunctive synthesis. The search for the unconditioned in the form of conjunctive synthesis can result only in the conjunction of all the objects of experience, which is called the world. Kant may claim that the concept of God is formed in the search for the unconditioned condition for the conjunction of all the objects of experience into one world. But this claim could not be limited to the conjunctive synthesis alone: There would be as much reason to claim that the concept of God is formed in the search for the unconditioned condition for holding together all the phenomenal objects into one substance or for sustaining all the phenomenal events in one causal chain. Thus there can be no special connection between the conjunctive synthesis and the genesis of the idea of God.

The only claim that can stand as a plausible assertion is the claim that the search for the unconditioned condition in the form of the hypothetical synthesis is the process for the formation of the concept of the world. This should come as no surprise because, as we have already pointed out, all forms of synthesis are methods of constructing the objects of experience. Since the form of the hypothetical synthesis is the method of establishing the causal nexus, the search for the absolute in the form of that synthesis should result in the concept of the world as the totality of the phenomenal causal chains.

Our assertion that not only the hypothetical synthesis but

any other form of synthesis can be used for the formation of the concept of the world can be supported by Kant's construction of the antinomies of pure reason. If the hypothetical synthesis were the only basis for the formation of the concept of the world, the causal category should have the exclusive government of all the antinomies. But Kant's four antinomies are rooted not only in the causal synthesis but also in the quantitative, the qualitative, and the modal syntheses. Thus the hypothetical synthesis can claim no special role in the formation of the concept of the world, that is, no role that other forms of synthesis cannot claim also.

While all the forms of synthesis participate in the antinomies, none of them participates either in the paralogisms or in the proofs of the existence of God except in the cosmological proof. This should confirm our previous claim that the forms of synthesis have no special role to play in the formation of the concepts of the self and God. The cosmological proof of God's existence is linked with the notion of synthesis because this proof is a continuation of the antinomies. That one proof of God is connected with the notion of synthesis, while the other proofs are not, should reveal one significant point about the formation of the concept of God, namely, that there are many ways of forming it. Kant naïvely assumes that all three proofs of the existence of God employ the same concept of God and that this concept can be formed only in one way. The concept of God that has been formed as the ultimate efficient cause of the world must be different from the concept of God that has been formed as the ultimate final cause of the world. That there are many ways of forming many concepts of God can, mutatis mutandis, be said about the formation of the concept of the self and the world.

Kant's derivation of the pure concepts of reason thus turns out to be a highly dubious operation. No wonder that it is usually dismissed as an outrageous architectonic manipulation.[1] But we should not overlook the momentous idea with which Kant may be struggling in his clumsy architectonic maneuvers. In Chapter 7 we have seen that he entertained two views of the human intellect: the formal and the material view. We have pointed out that the formal view is truly Kant's own while the material view is essentially the continuation of the rationalistic view of intellect. It should thus be reasonable to expect that he also entertaned two views of pure reason: (1) the material view that pure reason is ab initio equipped with a set of primitive material concepts and (2) the formal view that pure reason has ab initio no material concepts but only a set of primitive formal concepts.

Kant expresses the material view of reason of his pre-Critical period when he compares the pure concept of reason with Plato's ideas. (A 313 = B 370) He stresses that Plato's ideas are not mere abstract concepts for the determination of objects, but archetypal universals that exist also as individuals. (A 319 = B 374) The ideas cannot of course exist in the phenomenal world but only in the noumenal world. Kant goes on to distinguish the pure concepts of reason from the pure concepts of understanding not only on the basis of their cognitive functions but also on the basis of their existential import. While the pure concepts of understanding are the abstract entities for the cognition of the phenomenal objects, he holds, the pure concepts of reason are the concrete entities existing in the noumenal world. Since the pure concepts of reason share all the distinguishing characteristics of Plato's ideas, he recommends that the exalted name of 'idea' be used exclusively for the pure concepts of reason.

Kant suggests one more exalted term that may fit the privileged status of the pure concepts of reason. This is the term 'principle.' (A 300 = B 356) If 'ideas' refers to the archetypal function of the pure concepts of reason, 'principle' refers to their cognitive function. Since the pure concepts of reason are individuals, to have them is to have intellectual intuition of their existences. Therefore the pure concepts are a special class of universals that can produce knowledge without the aid of the sensible intuitions. Kant designates this special class of universals as the 'principle.' He says, "Knowledge from principles is, therefore, that knowledge alone in which I apprehend the particular in the universal through concepts." (A 300 = B 357) He takes pains to insist that pure understanding can produce no principles in this strict sense of 'principle' and that the a priori principles of understanding are called principles only in "a comparative sense." (A 300 = B 357 f.)

As long as Kant holds this material view of pure reason, he can see no need to explain the formation of the pure concepts of reason. It requires only the doctrine of intellectual intuition —exactly the point made in Chapter 7 as regards the material view of pure understanding. The "knowledge from principles" or the "apprehension of the particular in the universal" is the simple cognition of the intuitive intellect. Consequently there is no need for the formation of those concepts. The need for their formation arises only with the repudiation of the doctrine of intellectual intuition. Once this doctrine is rejected, pure reason cannot be claimed to have any material concepts as a part of its innate nature. In Chapter 7 we pointed out that the innate possession of material concepts can never be explained without invoking the power of intellectual intuition.

With the repudiation of intellectual intuition, only formal concepts can be legitimately claimed as the innate possessions of pure reason. This is Kant's formal view of reason in his Critical period. Within this formal view of reason, Kant cannot avoid the need to explain how pure reason comes into possession of its a priori material concepts. Since he begins with the assumption that formal concepts are the only innate possessions of pure reason, he seems to believe that pure reason must use its formal concepts in obtaining its material ones. This is precisely the position adopted with regard to the formation of the phenomenal categories. In implementing this doctrine, he has to begin with the identification of the formal concepts of pure reason; these he identifies with the forms of syllogism. This identification is guided by the same idea that has led him to identify the formal concepts of pure understanding with the forms of judgments.

Kant does not appear to feel the same confidence in his identification of the formal concepts of pure reason with the forms of syllogism that he has felt in his identification of the formal concepts of understanding with the forms of judgment. He does not make the outright claim that pure reason must have three formal concepts because there are three forms of syllogism. He may have seen that this claim cannot be sustained because the differentiation of the three forms of syllogism depends on the formal concepts of pure understanding. It is the three relational categories that differentiate the categorical, the hypothetical, and the disjunctive forms of syllogism from one another. So the three forms of syllogism seem to embody the three formal concepts of pure understanding rather than the formal concepts of pure reason.

Kant may have assumed that the forms of syllogism at least embody the formal concept of the condition for the conditioned and that this formal concept properly belongs to pure reason rather than to pure understanding. Even this is an unacceptable view. The formal notion of the condition for the conditioned should also belong to pure understanding. The logical concept of ground and consequence is precisely the notion of the condition for the conditioned. For this reason, all syllogisms can be expressed in the hypothetical form. 'All men are mortal' and 'Caius is a man,' therefore 'Caius is mortal,' is a syllogism whose logical chain can be expressed by the 'if–then' connective: 'If all men are mortal' and 'If Caius is a man,' then 'Caius must be mortal.' Thus it is impossible for Kant to claim the notion of the condition as a formal concept of pure reason.

Kant also tries to find a formal concept of reason in the concept of the unconditioned condition or the absolute. This attempt may appear to be a little more reasonable than his other attempts, if we assume that all the pure concepts of understanding are concepts of finite or conditioned entities. But we cannot legitimately make this assumption. One of the pure concepts of understanding is the concept of totality, and we have no reason to assume that this concept is incapable of handling the absolute. Kant himself sometimes equates the unconditioned condition with the totality of conditions. (A 322 = B 378 f.) According to this, the concept of the unconditioned condition or the absolute can be formed with the two pure concepts of understanding: the concept of totality and the concept of ground and consequence. So the concept of the unconditioned condition cannot be identified as uniquely a formal concept of pure reason.

I have tried to show how Kant never succeeded in his various attempts to specify the formal concepts of pure reason. His failure was inevitable because it is impossible to distinguish between the two kinds of formal concepts. It is indeed permissible to distinguish between two kinds of material concepts, provided there are two kinds of world. One kind of material concepts would be for the phenomenal world and the other kind for the noumenal world. We could have two different kinds of formal concepts only if there were two different worlds governed by two different formal logics. The formal concepts of pure reason could be different from the formal concepts of pure understanding, only if the formal logic of the noumenal world were different from the formal logic of the phenomenal world. Since this hypothesis is incompatible with the universal validity of formal logic, it is impossible to recognize more than one set of formal concepts. If there is only one set of formal concepts, it is senseless to try to distinguish between the formal concepts of reason and those of understanding. This explains Kant's failure in his various attempts to specify the formal concepts of pure reason as distinct from the formal concepts of pure understanding.

It is not always success, but sometimes failure, that brings us benefit. If Kant had succeeded in his identification of the formal concepts of reason, he would surely have tried to extend the concept-conversion theory from the domain of understanding to that of reason. Since he feels no confidence in the identification of the formal concepts of reason, he never thinks of espousing the implausible theory of concept-transformation in the domain of reason. All his remarks on the genesis of the ideas of reason clearly converge on the concept-formation theory. Thus his momentous concept-formation theory comes to receive a fair representation in the Transcendental Dialectic.

Kant cannot give adequate expression to his concept-formation theory as long as he operates under the erroneous assumption that formal concepts should be the basis for the formation of material concepts. But he finally succeeds in freeing himself from this assumption on one occasion and tries to explain the formation of the pure concepts of reason without invoking the three forms of syllogism:

> The relations which are to be universally found in all our representations are (1) relation to the subject; (2) relation to objects, either as appearances or as objects of thought in general. If we combine the subdivision with the main division, all relation of representations, of which we can form either a concept or an idea, is then threefold: (1) the relation to the subject; (2) the relation to the manifold of the object in the [field of] appearance; (3) the relation to all things in general. (A 334 = B 391)

Here Kant makes no mention of the forms of syllogism or any other formal concepts. He introduces the pure concepts of reason in the context of representations or experience rather than in the context of formal concepts. In our examination of Kant's derivation of the phenomenal categories, we pointed out that the domain of intuitions or experience is the only proper place for the formation of material concepts. Thus Kant assembles almost all the essential conditions for the formation of the pure concepts of reason and does fully practice the concept-formation theory although he may not preach it.

I do not mean to say that Kant has finally given an adequate account of the formation of the three concepts of reason. His account is still underdeveloped. For example, he has not even linked the third concept with the concept of God. He says that the third concept of pure reason is the concept of subject and object together. There is no reason to expect to obtain the concept of God by combining the subject and the object of experience into one. But he gives a better account of the formation of the concepts of the subject and the object because he frees it from the logical notion of the unconditioned condition. The concept of the unconditioned is in fact incompatible with the concepts of the self and the world. Kant has already argued in the Transcendental Analytic that the subject and the object are the necessary conditions for constituting each other and that the self and the world are inseparable from each other.

How Kant accounts for the formation of each individual concept of reason is a matter of details. Much more important than this is the matter of principle: Kant argues for the formation of the pure concepts of reason and rightly locates the matrix of their formation in the context of experience. We can take this point as evidence to confirm our view that Kant was groping for the concept-formation theory in the transcendental schematism when he tried to express it in the form of the concept-transformation theory.

It must be stressed that the formal view of reason cannot admit the distinction between reason and understanding. In the material view of reason, reason and understanding can be distinguished from each other by the nature of their a priori material concepts. We have seen that the formal view of reason can admit no a priori material concepts but only a priori formal concepts as the innate possessions of intellect and that there can be only one set of formal concepts. Since reason and understanding must share one set of formal concepts, their distinction becomes a distinction without difference, or rather a pre-Critical distinction that can no longer be substantiated with any real difference in the fully Critical context. Kant comes very close to repudiating this pre-Critical distinction when he claims reason to be a mere extension of understanding. (A 408 f. = B 435 f.)

Once the distinction between reason and understanding ceases to be the distinction between two kinds of intellectual faculties, there is not a difference of kind but only of degree between the concepts of reason and those of understanding. It would no longer be legitimate to claim a generic demarcation between the immanent and the transcendent concepts, but only a distinction of degree on many different levels. For example, the mathematical and the dynamical categories do not enjoy immanence on the same level. Perhaps Kant's recognition of this was one of the reasons that led him to equate the distinction between the mathematical and the dynamical principles with that between the constitutive and the regulative principles.

It should also be pointed out that the three concepts of reason do not enjoy transcendence on the same level. Even if we take Kant's single criterion of *sense-exhibitability* for immanence, we can see that the three pure concepts of reason are transcendent in three different ways. The concept of God can be exhibited in senses neither in part nor in whole. The concept of the world can be at least partially exhibited in senses, although it cannot be exhibited in its totality. The concept of the self cannot even partially be exhibited in senses insofar as it refers to the subject of experience. But the concept of the self refers to no noumenal entities, as does the concept of God. Thus the three concepts of reason transcend the phenomenal world on three different levels.

By converting the distinction between understanding and reason from the distinction of kind into that of degree, we should not expect to deprive the pure concepts of reason of their special status or to prevent them from generating all the dialectical problems of pure reason. We must still recognize the unique status for the pure concepts of reason, not because they belong to a special faculty but because they are the limiting concepts of experience or the limits of experience. Since the pure concepts of reason are the limiting concepts of experience, they are bound to generate dialectical problems. For those problems are the same problems that arise when we step beyond the limits of experience. Thus, within the theory of one continuous intellect, we can give a functional account of the unique status that rightly belongs to the pure concepts of reason and the special problems that can be generated only by their abuse. This functional account is much more cohesive and simple than the genetic account based on the generic distinction between reason and understanding.

Kant says that the three pure concepts of reason are the sources for the three different types of transcendental inferences, namely, transcendental psychology, transcendental cosmology, and transcendental theology. In the following three chapters, we shall explore these three provinces of transcendental inference. In all these three provinces, Kant gives the impression that his chief aim is to expose the fallacy of the dogmatic conclusions in the rationalists' dialectical inferences. Since we are no longer as interested in the refutation of the rationalists' transcendental illusions as he was, we need not devote ourselves to his professed chief aim.

Under the shadow of the negative function of refuting the dogmatic sciences of rationalists, Kant performs the positive function of elaborating on his own doctrines of the self, the world, and God. He renders this positive function because he often bases his criticisms of the rationalistic doctrines on his own doctrines of the same subject matter. His exposition of his own doctrines, however, is never systematic but always notoriously fragmentary because he touches on them only when it is demanded by his critical function. So we must take special pains in assembling his scattered remarks and constructing a cohesive account of his doctrines of the self, the world, and God.

Chapter 10

Transcendental Psychology

Kant distinguishes rational psychology from empirical psychology. (A 342 f. = B 400 f.) Like any other empirical discipline, empirical psychology is constructed on the evidences of intuitions and conforms to Kant's canon of experience. But rational psychology defies his canon because it is alleged to be constructed on pure thought alone. This pseudo-science claims to deduce a set of a priori synthetic propositions about the nature of the soul or the self from one nonempirical premise: "I think." Furthermore, those a priori propositions are claimed to reveal the nature of the soul even beyond the phenomenal world. Since these claims constitute some of the salient rationalistic doctrines that run counter to the major tenets of transcendental idealism, Kant feels a special need to expose their fallacy.

The knowledge claim of rational psychology can be expressed in one sentence: The soul is a simple substance that cannot perish. But Kant divides it into four propositions for the architectonic purpose of fitting it into the fourfold division of the categories: (1) The soul is a substance; (2) the soul is simple; (3) the soul is numerically identical over different times; and (4) the soul can have no real but only an ideal relation to external objects. No doubt, as Kemp Smith points out, this architectonic arrangement is arbitrary.[1] But we have nothing to gain by criticizing Kant's arbitrary architectonic maneuvers because Kant does not claim to achieve anything by them. Architectonism can gain significance only when it is claimed to be an indispensable instrument for a certain task or an integral feature of some substantive argument. Such was the case with the Metaphysical Deduction. Since the architectonism in the fourfold division of the Paralogisms is no more than a dispensable expository device, its arbitrariness should not be allowed to distract our attentions from Kant's substantive arguments.

Kant maintains that the four a priori synthetic assertions of rational psychology have been deduced as the conclusions of illicit syllogisms. For this reason he calls them Paralogisms. A paralogism is an illegitimate syllogism whose middle term does not retain the same meaning in the transition from the major to the minor premise. (A 402) If the middle term of a syllogism is not univocally used, the syllogism cannot secure its distribution and cannot establish the validity of its deduction. Thus a paralogism is a sophistical inference paraded under the cover of the ambiguity of its middle term. The alleged dialectical inferences of rational psychology commit not only the logical error of abusing their middle terms, but also the material error of extending their arguments from the domain of phenomena to that of noumena. For that reason, they are called transcendental paralogisms. We will now review Kant's criticism of these paralogisms as it is formulated in the first edition.

THE FIRST PARALOGISM

> That, the representation of which is the *absolute subject* of our judgments and cannot therefore be employed as determination of another thing, is *substance.*
> I, as a thinking being, am the *absolute subject* of all my possible judgments, and this representation of myself cannot be employed as predicate of any other thing.
> Therefore I, as thinking being (soul), am *substance.* (A 348 ff.)

Kant gives two different criticisms of this Paralogism because he operates with not one but two conceptions of the self. He conceives the self sometimes as the individual subject and sometimes as the transcendental subject. The individual subject is an existential entity in the phenomenal world, but the transcendental subject does not have a phenomenal existence. In the Transcendental Analytic Kant has argued that the transcendental ego or apperception is the necessary condition for constituting the phenomenal world. The transcendental subject is therefore coextensive with the entire phenomenal world. While the individual subject is a real entity, the transcendental subject is an ideal entity. Kant does not announce that he is using these two different notions of the self in his criticism of rational psychology.

Kant admits the substantial nature of the self when he conceives it as an individual subject. He says, "Everyone must, therefore, necessarily regard himself as substance, and thought as [consisting] only [in] accidents of his being, determinations of his state." (A 349) By 'everyone' Kant refers to every individual subject. He can find no fault with this substantial conception of the self as long as it is confined within the phenomenal world. He maintains that it becomes abused when it is used to deduce the nature of the soul beyond the phenomenal world, that is, the argument that the soul cannot perish because it is a simple substance. (A 349)

The substance that is conceived as indivisible and hence imperishable is not the substance of the phenomenal but of the noumenal world. The error of the First Paralogism lies in its abuse of the middle term 'substance': it is used to mean the phenomenal substance in the premises and the noumenal substance in the conclusion. Through this equivocal usage of 'substance,' the First Paralogism commits not only the logical error of having an undistributed middle term but also the material error of drawing a noumenal conclusion from phenomenal premises. Hence it is a transcendental paralogism.

Kant does not recognize the substantial nature of the self when he conceives it as the transcendental subject. He maintains that the category of substance cannot be applied to the self. (A 349 f.) Whereas the category of substance can be applied only to the objects of intuition, he argues, the self cannot be an object of intuition. Unlike the individual subject, the transcendental subject cannot be encountered as an object of intuitions because it is the pure thought which is coextensive with the totality of the objects of intuition.

Kant says that the self is not a real subject but a logical subject. (A 350) Unfortunately he does not explain the difference between these two types of subject. By 'the real subject' he apparently means the substantial or the permanent subject in the phenomenal world. By 'the logical subject' he may mean the subject which has been introduced not in the context of intuitions but in the context of thought. Whereas the individual subject can be introduced in the context of intuitions, the transcendental subject can be introduced only in the context of thought. For unlike the individual subject, the transcendental subject cannot be encountered as an object of intuitions. The transcendental subject can be introduced as a subject in the context of thought by defining it as the subject of all judgments. But these judgments should not be construed as actual occurrences in inner sense because such occurrent thoughts would constitute a context of intuitions. They would constitute a context of thought if they are construed as not actual but possible constituents of the phenomenal world. To put it in another way, the transcendental subject is introduced in the context of the entire phenomenal world, that is, as the subject of the phenomenal world. Since the phenomenal world is not an object of sense but an object of thought, it constitutes a context of thought rather than a context of sense.

Kant's thesis that the phenomenal world or the world of experience is a joint product of thought and sense should be understood in terms of the transcendental subject rather than of the individual subject. If this thesis were to be construed in terms of occurrent thoughts, the phenomenal world would be nothing more than the construction of an individual subject. Kant often stresses that the thoughts that constitute the phenomenal world are not actual but possible thoughts, because they are the thoughts of the transcendental subject. For example, he says,

> But it must not be forgotten that the bare representation 'I' in relation to all other representations (the collective unity of which it makes possible) is transcendental consciousness. Whether this representation is clear (empirical consciousness) or obscure, or even whether it ever actually occurs, does not here concern us. But the possibility of the logical form of all knowledge is necessarily conditioned by relation to this apperception *as a faculty.* (A 117, note *a)*

The transcendental subject is thus an ideal or a possible entity, which has been introduced as a logical condition for the constitution of the phenomenal world.

When Kant criticizes the First Paralogism in the context of the logical subject rather than in that of the individual subject, he maintains that the term 'subject' (or 'substance') is used to mean a logical subject in one of its premises and a real subject ('substance') in its other premises. By this equivocal use of the term 'subject' (or 'substance'), he argues, this Paralogism tries to deduce a synthetic proposition ('The self is a substance') from an analytical proposition ('The self is a subject of thought'). The latter proposition is analytical because its subject term (the self) has been introduced or defined as a subject of thought. But the former proposition is synthetic because the term 'substance' means a substantial subject. One is an existential assertion about an individual subject, while the other carries no existential significance.

Thus Kant presents two criticisms of the First Paralogism. In one of them he accuses the rationalists of confusing the phenomenal with the noumenal substance; in the other he accuses them of confusing substance with subject. He does not himself seem to see clearly the difference between these two errors and indicates his own confusion by using 'substance' and 'subject' interchangeably in his own formulation of the First Paralogism.

THE SECOND PARALOGISM

That, the action of which can never be regarded as the concurrence of several things acting, is *simple*.
Now the soul, or the thinking 'I', is such a being.
Therefore, [the soul is simple]. (A 351 ff.)

The Second Paralogism is an elaboration of the First because it asserts that the soul is not only a substance but a simple substance. Kant again treats this Paralogism from two different perspectives. When he conceives the self as an individual subject, he argues that the unity of the self is not a simple but a collective unity:

For the unity of the thought, which consists of many representations, is collective, and as far as mere concepts can show, may relate to the collective unity of the subject. Consequently, the necessity of presupposing, in the case of a composite thought, a simple substance, cannot be demonstrated in accordance with the principle of identity. (A 353)

Thus the subject of occurrent thoughts may be a unitary subject but not a simple one.

Kant also criticizes the Second Paralogism as a paralogistic deduction from the notion of the self as the transcendental subject. (A 354) He says that the transcendental apperception has been introduced as a logical subject to establish or explain the unity of experience. He maintains that the error of the Second Paralogism lies in its attempt to deduce the substantial simplicity of the individual subject from the logical unity of the transcendental subject.

At this point Kant goes into an interesting digression. (A 357 ff.) He briefly touches on the relation of the individual subject to material objects, which really belongs to the Fourth Paralogism. He observes that the simplicity of the soul is claimed in order to maintain its incorporeality. He says that the incorporeality of the soul can be maintained without resorting to its dubious simplicity. Since material objects are defined as the objects of outer sense, he holds, the self cannot be mistaken for a material object because it can appear only in inner sense. (A 357) But he is quick to warn against assuming an unbridgeable difference between thinking and material beings. He gives two reasons against such a dogmatic assumption. In the first place, the phenomenal subjects and the phenomenal objects may be appearances of the same noumena. (A 358) In the second place, some material objects may very well be agents of thought:

> I may further assume that the substance which in relation to our outer sense possesses extension is in itself the possessor of thoughts, and that these thoughts can by means of its own inner sense be consciously represented. In this way, what in one relation is entitled corporeal would in another relation be at the same time a thinking being, whose thoughts we cannot intuit, though we can indeed intuit their signs in the [field] of appearance. Accordingly, the thesis that only souls (as particular kinds of substances) think, would have to be given up; and we should have to fall back on the common expression that men think, that is, that the very same being which, as outer appearance, is extended, is (in itself) internally a subject, and is not composite, but is simple and thinks. (A 359 f.)

This passage introduces Kant's third notion of the self: The self as the subject of extension or the physical agent. This notion of the self may be considered as the extension of the notion of the self as the individual subject. Up to this point, the individual subject has been considered only as the subject of occurrent thoughts, which is an object of inner sense. To bring together all these different notions of the self is going to be one of the most difficult problems in transcendental philosophy.

THE THIRD PARALOGISM

> That which is conscious of the numerical identity of itself at different times is in so far a *person*.
> Now the soul is conscious, etc.
> Therefore it is a person. (A 363 ff.)

As an individual subject, Kant admits, everyone is conscious of one's personal identity in one's inner sense. But he wants to add that this internal awareness of one's personal identity cannot be experienced by an external observer:

> In my own consciousness, therefore, identity of person is unfailingly met with. But if I view myself from the standpoint of another person (as object of his outer intuition), it is this outer observer who first represents *me in time,* for in the apperception *time* is represented, strictly speaking, only *in me*. Although he admits, therefore, the 'I', which accompanies, and indeed with complete identity, all representations at all times in *my* consciousness, he will draw no inference from this to the objective permanence of myself. For just as the time in which the observer sets me is not the time of my own but his sensibility, so the identity which is necessarily bound up with my consciousness is not therefore bound up with his, that is, with the consciousness which contains the outer intuition of subject. (A 362 f.)

This Paralogism is also criticized from two perspectives.

Here Kant introduces the standpoint of an external observer for the first time. He may introduce this novel element in order to stress the connection between the individual subject and his body, because he regards the body as an integral feature of the individual subject. From the vantage point of an external observer, he argues that the internal consciousness of one's personal identity cannot assure the identity of one's body. That is, the error of this Paralogism lies in confusing the identity of one's consciousness with that of one's person, which is conceived as having both mind and body.

When Kant criticizes the Third Paralogism in the context of the transcendental subject, he does not recognize the consciousness of its identity as an item of experience. Instead of the consciousness of identity, he recognizes only the identity of the consciousness as a formal condition of experience. He says, "The identity of the consciousness of myself at different times is therefore only a formal condition of my thoughts and their coherence, and in no way proves the numerical identity of my subject." (A 363) That is, the coherent experience of a sane person does not prove his personal identity any more than the incoherent experience of an insane person proves his personal disidentity. The notion of the identity of the transcendental subject is the notion of a logical identity which has been introduced in the context of thoughts; the notion of the identity of the individual subject is the notion of a real identity which has been introduced in the context of senses. It is in the confusion of these two types of identity that Kant now claims to locate the error of the Third Paralogism.

THE FOURTH PARALOGISM

> That, the existence of which can only be inferred as a cause of given perceptions, has a merely doubtful existence.
>
> Now all outer appearances are of such a nature that their

existence is not immediately perceived, and that we can only infer them as the cause of given perceptions.

Therefore the existence of all objects of the outer senses is doubtful. This uncertainty I entitle the ideality of outer appearances, and the doctrine of this ideality is called *idealism,* as distinguished from the counter-assertion of a possible certainty in regard to objects of outer sense, which is called *dualism.* (A 366 ff.)

This Paralogism is quite different from the others because it is not really concerned with the contention of rational psychology that the soul is an indivisible and indestructible substance. Kemp Smith is probably right in holding that Kant made up the Fourth Paralogism only to meet the requirements of his architectonic.[2] Since this Paralogism is not concerned with the nature of the soul as an indivisible substance, Kant's formulation of it does not even use the term 'substance,' which functions as a pivotal term in the transcendental inferences of the other Paralogisms.

We have seen that Kant criticizes the first three Paralogisms from the perspectives of both individual and transcendental subjects. The difference between these two perspectives has been associated with his usage of two seemingly equivalent terms, 'substance' and 'subject': that is, 'substance' is used to refer to the individual subject and 'subject' to the transcendental subject. Neither term is used in the formulation of the Fourth Paralogism, and Kant's criticism of it can be read either in the context of the individual subject or in that of the transcendental subject.

The contention of the Fourth Paralogism is the idealistic position on the relation of mind and body: The consciousness of external objects is never immediate and always uncertain, while that of the self is always immediate and certain. This position can be deduced from the monadic conception of the soul, which has been the target of Kant's criticisms in the first three Paralogisms. If the soul is an indivisible, unitary substance, it cannot have any real relation with any external objects or rather cannot have any immediate awareness of anything outside itself. This was in fact Leibniz' doctrine.

Kant tries to refute this idealistic contention by clarifying the meaning of 'external objects.' If the expression 'external objects' were to mean the objects which are external to the mind, he admits, the mind cannot reach them except through probable inferences. He observes that the expression 'external objects' can mean either the noumenal objects or the material objects. (A 373) Whereas the former are outside the mind, he argues, the latter are merely representations in the mind because they are the objects of outer sense. Since the objects of outer sense are as much in the mind as the objects of inner sense, he concludes, both types of objects are equally immediate objects of consciousness.

The thesis that the entire phenomenal world has only a representational being in consciousness surely sounds like Berkeleyan subjective idealism if it is construed in the context of the individual subject. In order to avoid this misunderstanding, Kant appears to treat the Fourth Paralogism not from the perspective of the individual subject but only from that of the transcendental subject. He does not want to have his idealism mistaken for subjective idealism and takes pains to establish the distinction. (A 369 ff.) He calls his idealism transcendental and subjective idealism empirical. Unfortunately, his explanation of their differences is far from clear and adequate; it may therefore be profitable for us to try to improve upon his explanation.

We may define transcendental idealism in the context of the transcendental subject and empirical idealism in the context of the empirical consciousness. Transcendental idealism may be defined as the doctrine that material objects are representations in the transcendental consciousness; empirical idealism may be defined as the doctrine that material objects are representations in the empirical consciousness. Now we have to be clear about the difference between transcendental and empirical consciousness. In the Transcendental Analytic, Kant equates the former with the pure understanding and the latter with the consciousness of empirical sensations. (A 119; B 139 f.) He also gives a negative characterization of empirical consciousness: It does not involve the pure understanding and its categories. He also stresses the objectivity of transcendental consciousness and the subjectivity of empirical consciousness. Although these distinctions and characterizations are not fully satisfactory, let us accept them provisionally.

We can now explain in terms of these two types of consciousness Kant's oracular pronouncements that transcendental idealism is at the same time empirical realism and that transcendental realism is bound to lead to empirical idealism. (A 371) Since transcendental idealism holds external objects to be representations in transcendental consciousness, it is equivalent to asserting that their existence is independent of any empirical consciousness. This is the contention of empirical realism. Since transcendental realism holds external objects to be external to the transcendental consciousness, it is equivalent to asserting that no external (material) objects can be immediately present to the transcendental consciousness. Hence there can be no transcendental consciousness of the external world. This leaves only the possibility of the empirical consciousness. If so, the objects of immediate awareness can have representational being only in empirical consciousness. This is the contention of empirical idealism.

Kant's assertion that the pure intuitions of space and time have empirical reality and transcendental ideality can be also understood in the context of the two kinds of consciousness. (Cf. A 28 = B 44; A 36 = B 52) That space and time are transcendentally ideal means that their existence is dependent on transcendental consciousness. That they are empirically real means that their existence is independent of the empirical consciousness. To put it another way, they are representations of transcendental consciousness but not of empirical consciousness.

Kant's refutation of idealism in the second edition is quite different from his refutation in the first edition. (Cf. B 274 ff.) Whereas he argued in the first edition for the equality of the objects of inner and outer sense in their immediacy, he argues in the second edition that the awareness of external objects is a necessary condition for the possibility of the consciousness of oneself. He begins this argument with the premise that the consciousness of oneself is the consciousness of one's existence as determined in time. (B 275) He goes on to claim that the determination of one's existence in time requires the perception of the permanent substances. Since the permanent substances are none other than external or material objects, he concludes, the awareness of external objects is the necessary condition for the possibility of the self-consciousness.

The striking feature of this refutation is the assertion that the self cannot be an object of immediate consciousness and that it can be conscious of itself only as the consciousness of external objects. The problematic point about this assertion is the function of external objects for self-consciousness. We can readily accept the assertion that the self can be conscious of itself only reflexively and never immediately. Hume has already made this observation: "I never can catch *myself* at any time without a perception."[3] Kant's claim is much stronger than Hume's. Kant maintains that the perceptions requisite for self-consciousness must be the perceptions of external objects.

In his second refutation of idealism, Kant does not specify whether by 'self-consciousness' he means the empirical or the transcendental consciousness. But his second refutation should not be read in the context of the empirical consciousness because he elsewhere characterizes empirical consciousness as the consciousness of subjective sensations and because he recognizes the possibility of self-awareness not for the empirical but only for the transcendental consciousness. (Cf. A 108; A 121 f.; B 139 f.) Kant himself would admit that no stronger claim than Hume's can be made for empirical consciousness.

In the Transcendental Analytic Kant has argued that the transcendental apperception and the phenomenal world are inseparable from each other. Since the phenomenal world is the public world of material objects, he can argue, transcendental consciousness is impossible without the existence of the external world. Since the phenomenal world is governed by the First Analogy along with the other a priori principles of understanding, he can further maintain, the permanence (or substantiality) of external objects is the necessary condition for the possibility of self-consciousness. (Cf. B 275) Thus Kant's refutation of idealism in the second edition stands on the a priori truths that are supposedly established in the Transcendental Analytic. Furthermore, it stands on the unexplained assumption that no substantial or permanent objects can ever exist in the self ("This permanent cannot, however, be something in me"). (B 275)

While Kant's refutation of idealism in the second edition is formulated in the context of the Transcendental Analytic, his refutation in the first edition is formulated in the context of the Transcendental Aesthetic.* For this reason, the latter refutation is chiefly a reiteration of Kant's claims presented in the Aesthetic. (Cf. A 28 ff. = B 44 f.; A 35 f. = B 52 f.) Since Kant's two refutations of idealism are presented in two different contexts, they follow two different lines of argument. One of them presupposes the truths of the a priori principles of understanding; the other presupposes the doctrine of a priori intuitions. The weakness of the former refutation is that Kant has had little success in proving the truths of a priori principles; the weakness of the latter is that the doctrine of a priori intuition is implausible.

*This point will be further clarified later in this chapter.

In our examination of the Paralogisms of the first edition, we have uncovered three kinds of subjects or consciousness: (1) the transcendental subject, (2) the empirical subject, and (3) the individual subject. We must raise the question: How are these three notions of subject or consciousness related to one another? Since Kant neither raises nor answers this question, let us try out the following hypothesis: Every individual subject has two components, the transcendental and the empirical.* Let us further assume that the empirical component is the empirical subject and that the transcendental component is the transcendental subject. This would mean that there are as many empirical and as many transcendental subjects as individual subjects.

The above hypothesis produces one troublesome consequence. If there are as many transcendental subjects as individual subjects, there must be as many phenomenal worlds as there are individual subjects, because the phenomenal world is said to have only a representational being in the transcendental subject. This is precisely the way most of Kant's contemporaries read the first edition Paralogisms and consequently they came to believe that Kant was propounding a form of subjective idealism.

Kant rewrote the entire Paralogisms for the second edition in order to dispel the suspicion that he had been advocating a version of subjective idealism. There he restates his criticisms of rational psychology only in the context of the transcendental

---

*In our examination of the Paralogisms of the first edition, it was said that Kant operates with two notions of the subject—the individual and the transcendental. We can now see that this was inaccurate. It should have been said that Kant examines the Paralogisms as doctrines concerning both the transcendental and the empirical features of the individual subject. We adopted the inaccurate nomenclature only provisionally, as a convenient framework for exposition, because then we had not yet elaborated on the intricate relation of Kant's different notions of the subject.

subject and at the same time repeatedly stresses its *ideality:* The transcendental subject is not a real but a logical or ideal entity. (B 407 ff.) If the transcendental subject is an ideal entity, he may have thought, it can be maintained that there is only one transcendental subject and consequently there is only one phenomenal world.

Since Kant is, in the second edition, overly concerned with the *ideality* of the transcendental subject, he says almost nothing about the individual subject. Consequently, he fails to join the issue with the rationalists, because he criticizes their assertions only in the context of the transcendental subject whereas their assertions have been formulated in the context of the individual subject. The central point of his criticism is that they have mistaken a logical entity (the transcendental subject) for a real entity (the individual subject). But the rationalists have been concerned not with the logical but with the real subject; they have argued for the immortality of not the former but the latter.

Since Kant's criticisms of rational psychology are not conducted in the same context in which it had been originally formulated, his criticisms can be branded as *para-criticisms.* He has called the arguments of rational psychology *paralogisms* (para-syllogisms) on the ground that their pivotal terms are not allowed to retain the same meanings. His criticisms can be justifiably called para-criticisms because the pivotal terms, such as 'subject' and 'consciousness,' are not given the same meanings in his criticisms that they had in the rationalists' arguments. Thus the second edition Paralogisms has little value as a refutation of rational psychology, but it has the virtue of focusing our attention on his thesis that the transcendental subject is not a real (or individual) but a logical (or ideal) entity.

Whether the transcendental subject is construed as an individual or an ideal subject, Kant always regards its essential nature as its capacity to transcend its subjectivity and attain objective knowledge. That is, the transcendental subject is the subject of *transcendence*. Although this is the central theme in Kant's doctrine of subject, he never renders a satisfactory account of how the transcendental subject transcends itself. So we must take upon ourselves the task of constructing Kant's doctrine of transcendence.

First of all, we must be clear about the meaning of the expression 'the transcendental subject,' which in turn requires clarification of the meaning of 'transcendental.' Here we will not go into the complex pre-Kantian history of this ancient term but confine ourselves to its Kantian usage. As a uniquely Kantian expression, 'transcendental' appears in the following three general contexts: *transcendental* vs. *transcendent, transcendental* vs. *empirical,* and *transcendental* vs. *logical.* By 'the transcendent' Kant means the supersensible or that which transcends the phenomenal world. In a few cases he uses 'transcendental' simply to mean 'transcendent' and these few occasions only reflect his momentary carelessness. His real intent is to maintain an emphatic distinction between the two terms. When he uses 'transcendental' in contrast to 'empirical,' he gives the former term the meaning of 'a priori.' This is the best-known meaning of 'transcendental.' The contrast of 'transcendental' vs. 'logical' is not so well known as the other two, but this third context reveals another significant meaning of 'transcendental.'

The least-known meaning of 'transcendental' is equivalent to the meaning of 'real' or 'material.' When Kant distinguishes the logical or formal functions of understanding and reason from their real or material functions, he calls the latter the transcendental functions. (A 79 = B 105; A 299 = B 355) When he distinguishes logical possibility from real possibility, he calls the latter transcendental possibility. (A 244 = B 302) He uses 'transcendental' in the same manner in his distinction between logical and transcendental paralogisms. (A 341 =

B 399) This is also the case in the distinction between logical and transcendental reflection in the Amphiboly. Logical reflection is the comparison of concepts alone; transcendental reflection is the comparison not of concepts but of objects. (A 261 = B 317) 'Transcendental' is thus interchangeable with 'material' and 'real.'

Now that we are confronted with two quite disparate usages of the term 'transcendental,' we cannot but wonder why Kant came to use this term to mean a priori in some cases and real or material in others. This rather strange dual usage of 'transcendental' appears to reflect two different views Kant entertained about the means of transcendence: (1) that the subject can transcend itself by means of a priori truths or knowledge and (2) that the subject can transcend itself by the real or material use of its intellect. For an adequate understanding of these two views of transcendence or objectivity, we must place them in the context of the Cartesian tradition.

Ever since Descartes' *Meditations,* it had been taken for granted by the rationalists that the objects of senses are private to each subject and that the sensible world can never become an objective domain. Hence, all rationalists tried to secure the domain of objective discourse in the supersensible world.

Kant took a long time in freeing himself from this metaphysical dogma of objectivity. In the *Träume* he shows the first sign of revolt against it by claiming the senses as the ground of objectivity. But he fails to sustain this revolt in the *Dissertation* where he admits the subjectivity of the sensible world and the objectivity of the intelligible world. *(Dissertation* § 4) But he is compelled to repudiate this position when he takes the stand in his Critical period that the intelligible world is not even knowable.

One of Kant's main tasks during the Critical period was to resuscitate the *Träume* position and securely establish the domain of objectivity in the sensible world. His doctrine of the transcendental subject was the focal point in this endeavor, because it was meant to be the subject of objective phenomena or experience. Thus the doctrine of the transcendental subject is inseparable from that of experience and constitutes an integral element of the Transcendental Analytic. For this reason, it is impossible to confine the problem of transcendental consciousness to the Transcendental Dialectic. But Kant never gives his doctrine of the transcendental subject a decent chance of formal exposition in any part of the Transcendental Logic, because he does not regard it as one of the proper topics of the Analytic and because in the Dialectic he is chiefly concerned with the negative task of refuting rational psychology rather than with the positive task of propounding his own doctrine. Thus the focal point in his doctrine of experience is left in a terrible obscurity.

Of course, Kant repeatedly identifies the transcendental subject with the pure understanding. But his identification cannot give us a complete specification of its nature. Since consciousness is always a consciousness of something, it is impossible to gain a complete understanding of transcendental consciousness without knowing the nature of its objects. Kant's two views of a priori knowledge are his two ways of specifying the contents of transcendental consciousness. We have seen that his postulational view presupposes the independent existence of empirical objects while his axiomatic view does not. According to the latter view, the phenomenal objects constituted through the pure synthesis are said to form the objective contents of transcendental consciousness. According to the postulational view, these objective contents are said to be the independently existing empirical objects. It may be profitable for us, from the standpoint of consciousness, to see why Kant has entertained these two views of phenomenal objects.

As a preliminary to this inquiry, let us distinguish between two types of subjects, which may be called the monadic and the nonmonadic subjects. By the former is meant the Leibnizian subject, the contents of whose consciousness are absolutely private to it; by the latter is meant the subject the objects of whose consciousness can be shared with other subjects.

Let us note that the term 'objectivity' cannot have the same meaning for monadic and nonmonadic subjects. For the latter, 'objectivity' means the accessibility to more than one consciousness: an object that is accessible to any nonmonadic subjects is objective. This meaning of 'objectivity' cannot be retained for monadic subjects because no two can perceive one common object. They can at best have some similar perceptions. As Leibniz puts it, their experiences "do not therefore have to be perfectly alike, but it is enough that they should be proportional; as several spectators believe that they are seeing the same thing, and in fact understand each other, although each sees and speaks according to the measure of his view."[4] Thus Leibniz holds that his monadic subjects can never have truly objective experience or knowledge in the phenomenal world.

Leibniz believes that true objectivity can be found only in the intelligible world because his monadic subjects can have absolutely identical apperceptions in the realm of essences or truths of reason. That is, since truths of reason are necessary truths, the monadic subjects which have a clear and distinct comprehension of them would necessarily gain intersubjective agreements. Thus the monadic conception of the Leibnizian subjects demands *necessity* or *necessary truths* as the ground for true objectivity.

Leibniz' monadic conception of the human subject was not an exception but a general rule accepted by all rationalists beginning with Descartes. It is because of this conception that Descartes claimed to find objectivity or certainty only in the domain of clear and distinct ideas. Kant also labors under this monadic conception of the human subject when he claims the necessity and universality of a priori synthetic judgments as the ground for the objectivity of our experience in the *Critique*.

The axiomatic necessity of his axiomatic program is meant to provide the ground of objectivity in the phenomenal world, just as Leibniz' necessary truths are claimed to do for the noumenal world. It is fairly certain that his axiomatic program has been conceived in the context of monadic subjects, each of which must form its own phenomenal world. Thus the object-formation theory is deeply rooted in the monadic idealism and the axiomatic necessity of a priori truths is meant to establish the intersubjective communion among the monadically constituted phenomenal worlds.

Kant's postulational program, on the other hand, must have been conceived in the context of the nonmonadic subjects. The empirical objects whose independent existence is presupposed by this program are public objects, which can be shared by many nonmonadic subjects. No doubt, the domain of public objects cannot provide objective experience if different subjects are to confront it with different systems of categories. Therefore a common categorial system is indispensable for the objective experience of the nonmonadic subjects. But there is no need to demand that the categories be of a priori origin or that they produce some axiomatically certain primitive propositions. Hence in the postulational program Kant can accept the concept-formation theory in accounting for the genesis of his categorial system and can adopt functional necessity in place of axiomatic necessity.

From these considerations, we may assume that Kant's transcendental subject has been conceived once as monadic and once as nonmonadic. The monadic transcendental subject is the transcendental (meaning a priori) subject, which can transcend itself and attain objectivity by means of a priori truths or knowledge; the nonmonadic transcendental subject is the transcendental (meaning real or material) subject, which can transcend itself and attain objectivity by the real or material use of its intellect. Thus the two disparate meanings of 'transcendental' reflect Kant's two views of subjectivity and objectivity, which are presupposed by his two programs of transcendence.*

It should, however, be acknowledged that his transcendental subject is seldom construed nowadays as a monadic one. Therefore we must assemble some evidence in support of our view. We can locate our most reliable evidence in Kant's doctrine of space and time, namely, that space and time are the forms of intuitions. Of all the possible interpretations which have been placed on this doctrine, the most obvious one construes it to mean that space and time are the ways in which the transcendental subject is affected by the transcendent objects. Kant clearly expresses this view when he calls space and time the forms of our receptivity or rather our "capacity to be affected by objects." (A 26 = B 42; A 33 = 49) If space and time are really the forms of affection, every subject must have its own space and time since no two subjects can be affected through the numerically identical set of forms. Thus Kant's doctrine of formal intuitions implies that space and time are private to each subject.

---

*We can now functionally explain how one transcendental subject is related to many individual subjects. In the context of monadic subjectivity, every individual subject can function as a transcendental subject in so far as it is in possession of one common set of primitive a priori truths. In the context of nonmonadic subjectivity, every individual subject can function as a transcendental subject in so far as it confronts one public world. In either case, many individual subjects can be said to participate in one transcendental subject, or, conversely, the latter can be viewed as present in the former. It is probably this one-and-many relation that Kant tried to express by the *ideality* of the transcendental subject and the *plurality* of individual subjects. The neo-Kantians have taken the ideality of the transcendental subject in the Platonic sense of ideality and have understood its participation in many individual subjects also in the Platonic sense of participation. This neo-Kantian interpretation may be acceptable for the monadic transcendental subject, but certainly not for the nonmonadic transcendental subject.

In the *Inaugural Dissertation,* where the formal view of space and time is originally proposed, Kant readily recognizes the subjectivity or privacy of formal intuitions. (*Dissertation* § 14, 5; § 15, D) That he carries over this view to the *Critique* can be established by his doctrine of sensations, in which he still maintains his previous view that all sensations are private to each subject. (A 28 f.; B 44) Since space and time are said to be the forms for receiving these private sensations, he must admit that space and time are as private as the sensations. For it is implausible to claim that private contents are given through public forms.

If space and time are private intuitions, they can provide the ground of objectivity only by virtue of their a priori origins. That is, only to the extent that space and time as pure intuitions provide the ground of necessary truths, the different monadic subjects can have experiences that are numerically different but qualitatively identical. Thus it is the monadic conception of the human subject that forces Kant to seek the ground of objectivity in the *purity* of a priori intuitions in his axiomatic program.

In contrast to this, his postulational program requires public space and time. In Chapter 8, we have seen that this program presupposes the independent existence of empirical objects. Empirical objects cannot have independent existence unless they are placed in space and time whose existence is independent of individual subjects. Such space and time are public entities. If space and time are public, they are bound to function as the objective framework for all nonmonadic subjects. Furthermore, their objectivity can have nothing to do with their genetic character, i.e. whether they are a priori or a posteriori. This confirms our contention in Part II of this volume that the doctrine of pure intuitions is required only for the axiomatic program.

It is always difficult to determine whether Kant's statements on the transcendental subject should be construed in the context of the monadic or the nonmonadic subject. The Paralogisms in the first edition is a typical example to illustrate this textual difficulty. Most of Kant's critics read it in the context of the monadic subjects, whereas Kant himself had meant it to be understood in the context of the nonmonadic subjects. Hence his indignation about the charge of subjective idealism. But this charge was well deserved because he had presented his doctrine of the transcendental subject in the context of the individual subject, which his contemporaries, being rationalists, had taken for granted as monadic.

It is highly probable that Kant did write the first edition Paralogisms while he was nurturing both the monadic and the nonmonadic conceptions of subject without fully realizing their differences. It is also possible that he was forced by the charge of subjective idealism into clearly recognizing these differences and rejecting the monadic conception in favor of the nonmonadic. The latter doctrine requires the existence of one phenomenal world, which can be shared by all individual subjects. Kant must have thought that this requirement could be met by the ideality of the transcendental subject without repudiating the representational character of the phenomenal world. Thus, as we have seen, he plainly stressed, in the second edition Paralogisms, that the transcendental subject is not a real but an ideal entity. The phenomenal world cannot be taken to be a private object of any monadic consciousness, he must have thought, if its representational being is grounded not in a real but in an ideal subject. Thus he must have concluded that the phenomenal world can be accepted as a public object for the nonmonadic subjects, although it is still claimed to have only a representational being in the transcendental subject.

The difference between the two versions of Kant's refutation of idealism can also best be specified in terms of his two different conceptions of subjectivity. Whereas the refutation in the first edition can be read either in the context of the monadic subject or in that of the nonmonadic subject, the refutation in the second edition makes sense only when it is read in the context of the nonmonadic subject. The central point of Kant's involved argument in the latter refutation is the simple claim that the objective consciousness is possible only when it confronts the public empirical objects ("the permanent"), precisely because the objective consciousness is simply the consciousness of the public empirical objects.

Earlier in this chapter we noted that the refutation of idealism in the first edition is formulated in the context of the Transcendental Aesthetic and that the refutation in the second edition is formulated in the context of the Transcendental Analytic. Now we can give a little more precise characterization of their difference. The second refutation is formulated in the context of the postulational program of the Analytic because it presupposes the independent existence of public empirical objects. The first refutation is formulated in the context of the axiomatic program because the Transcendental Aesthetic is an integral feature of the axiomatic program. Therefore, we may say that the first refutation belongs to the axiomatic program and that the second refutation belongs to the postulational program.

Thus Kant's doctrine of the transcendental subject turns out to be a form of direct realism when it is construed as a doctrine of the nonmonadic subject, while it also turns out to be a form of subjective idealism when it is construed as a doctrine of the monadic subject. In the latter interpretation, Kant's notion of the transcendental subject is simply an extension of Leibniz' notion in exactly the same sense that Kant's axiomatic program is an extension of Leibniz' program. In both cases, Kant faithfully accepts the Leibnizian method and tries to achieve in the phenomenal world what Leibniz is reputed to have been able to achieve only in the noumenal world. But, in the nonmonadic conception of the transcendental subject, Kant makes a decisive break with the Leibnizian camp just as he does in his postulational program.

At any rate, it should never be forgotten that the transcendental subject is the subject of transcendence, that transcendental logic is the logic of transcendence, and that the axiomatic and the postulational programs are Kant's two programs of transcendence.

Chapter 11

Transcendental Cosmology

Kant characterizes rational cosmology as a set of dialectical inferences about the ultimate nature of the world. This pseudo-science is literally dialectical: Every one of its assertions is matched by a counter-assertion. Thus rational cosmology dialectically generates several pairs of mutually conflicting assertions, called the antinomies of pure reason. Kant claims that the thesis and the antithesis of each antinomy can be supported by equally cogent arguments. We will now see the claims and counterclaims of the four Antinomies and the various arguments advanced in their support.

THE FIRST ANTINOMY (A 426 ff. = B 454 ff.)

Thesis	Antithesis
The world has a beginning in time, and is also limited as regards space.	The world has no beginning, and no limits in space; it is infinite as regards both time and space.

The thesis of the First Antinomy argues for the finitude of the world in space and time. In the proof of the thesis, Kant first argues for the temporal finitude of the world and then applies the same argument to its spatial finitude. To prove that the world must have had a definite beginning in time, he argues that it is absurd to conceive the world without a beginning. If the world had had no beginning, he claims, an eternity must have elapsed. The elapse of an eternity requires an infinite number of syntheses. But the infinite number of syntheses is an infinite series that can never be completed: "Now the infinity of a series consists in the fact that it can never be completed through successive synthesis." (A 426 = B 454) Therefore the world must have had a beginning. Unlike time, Kant recognizes, space does not exist as a series. But he argues that space as a whole can be known through the acts of synthesis. Since an infinite space would require an infinite number of syntheses, he concludes, an infinite space is as impossible as an infinite time. Therefore the world must be limited in space.

The proof of the thesis rests on the premise that an infinite series can never be completed. This premise appears to resemble the proposition that an actual infinite is impossible. But Kant takes pains to dissociate the former from the latter. He maintains that the proof of the thesis does not appeal to the dogmatic notion that the concept of an actual infinite is self-contradictory. (A 430 = B 458) He says that an actual infinite appears to be self-contradictory if it is erroneously conceived as a summation of successive units. Since more units can be added on to any series of units, he argues, the infinite conceived as a series of units should be as contradictory as the concept of the greatest cardinal number. (A 430 = B 458)

Kant is a little more explicit on the question of infinity in the *Inaugural Dissertation. (Dissertation* § 1, note) There he argues that an actual infinite is impossible for the human intellect, which can apprehend it only as a summation of successive units. He also argues that an actual infinite is possible for the intellect which can apprehend it in one glance without going through the process of successive synthesis. He further intimates that even human intellect might be able to apprehend an actual infinite if it were freed from the requirement that its successive synthesis must be completed in a finite time. He appears to think that the human intellect cannot apprehend an actual infinite because of the two features of its finitude: (1) the unit of its synthesis is finite and (2) it is given only a finite span of time for apprehension. He clearly believes that an actual infinite can be apprehended by an intellect which is not encumbered with both of these limitations of the human intellect.

Since the question of infinity is inseparable from the question of the subject, we cannot determine the validity of proof for the thesis of the First Antinomy without determining the nature of the subject that is presupposed for the argument. But this is an ambiguous point difficult to determine: The subject involved may be construed either as the individual (actual) human subject or as the transcendental (ideal) subject. This is the same ambiguity that we have encountered in the four Paralogisms of the first edition. This ambiguity appears not only in the First Antinomy but runs through all four. Unfortunately we cannot avoid certain difficulties whether we construe the subject presupposed for the Antinomies either as the individual human subject or the transcendental subject.

Since the four Antinomies are supposed to be the products of rational cosmology, which had been formulated before the emergence of the transcendental philosophy, it would be anachronistic to assume that their assertions and counter-assertions had been formulated in the context of the transcendental subject. But it is equally difficult to assume that they had been formulated in the context of the individual human subject, because the subject involved is supposed to be the agent of synthesis. The pre-Kantian rationalists could not have conceived the individual human subject as an agent of synthesis; this conception appears to have emerged as uniquely Kantian. Kant often states that the four Antinomies are the inevitable products of human reason as such, rather than the peculiar products of some eccentric school. Even this point does not help us at all in resolving the ambiguity in question. Since we cannot resolve this ambiguity to our satisfaction, we will try to construe the proof of the thesis in the context of the individual subject as well as in that of the transcendental subject.

The argument that an infinite series can never be completed by the synthesis of an individual human subject because it is limited by its finite unit of synthesis and its finite span for apprehension, is valid when it is construed in the context of the individual subject. But this proof exacts a high price—the acceptance of subjective idealism. When the proof is construed in the context of the individual human subject, it demands the presupposition that the entire world is just a representation in an individual subject. This subjective idealism entails the finitude of the world. The proof of the thesis becomes analytical: The finitude of the world in time is proved by the definition of the world as a finite construction of the individual subject.

Let us see whether the proof of the thesis can be accepted in the context of the transcendental subject. We have seen in the last chapter that the transcendental subject is an ideal subject that cannot be exhausted by any number of individual subjects, so we should be careful in attributing the limitations of individual subjects to the transcendental subject. We can very well admit that the unit of synthesis for the transcendental subject is finite. But it is difficult to assume that the transcendental subject is also limited by a finite span of time for its apprehension. The individual human subject can have only a limited span of time for its apprehension because its life is bounded by the two events of birth and death. The span of time which can be assigned to the transcendental subject cannot be bounded by these two events, because it can neither be born nor die. The only two events that can bound the period of its apprehension are the beginning and the end of the world.

An infinite series can never be completed by the synthesis of the transcendental subject if it is given only a finite span of time, but it can be completed if it is given an infinite span of time. Whether the transcendental subject should be given a finite or an infinite span of time for its apprehension cannot be determined without the prior determination of whether the world has had a finite or infinite period of existence, because the life of the transcendental subject must be coextensive with the life of the world. So the argument that an infinite series can never be completed, even for the transcendental subject, cannot be maintained without presupposing that the world has had a finite period of existence and that the transcendental subject has been allowed a finite span for constructing it. Thus the proof turns out to be circular when it is construed in the context of the transcendental subject.

If we presuppose the temporal infinitude of the world, we can attribute an infinite span of time to the transcendental subject for its apprehension. For this infinite transcendental subject, every moment should be the conclusion of an infinite series of temporal syntheses. The argument that an eternity can never elapse, can hold only for the transcendental subject that is conceived as the subject of a finite temporal world. An eternity must elapse every moment in the world that has had no beginning.

The proof of the finitude of the world in space takes the same form as the proof of its finitude in time. Although the parts of space are coexistent or simultaneous with one another, Kant says, they can be apprehended only through the acts of synthesis. Since an infinite series of syntheses is impossible to complete, he argues, the world cannot be infinite in space. Since the subject that is presupposed for the synthesis of space can be also regarded either as an individual subject or the transcendental subject, the proof for the spatial finitude of the world can be also interpreted in two different ways. Whether the proof is construed in the context of the individual human subject or the transcendental subject, it can be established only on the premise that the subject involved be given only a finite span of time for its synthesis. But once this premise is accepted, the proof becomes circular or analytical.

When Kant comes to prove the antithesis of the First Antinomy, he begins with the premise that space and time are infinite. If the world has had a definite beginning in time and has a definite boundary in space, he argues, the world must be bounded by an empty time and an empty space. (A 427 = B 455) Then he tries to show that there can be neither an empty time nor an empty space. He claims that the beginning of the world cannot be preceded by an empty time because nothing can come into being in an empty time. He also claims that the extension of the world cannot be limited by an empty space because then the world would be related to a nonentity, or no object. It is interesting to note that Kant tries to establish these two claims on the Leibnizian principles rather than on his own. He tries to establish the former point by appealing to the principle of sufficient reason rather than to his own principle of causation. He tries to establish the latter point by appealing to the relational theory of space rather than to his own formal theory of space. He may have done this because he wanted to present these arguments as the products of the Leibnizian rational cosmology.

The proof of the antithesis is dubious not only because it rests on the dubious principles of the Leibnizian cosmology but particularly because it presupposes the infinitude of space and time. The infinitude of space and time should not be presupposed because it is one of the very items to be proved. The proof is bound to be circular to the extent that one of the items to be proved is used as a premise.

The presupposition of the infinitude of space and time in the proof of the antithesis has one adverse effect on the construction of the First Antinomy as a whole. A thesis and its antithesis must stand on the same premise in order to constitute an antinomy. If they were to stand on different premises, they would fail to join the issue and could not come into a real conflict. Since Kant has already presupposed the finitude of the world in the proof of the thesis of the First Antinomy, he is eliminating the basis for its conflict with its antithesis by presupposing the infinitude of space and time for the proof of the antithesis.

THE SECOND ANTINOMY (A 434 ff. = B 462 ff.)

Thesis	Antithesis
Every composite substance in the world is made up of simple parts, and nothing anywhere exists save the simple or what is composed of the simple.	No composite thing in the world is made up of simple parts, and there nowhere exists in the world anything simple.

This Antinomy is concerned with the ultimate nature of physical matter. Both the thesis and the antithesis assume that material substances are composite entities. The point of disputation is whether or not these composite entities are composed of the simples or the indivisibles. The proof of the thesis rests on the definition of the composite as an accidental aggregation of simple substances. (A 434 = B 462) Since the composite is the composite of the simples, Kant argues, composite entities must be composed of the simples. Thus the proof turns out to have a definitional certainty.

The proof of the antithesis consists of two arguments. The first is based on the nature of space. (A 435 = B 463) Since space is infinitely divisible, Kant argues, matter which occupies space should also be infinitely divisible. As we have shown in Chapter 6, this is an illegitimate a priori inference made from the nature of pure intuitions to that of empirical intuitions. Kemp Smith says that this inference has been eventually rejected by Kant himself in his *Metaphysical First Principles of Natural Science* ("the infinite divisibility of matter is very far from being proved through proof of the infinite divisibilty of space").[1]

The second argument for the antithesis is based on the nature of perceptual experience. (A 437 = B 465) Kant claims that the existence of the absolutely simple can never be established because the absolutely simple cannot be encountered in possible experience. In the proof he does not explain why the simples can never be encountered in perception. In the Observation on the Second Antinomy he says that the perception of the absolutely simple is impossible due to the laws of sensibility. But he does not explain what he means by the "laws of sensibility." There can be two kinds of laws of sensibility, the a priori laws about pure intuitions and the a posteriori laws about empirical intuitions. Kant however cannot invoke the a posteriori laws because no empirical claims can be accepted in the transcendental arguments of rational cosmology. Hence the laws of sensibility to which he appeals must be the a priori laws of pure intuitions. The only a priori law of sensibility that is relevant to the Second Antinomy appears to be the law that pure intuitions are infinitely divisible. If so, the second argument for the antithesis is no different from the first argument.

THE THIRD ANTINOMY (A 444 ff. = B 472 ff.)

Thesis	Antithesis
Causality in accordance with laws of nature is not the only causality from which the appearances of the world can one and all be derived. To explain these appearances it is necessary to assume that there is also another causality, that of freedom.	There is no freedom; everything in the world takes place solely in accordance with laws of nature.

This Antinomy is concerned with the dialectical problem of freedom and necessity. Kant tries to prove the thesis by a dialectical method: The causal principle in its unlimited application falls into self-contradiction. If the causal principle has absolute universality, he argues, it should be impossible to give a complete causal account of any event because such an account would result in an infinite series. (A 446 = B 474) This argument presupposes the impossibility of completing an infinite series, but we have seen in the First Antinomy that Kant could give only a circular proof of this presupposition. Granting the impossibility of completing any causal account, it is still difficult to see how the causal principle must fall into self-contradiction when it is employed without restrictions. The only thing we can be certain of is that every causal account must be incomplete, but no incomplete causal account can result in the self-contradiction of the causal principle. Thus the alleged self-contradiction evaporates.

The proof of the antithesis is based on the Second Analogy. Kant argues that there can be no freedom because its existence would nullify the causal principle and endanger the possibility of experience. Unfortunately we have already seen that Kant has never succeeded in proving the causal principle. Thus the proof of the antithesis is as unconvincing as the proof of the thesis.

THE FOURTH ANTINOMY (A 452 ff. = B 480 ff.)

Thesis	Antithesis
There belong to the world, either as its part or as its cause, a being that is absolutely necessary.	An absolutely necessary being nowhere exists in the world, nor does it exist outside the world as its cause.

This Antinomy is concerned with the controversy over necessary vs. contingent being. The arguments in this Antinomy are confusing because 'the necessary being' and 'the contingent being' are not used in their traditional sense. By 'the necessary being' Kant means not that which cannot not exist, but that which exists freely or without being causally determined. By 'the contingent being' he means not that which need not exist, but that which exists conditionally or whose existence is causally determined. A necessary being in its traditional sense may be a free being, but every free being need not be a necessary being. A free being may very well be contingent in its traditional sense. Every causally determined being may be contingent in its traditional sense, but not every contingent being need be causally determined. These discrepancies between Kant's usage and traditional usage of the central terms constitute a source of confusion for the arguments in the Fourth Antinomy.

Since Kant redefines 'a necessary being' and 'a contingent being' in terms of freedom and causation, the Fourth Antinomy becomes a repetition of the Third Antinomy. For this reason, some commentators do not even bother to examine the claims and the counter-claims of this Antinomy.[2] The proofs of the thesis and the antithesis of the Fourth Antinomy appear to be quite different from the proofs of the thesis and the antithesis of the Third Antinomy, if 'the necessary being' and 'the contingent being' are assumed to have their traditional meanings. Once these terms are understood to have Kant's own stipulated meanings, the proofs in the two Antinomies turn out to be substantially the same.

It would be well, however, to recognize one noteworthy difference between the Third and the Fourth Antinomies. Whereas the Third Antinomy allows its controversy to extend beyond the phenomenal world, the Fourth Antinomy emphatically prohibits such an extension of its arguments. Kant insists that the Fourth Antinomy is confined exclusively to the phenomenal world. (A 452 = B 480; A 455 = B 483) In the Fourth Antinomy he appears to be motivated by the desire to maintain a clear demarcation between rational cosmology and rational theology. He expresses this desire at the beginning of his Observation on the Fourth Antinomy. (A 456 = B 484) The same desire appears to have influenced him in his decision to use 'the necessary being' and 'the contingent being' in a nontraditional sense. If these terms are allowed to retain their traditional meanings, the Fourth Antinomy would inevitably encroach on the domain of rational theology.

Kant's decision to maintain a clear demarcation between the three branches of the Transcendental Dialectic is quite unfortunate. We have already seen why the notion of the transcendental subject cannot be adequately formulated without introducing the notion of the world. We have also seen why the validity of some arguments in the Antinomies cannot be determined without clarifying the notion of the subject involved. From these we can expect some of the theological problems to be bound up with the problems of the self or the world. The Fourth Antinomy is concerned with one of these transcompartmental problems, but Kant forces it into one compartment. Thus the problem in question is not allowed to retain its organic ties with other problems. Kant's penchant for clear demarcation often disrupts the organic connections among different philosophical problems.

Now that we have seen the arguments and the counterarguments in the four Antinomies, we will next examine Kant's resolution of these dialectical issues. Before going into this examination, we must stress that Kant has not been able to provide cogent arguments in support of the conflicting claims of the four Antinomies. Notwithstanding his claim that the proofs of the theses and the antitheses involve neither the dubious tricks of sophists nor the bad faith of dogmatists, most of the proofs are based either on some definitions which render the proofs circular or analytical, or on some presuppositions which are themselves in need of proof. Hegel justly says that Kant's proofs are plain assertions in disguise.[3] Cassirer advises us simply to ignore the proofs.[4]

We cannot therefore accept Kant's thesis that the claims and the counter-claims of the four Antinomies are the inevitable products of sound theoretical reason. There is no reason to assume that sound reason is bound to fall into the trap of self-contradiction. Whenever we can deduce incompatible conclusions from one set of premises, we have the logical certainty that the incompatibility of the former is derived from that of the latter. As we have seen, Kant's antinomies really derive their dialectical conflict from the logical conflict of their incompatible premises or assumptions.

Kant presents his transcendental idealism as the key for resolving all the antinomies of pure reason. (A 490 = B 518) He says that the general premise for the genesis of all the Antinomies is the principle that "if the conditioned is given, the entire series of conditions is likewise given." (A 497 = B 525) He holds that this principle is true of things in themselves but not appearances. (A 498 = B 526) He reminds us that appearances have no independent existence and that they can exist only in the agent of synthesis. Since the world of appearances is a product of synthesis, he argues, the existence of the conditioned in the phenomenal world cannot entail the existence of all its conditions. Given the conditioned, he admits, its conditions can always be constructed in a regressive synthesis. He insists that those conditions can never be assumed to have existence independent of the regressive synthesis. (A 499 = B 527) In short, appearances and things in themselves have different modes of existence. The confusion of these modes of existence generates all the antinomies about the nature of the world; the clarification of this confusion is the key to their resolution.

Kant maintains that the principle of the excluded middle does not hold in the phenomenal world as it does in the noumenal world. If the principle of the excluded middle were to be valid of the Antinomies, he says, either the thesis or the antithesis of each Antinomy must be true. That is, it would be impossible for both of them to be false or true at the same time. He wants to show that the theses and the antitheses in the First and the Second Antinomies are both false and that the theses and the antitheses in the Third and Fourth Antinomies can both be true. Let us see how he substantiates this point.

Kant resolves the First Antinomy by holding that the world is neither finite nor infinite in space and time. Since the spatial and temporal syntheses of the world can be extended indefinitely, he argues, the age and the extent of the world are indefinite. In order to stress the difference between the infinite and the indefinite, he introduces two technical expressions: the *regressus in indefinitum* and the *regressus in infinitum*. (A 520 = B 548) While the latter implies an actual infinite, the former signifies a potential infinite or rather the regress that can be extended beyond any finite stage. Kant holds that the regressive synthesis of the phenomenal world is not the *regressus in infinitum* but the *regressus in indefinitum*. He resolves the Second Antinomy in the same manner; that is, the division of physical matter can result neither in a finite series nor in an infinite series because its division can be carried out only to the extent that the regressive synthesis can be executed.

Kant tries to resolve the Third Antinomy by the conjunction of the phenomenal and the noumenal worlds: The thesis is true of the noumenal world, while the antithesis is true of the phenomenal world. If the thesis and the antithesis were to be asserted of the phenomenal world alone, at least one of them should be false. But they need not conflict if each is assigned its proper domain. Kant's resolution of this Antinomy may be called a perspectival resolution: One and the same series of phenomena can be regarded as causally determined or as freely initiated, depending on whether it is viewed from the perspective of the phenomenal world or from that of the noumenal world.

Kant also gives a perspectival resolution to the Fourth Antinomy: The thesis is true from the perspective of the noumenal world and the antithesis is true from the perspective of the phenomenal world. There is one thing noteworthy about his resolution of the Fourth Antinomy: He restores the traditional meaning of 'necessary existence.' We have seen that Kant, in the arguments of the Fourth Antinomy, uses 'necessary being' not in its traditional sense but in the sense of 'the causally independent being.' In the beginning of the resolution of the Fourth Antinomy, he says that "We are concerned here, not with unconditioned causality, but with the unconditioned existence of substance itself." (A 559 = B 587) He goes on to argue that necessary beings can never exist in the phenomenal world because everything in it is alterable and changeable. Since necessary beings can exist only in the timeless world, he maintains, we should admit the possibility of the noumenal world. Thus Kant uses the Fourth Antinomy to argue for the existence of the noumenal world.

Kant should have guarded against one point in the resolution of the Third and the Fourth Antinomies; he should not have asserted the truths of the antitheses without qualification. These antitheses claim the existence of actual infinities, if they are asserted without qualifications. But that would contradict Kant's resolution of the First and Second Antinomies, which rejects an actual infinite. Therefore he should have said that the antitheses of the Third and the Fourth Antinomies should be understood to assert only the *regressus in indefinitum* rather than the *regressus in infinitum.*

Kant's resolutions of the four Antinomies amount to asserting the following picture of the world. The world consists of two layers, the phenomenal and the noumenal. The phenomenal world is the domain of necessity; the noumenal world is the domain of freedom. The domain of freedom consists of necessary beings; the domain of necessity consists of contingent beings. Every event can be viewed in two different contexts, that is, as belonging to the phenomenal world and also to the noumenal world. As far as the phenomenal world is concerned, it exists only as an indefinite whole, which is constructed by synthesis. The act of synthesis takes two main forms, the synthesis of dividing the content of the phenomenal world and the synthesis of extending its temporal and spatial boundaries. Since these two forms of synthesis can be carried on to an indefinite extent, the phenomenal world can be neither finite nor infinite.

Let us now try to assess Kant's cosmology. We will begin with his picture of the phenomenal world. We may call it *indefinitism* in contrast to *finitism* (the world is finite) and *infinitism* (the world is infinite). As many critics have pointed out, this indefinitism comes into conflict with Kant's doctrine of space and time as presented in the Transcendental Aesthetic. Kant's indefinitism presents the picture of space and time as a *compositum,* whereas the Aesthetic has presented the view of space and time as a *totum.* (Cf. A 25 = B 40; A 32 = B 48; A 438 = B 466) This conflict can be resolved by distinguishing two domains of phenomenal existence: Space and time are given in intuitions as a *totum* but they are experienced in thought as a *compositum.* This resolution assumes that space and time are given as actual infinities in the domain of intuitions. In fact, this assumption appears to be indispensable as a premise for Kant's indefinitism. Without assuming the infinity of space and time, he cannot claim that the spatial and temporal syntheses of the world can be extended indefinitely. If space and time are assumed to be finite intuitions, the temporal and the spatial syntheses of the world should come to an end at some point.

Some may be tempted to say that Kant need not be forced to the choice between the finitude and the infinitude of space and time because he can extend his indefinitism to his doctrine of pure intuitions. That is, Kant can say that space and time are given as indefinite rather than infinite wholes. This would be a charming way to resolve the dilemma, but it is not available to Kant. We should remember that he has introduced his indefinitism in the domain of thought and that it cannot be extended to the domain of senses. Indefinitism is acceptable in the domain of thought because the domain of thought is the domain of synthesis. That is to say, the domain of thought can be indefinitely extended because the synthesis of understanding can be carried on indefinitely. But intuition cannot be an agent of synthesis; the sense world as merely given cannot be a domain of synthesis. Hence we cannot apply Kant's indefinitism to space and time as intuitions. Since indefinitism is inapplicable to intuitions as merely given, Kant must choose between finitism or infinitism in his doctrine of space and time as pure intuitions.

At this point, it is important to stress that the phenomenal world can be viewed in two ways: (1) as given in senses only (merely sensed) and (2) as not only given in senses but also as understood in thought (fully experienced). The distinction between these two perspectives cannot be rejected as long as Kant's distinction between sense and thought is retained. Let us keep firmly in mind that Kant's indefinitism is valid only for the second type of world, the world that is not merely given in senses but is also known in thought. We have yet to determine whether Kant would hold finitism or infinitism about the world which is only given in senses. He cannot maintain finitism for the merely *sensed* world because the doctrine of finite intuitions would not allow him to maintain his indefinitism for the fully *experienced* world. Thus he is compelled to accept infinitism as far as the merely *sensed* world is concerned.

The most devastating criticism of Kant's indefinitism, however, is that it can be maintained only for the individual subjects and not for the transcendental subject. We have already seen why Kant must accept the doctrine of infinite space and infinite time. As far as the individual subjects are concerned, we can see that the world could be neither finite nor infinite. But we cannot admit the same limitations for the transcendental subject, since it is neither born nor dies, and its synthesis cannot be limited by temporal conditions. The synthesis of an individual subject must take some time because it is an actual event in time. But the synthesis of the transcendental subject cannot be regarded as taking up any span of time because it is not an actual but only an ideal, or possible, event. If its synthesis is not burdened by temporal conditions, there can be nothing to prevent the transcendental subject from constructing or experiencing an infinite world, as long as its intuitions are infinite.

There is only one way to limit the world of the transcendental subject to an indefinite size and this is to provide the transcendental subject with an indefinite domain of intuitions. But it is impossible to maintain the doctrine of indefinitism for the domain of intuitions without conceding the power of synthesis to the faculty of intuitions, because indefinitism is possible only as an indefinite extension of synthesis. Once we concede the power of synthesis to the faculty of sensibility, we can no longer maintain the distinction between intuition and intellect. For, with the power of synthesis, sensibility would cease to be receptive and would become as spontaneous as understanding. Thus the doctrine of Kant's indefinitism cannot be extended to the domain of intuitions and to the world of the transcendental subject without eliminating the foundations of transcendental idealism.

We thus have to conclude that Kant can maintain his indefinitism not for the transcendental subject but only for the individual subject. But even for the individual subject, Kant's indefinitism requires some qualifications. In the previous chapter we have seen that there are two components in the individual subject, the transcendental and the empirical. Insofar as the individual subject participates in the transcendental subject, the former must have an infinite world if the latter has an infinite world. So indefinitism cannot be maintained even for the individual subject as a whole. The only subject for which indefinitism is admissible is the empirical subject or rather the empirical component of the individual subject. This means that the world is neither finite nor infinite, but is indefinite only insofar as the world is considered as an object of actual exploration or of empirical construction.

If we do not place such limitations on Kant's indefinitism, his doctrine of the world would be indistinguishable from subjective idealism. The assertion that the totality of the world can exist only in the regressive synthesis is, after all, plainly a subjective idealism. If this assertion were not limited to the empirical subject, the transcendental subject would be a gratuitous entity in the formation of the transcendental cosmology and transcendental idealism would be indistinguishable from subjective idealism. No wonder, then, that Cassirer and many others have voiced a strong suspicion that Kant has propounded a Berkeleyan view of the world in the Transcendental Dialectic.[5]

We have so far criticized Kant's indefinitism only in the context of the First Antinomy. Although Kant again invokes his indefinitism in the resolution of the Second Antinomy, he feels a considerable hesitation in doing so. (A 524 = B 552) He feels something intuitively strange in claiming that the parts of physical matter can exist only in the regressive synthesis. But he finally overcomes this intuitive discomfort and extends his indefinitism to the nature of physical matter. There is no need to examine this extension of his indefinitism because our criticism of indefinitism is equally applicable to it.

We now come to the relation of the phenomenal and noumenal worlds. Kant's resolution of the Third Antinomy resembles Leibniz' reconciliation of freedom and necessity. Leibniz holds that there are two domains of discourse, the realm of matter or nature and the realm of spirit or grace.[6] He says that the realm of matter is governed by necessity (efficient causation) and that the realm of spirit is governed by freedom (final causation). Since these two realms are in preestablished harmony, he maintains, human behavior can be viewed both as a free action belonging to the realm of spirit and as a causally determined motion belonging to the realm of matter.

This is a double perspective theory: One event can be viewed from two different perspectives. Kant in effect tries to adopt Leibniz' double perspective theory without the doctrine of preestablished harmony.

Kant has not done anything seriously wrong in repudiating the doctrine of preestablished harmony, but in the Transcendental Analytic he already foreclosed the possibility of adopting Leibnizian double perspectivism. In order to adopt double perspectivism, Kant should have established two domains of meaningful discourse. But time and again in the Analytic Kant has stressed that the phenomenal world is the only domain of meaningful discourse and that we do not even understand the meaning of the assertions about the noumenal world. Even in claiming the transcendental freedom of the human subject, he admits that the human subject as a noumenal entity cannot be meaningfully placed in the context of actions in the phenomenal world. He says, "Inasmuch as it is *noumenon,* nothing *happens* in it. . . . No action begins *in* this active being. . . ." (A 541 = B 569) To be sure, Kant is modest enough to say that he is not proving the reality of freedom but only trying to establish its possibility. (A 558 = B 586) But possible freedom is not any less unintelligible than actual freedom when it is presented in the context of the noumenal world. Thus Kant's double perspectivism fails because one half of it is submerged in the domain of meaningless discourse.

In the resolution of the Fourth Antinomy, Kant makes special efforts to establish the possibility of the noumenal world. In fact he wants to use the existence of antinomies themselves as an evidence for the existence of the noumenal world. (A 506 = B 534) Since the phenomenal world inevitably produces a set of opposite claims, he holds, it cannot be a self-consistent object. Since self-contradiction can never be found in a real object or a thing in itself, he claims, the phenomenal world cannot be assumed to exist outside the mind. Since the phenomenal world has only a representational being, he thus concludes, there must be a noumenal world that is the ground of the phenomenal world.

This is a dialectical argument for the existence of the noumenal world; it can be validated by the premise that Kant has succeeded in formulating cogent proofs for all the theses and antitheses of the four Antinomies. But we have seen that he cannot be credited with such a success, and hence his dialectical argument for the existence of the noumenal world cannot even get off the ground.

There is nothing against the introduction of the noumenal world, except that it seems of little value as long as it is kept as a domain of meaningless discourse. Moral freedom does not become any more intelligible when it is placed in the context of the noumenal world, unless the noumenal world is rescued from the abyss of meaninglessness. That Kant cannot give an adequate account of moral freedom and moral acts is one more piece of telling evidence for the inadequacy of his theories of the subject and the world.

This inadequacy is not limited to Kant's doctrine of the moral subject. We should realize that the notion of freedom is as indispensable to Kant's theoretical subject as to his moral subject. He does not want to admit that the activities of the cognitive subject are governed entirely by the causal laws of the phenomenal world any more than he is willing to admit that the activities of the moral subject are likewise governed. (A 546 f. = B 574) It is quite misleading to take at its face value Kant's well-known remark that theoretical reason can establish only the possibility of human freedom and that only practical reason can establish its reality. But the *spontaneity* of the theoretical intellect is none other than the freedom of the cognitive reason. As long as the spontaneity of intellect is a necessary condition for cognitive activities, human freedom is as necessary a presupposition for theoretical as for practical reason. Neither intellectual freedom nor moral freedom can be meaningfully accommodated within transcendental idealism as long as the causal principle is given absolutely universal reign over the phenomenal world, and the domain of meaningful discourse has not been expanded so as to include the noumenal world. Thus Kant's doctrine of the world and the subject fails to give a proper account of our intellectual life as well as our moral life.

So far we have confined our attention to Kant's resolution of the Antinomies. In order to complete our investigation, we shall now determine how he understood the genesis of the Antinomies. He attributes their genesis to the conflict between understanding and reason:

> Such dialectical doctrine relates not to the unity of understanding in empirical concepts, but to the unity of reason in mere ideas. Since this unity of reason involves a synthesis according to rules, it must conform to the understanding; and yet as demanding absolute unity of synthesis it must at the same time harmonize with reason. But the conditions of this unity are such that when it is adequate to reason it is too great for the understanding; and when suited to the understanding, too small for reason. There thus arises a conflict which cannot be avoided, do what we will. (A 422 = B 450)

Kant believes that the dialectical antinomies cannot arise as long as the understanding is left alone in its empirical investigations and that they arise only when reason steps in with its ideas of the absolute totalities or the unconditioned conditions. He also believes that the two intellectual faculties are bound to come into conflict because one is the finite faculty of the conditioned and the other the infinite faculty of the unconditioned. In his view, the antinomies of pure reason are the manifestations of this inevitable inner conflict of human intellect.

Kant's diagnosis of the antinomies is not quite acceptable

as it stands. It oversimplifies the nature and extent of antinomies to maintain that they arise only in the context of absolute totalities or only in the domain of reason, which seeks the unconditioned conditions. Antinomies and paradoxes have been encountered in almost all scientific disciplines ranging from logic to nuclear physics and in almost every phase of their inquiries. In the *Critique of Judgment* Kant himself recognizes the antinomies which have nothing to do with the faculty of reason or its ideas of absolute totalities. Since antinomies are not limited to the problems of the unconditioned conditions, we should try to reformulate Kant's diagnosis and expand the scope of its coverage.

Let us begin with the distinction between the formal and the material antinomies. By 'the formal antinomies' is meant those which arise from confusion and carelessness and which can be eliminated by some logical purgation. By 'the material antinomies' is meant those that arise from the very nature of the subject matter and that cannot be resolved merely by logical clarifications. The formal antinomies can make no positive contribution to any inquiry, although their prevention and elimination are essential for any rational enterprise. As we shall soon see, however, the material antinomies render positive contributions to the development of an inquiry because they arise as one of its necessary phases.

Kant's fundamental error in handling his four Antinomies is to assume that all of them are formal rather than material. Before presenting their solution, he writes a section called The Absolute Necessity of a Solution of the Transcendental Problems of Pure Reason. (A 476 ff. = B 504 ff.) There he argues that the cosmological antinomies are not empirical problems and that they can be resolved once and for all without recourse to empirical evidences. He can make this claim because he views the antinomies as formal rather than material. He may have viewed them as formal because he assumed them to be the inner conflicts of human intellect (understanding vs.

reason). In any case, it is this formal view of the antinomies that misled Kant in his effort to resolve them.

The cosmological antinomies are material because they arise in the course of interpreting the ultimate nature of the universe on the basis of empirical evidence. Since they are material antinomies, they can be resolved not by formal but only by material inquiries. To be sure, mankind has not lived long enough to gather enough data with which to determine the ultimate nature of the universe. But there can be no doubt that the cosmological antinomies can be settled only by appealing to the cosmological evidence.

Now we come to the genesis of the antinomies. There is not much to be said about the genesis of the formal antinomies because they have been defined as products of confusion and carelessness. So we will confine our attention to the genesis of the material antinomies. Let us begin with the distinction between observation and interpretation. I submit that the material antinomies arise with the leap from one level to the other. The leap from observation to interpretation is bound to produce conflicting views because one set of observation sentences can always allow more than one interpretation. These antinomies perform indispensable functions in establishing an adequate interpretation of the observation sentences because the process of confirming an adequate interpretation is inseparable from the process of exposing the inadequacies of all the competing interpretations. Herein lies the constructive functions of material antinomies.

There are some material antinomies whose genesis cannot be readily attributed to a conflict of interpretations. For example, some antinomies may arise from two sets of conflicting observation sentences. This sort of antinomy is still a product of interpretation and will not arise as long as the two sets of observation sentences are kept apart from each other. It arises only when the two sets are related to a common subject matter, for to bring together two sets of observation sentences in the context of a common subject matter is also a function of interpretation. There may be complex as well as simple interpretations, and the constructive antinomies appear in every phase of interpretation.

This characterization of the antinomies can be regarded as a reformulation of Kant's characterization of them as the conflict between understanding and reason. Kant calls reason a faculty of inference. Since interpretation is one sort of inference, we may say that reason is the faculty of interpretation or that interpretation belongs to the domain of reason. Kant regards understanding as the faculty of experience or empirical synthesis. Since perceptual experience or empirical synthesis is much like observation, we may say that understanding is the faculty of observation or that observation belongs to the domain of understanding. Kant has said that antinomies do not arise as long as understanding is left alone to its empirical synthesis. We can say that antinomies do not arise as long as we stay on the level of observation. Kant has said that antinomies are bound to arise when human cognition moves from the level of understanding to that of reason. We can say that antinomies are bound to arise when we try to leap from the level of observation to the level of interpretation.

There is one technical point on which our version diverges from Kant's. Kant has said that antinomies are the conflicts between understanding and reason. But we should not say that antinomies are the conflicts between observation and interpretation because interpretations per se can never conflict with observations. Instead we should say that they are the conflicts between interpretations and interpretations.

Kant himself once regards the antinomies as conflicts in interpretations. In the Observation on the Fourth Antinomy he brings out the controversy between two famous astronomers on whether the moon does or does not revolve on its axis. (A 461 = B 489) On the basis of the same evidence that the moon always turns the same side towards the earth, the two astronomers produced exactly opposite inferences. Kant says that the same evidence can be used to support both inferences. He compares the antinomies to this sort of conflict in inferences or interpretations.

It is desirable to make one qualification about the distinction between observation and interpretation: The distinction is not meant to be watertight. Nowadays it is well recognized that any observation sentence can be an interpretation sentence. For this reason, the distinction in question should be taken as a flexible one. Since every judgment can be a function of interpretation as well as observation, it is more accurate to attribute the genesis of antinomies to judgment rather than interpretation. We have seen that the relation of observation to interpretations is always one-to-many, that is, every observation can be given more than one interpretation. This one-to-many relation reflects the nature of judgment or the relation of thought to sense. Since judgment is an attempt to characterize the nature of a particular through a universal, there is always some epistemic distance between a judgment and its object. Every object can be judged in more than one way, just as every observation can be interpreted in more than one way. Every judgment is bound to be challenged by other judgments, just as every interpretation is bound to be challenged by other interpretations. We may now characterize the material antinomy as the conflict among the competing judgments about the same object or set of objects.

We will now define the dialogical method as the method of inquiry that relies on the use of material antinomies. This method consists in inviting all possible interpretations about the subject matter, letting them freely compete with one another without prejudice, and then in choosing the most adequate interpretation as a consequence of fair debate. This method abstains from choosing any interpretations when evidence and arguments are not strong enough to warrant such a choice and will keep the issue open until sufficient evidence and convincing arguments can be assembled to reach a mature decision.

Kant has a high regard for this method of inquiry; he calls it the skeptical or polemical method. (A 424 = B 451; A 507 = B 535; A 738 ff. = B 766 ff.) It may not be advisable to use these two expressions, however, because they unfortunately have some misleading associations. The dialogical method can be called the dialectical method. It is also advisable to avoid this expression because it has been abused by Wolffians and Hegelians.

I am not pretending to propose a new method of inquiry. The dialogical method is in essence the method of inquiry that Peirce persistently advocated. Peirce propounded that any given sign can admit of alternative interpretations and that this one-to-many relation between a sign and its possible interpretants can take the form of an endless dialogue.[7] His dialogical method is rooted in his firm belief that all our thinking is in its essence dialogical. He says, "All thinking is dialogic in form. Your self of one instant appeals to your deeper self for his assent."[8] This is to say, our thinking is always a dialogue of interpretants whether it is carried on by one or many persons. Of course, Plato was the first to recognize the dialogical nature of our thought. He characterized our thinking as a dialogue of the soul with itself. It is this spirit of the dialogical inquiry that underlies Plato's dialogues.

Let us now contrast the dialogical method with the deductive method. By the latter is meant the method of inquiry that relies on deduction from first principles. The deductive method is exemplified by the scientific method as formulated by Aristotle and Descartes. Since this method must secure a set of indubitable principles which can function as the premises for its deductive inquiry, it must appeal to a special faculty of intellectual intuition that can vouch for the certainty of the first principles. In contrast to this, the dialogical method requires no such intuitive faculty because it never relies on any indubitable principles and because all its assertions are subject to constant criticism.

I have elaborated these two methods of inquiry in order to determine the nature of the method of inquiry that Kant employs in the Transcendental Analytic. His axiomatic program is clearly meant to exemplify the deductive method, while his postulational program is meant to embody the dialogical method. His a priori principles can be accommodated within either of the two methods: they can be considered as a set of indubitable premises for deduction or as a set of acceptable postulates attained in abduction. Kant reveals his staunch confidence in the deductive method when he expresses suspicion and contempt for the dialectical method. On the other hand, he acknowledges the significance of the dialogical method when he emphasizes the critical or skeptical spirit of inquiry in opposition to the dogmatic one.

We will now show why the dialogical method rather than the deductive method can embody the true spirit of the philosophy of Kant's Critical period. For this, we must go back to the medieval era. It was the audacious Abelard who resurrected the method of dialogical inquiry by advocating his method of questions and answers. In spite of the opposition of religious zealots, Abelard's method of disputation came to be accepted as an appropriate method of theological inquiry when the medieval world finally came of age. It was with Abelard's method of disputation that the Angelic Doctor constructed his *Summa Theologica,* the greatest monument of medieval theology.

Even when the method of disputation was accepted by medieval theologians, it was never given complete autonomy. As long as philosophy was made subservient to theology, the method of disputation was allowed the right of interrogation only under the authority of revealed truths. But as philosophy began to outgrow its medieval role of an obedient handmaiden and to reclaim the august title of the queen of all sciences, the method of disputation was bound to reject the religious authority and claim autonomy. The disquieting doubts that afflicted Descartes in his moments of meditation had been amassed by this method of disputation in its autonomous mature stage.

It was in order to save himself from such troublesome doubts that Descartes devised his deductive method. This method was intended to establish the intuitive authority of natural intellect and to let it take the place of the discredited authority of supernaturally revealed truths. Unfortunately Descartes' deductive method deteriorated into a dogmatic one in the course of post-Cartesian developments. Kant's Critical philosophy was an attempt to rescue the life of human reason from the shackles of dogmatic rationalists and thereby recover the critical spirit of free inquiry that had animated Plato's method of dialogical confrontation, Abelard's method of disputation, and Descartes' method of systematic doubt. Only the dialogical method can fulfill this critical spirit of free inquiry.

Chapter 12

Transcendental Theology

The unique feature of rational theology is that the object of its inquiry cannot be presupposed to exist. No one questions the existence either of the self or the world, but anyone can question the existence of God. For this reason, rational theology cannot simply presuppose the existence of God and proceed to determine the nature of God. It must settle the existence question before anything else. Kant says that rational theology has claimed three ways of establishing the existence of God: the ontological proof, the cosmological proof, and the physico-theological proof. He criticizes and repudiates all three as transcendental illusions. Before examining his criticism, it is desirable for us to have a clear understanding of Kant's conception of God.

Kant introduces the concept of God in several different contexts, which may be divided into two groups: the context of the possible and the context of the actual. When Kant introduces the concept of God in the context of the possible, he defines God as the sum total of all possibilities (A 572 f. = B 600 f.); that is, every entity derives its possibility from God. Apparently assuming the identity of the possible and the ideal, he calls the concept of God the ideal of pure reason or the archetype which everything imitates. (A 574 = B 602; A 578 = B 606)

Kant is not content with the notion of God as the sum of all possibilities; he also considers the notion of God as the source of all possibilities. (A 578 = B 606) Whereas the former notion may be a possible entity, the latter must be an actual entity. It is this latter notion of God that requires the context of the actual.

In the context of the actual, Kant presents three notions of

God: (1) as the substratum of all realities, (2) as the ground or cause of all realities, and (3) as the sum of all realities. (A 576 ff. = B 604 ff.) These three notions of God may be regarded as extensions of the three relational categories. Kant gives the name of *'ens realissimum'* to God, who has been introduced in these contexts of the actual or the real.

These various ways of introducing the concept of God brings out some important points about the concept-formation theory, which we have attributed to Kant. They confirm our previous contention that there is more than one way of forming the concept of God. We have already tried to expose the error in his claim that the disjunctive prosyllogism is the only way of forming the concept of God. We now see that Kant himself does not honor this claim in his own practice.

There is no reason to expect the different ways of forming the concept of God to produce the same concept. In fact Kant appears to produce as many concepts of God as there are methods of forming them. For example, the concept of God as the substratum of all realities is Spinoza's concept of God, while the concept of God as the ground or the cause of all realities is that of Leibniz. So the difference between various concepts of God is not trivial.

In Chapter 7 we have maintained that concepts can be formed only in confrontation with objects; this we may call the principle of confrontation. This principle is used in the three ways of forming the concept of God in the context of the actual. This is not to say that the concept of God is formed in confrontation with God. The principle is used indirectly because the concept is formed in confrontation with the objects of experience. Since these concepts of God are formed in the context of experience, it is quite natural that they turn out to be the extensions of some categories. Since these extensions go beyond the domain of experience, Kant once goes so far as to brand them all as mere fictions produced by transcendental subreption. (A 580 ff. = B 608 ff.)

Only the concept of God that is introduced in the context

of the possibles is not in conformity with the principle of confrontation. The concept of the possible that can be formed in confrontation with reality may be only the concept of some derivative possibility that is derived from some reality. But God cannot be the sum of derivative possibilities. Since all original possibilities are prior to all realities, the concept of God as the sum of all original possibilities cannot be formed in confrontation of some reality but must be intuited in its own right.

Since the concept of God as the sum of all primordial possibilities is an object of intellectual intuition, Kant compares it to Plato's ideas and calls it the archetype or the ideal of pure reason. This conception of God reflects Kant's material view of reason, which is expressed in the *Inaugural Dissertation* and which underlies the axiomatic program of the *Critique of Pure Reason*. The view that the concept of God is formed in confrontation with reality reflects Kant's formal view of reason, which underlies the postulational program of the *Critique*.

Kant does not regard all the different concepts of God as equally acceptable. Indeed, he prefers the concepts of God introduced in the context of the actual to those introduced in the context of the possible. He indicates this preference by adopting as the principal name of God *'ens realissimum'* rather than *'ens perfectissimum'* throughout his criticism of rational theology. The epithet of *ens realissimum* properly belongs to the God who is conceived as the sum or source of all realities, whereas the epithet of *ens perfectissimum* properly belongs to the God who is conceived as the sum of all original possibilities.

Kant never openly claims the notion of the greatest perfection as a constituent of the concept of the *ens realissimum*. As far as I know, only once does he refer to the greatest perfection of the *ens realissimum*. (A 613 = B 641) Even then he does so only casually. He may have made this casual reference simply under the force of the tradition that had associated the notion of the most perfect being with the ontological proof. Throughout his criticism of the ontological proof, he does not even mention the divine attribute of the greatest perfection. Even his famous thesis that existence is not a predicate is not called forth to contest the validity of this divine attribute. His *ens realissimum* can be regarded as the greatest being only on Spinoza's maxim that perfection and reality are one.[1]

Among the three concepts of the *ens realissimum,* Kant considers the concept of God as the ground of all realities as the best. (A 579 = B 607) Strangely, he fails to see any difference between God conceived as the sum of all realities and God conceived as the substratum of all realities. (A 578 = B 606) He disapproves of these two conceptions of God on the ground that they do not ensure the simplicity of the divine nature. (A 579 = B 607) Thus he comes to adopt Leibniz' conception of God in preference to Spinoza's. Kant's *ens realissimum* is the supreme reality from which all other realities are derived. (A 581 = B 609)

THE ONTOLOGICAL PROOF

Kant characterizes the ontological proof (A 592 ff. = B 620 ff.) as an attempt to deduce the existence of God from the concept of God. The concept of God is the only premise on which the ontological proof stands, and the denial of the existence of God is alleged to contradict this premise. Kant's refutation of the ontological proof rests on his contention that the denial of the existence of God can never produce the alleged contradiction. This contention is supported by the following arguments:

(1) The absolute or unconditioned necessity is applicable only to judgments but not to things and their existences. (A 593 ff. = B 621 ff.)

By 'the absolute or unconditioned necessity' Kant means that whose denial is impossible because it results in a contradiction. He maintains that this type of necessity can be found only in the analytical relation of concepts in a judgment or of judgments in a deductive inference, because only the denial of such an analytical relation can produce a contradiction.

Besides the analytical necessity, to be sure, Kant has recognized other necessities in the Transcendental Analytic: the necessity of mathematical judgments, the necessity of empirical thought in general, and causal necessity in particular. But these are not absolute necessities because their denial produces no contradictions; they are relative necessities because they are accepted only in relation to the possibility of experience. These synthetic necessities have nothing to do with the ontological proof, which relies solely on the logical principle of contradiction.

Kant is emphatic in his claim that absolute necessity is exclusively limited to the domain of conceptual relations. He says that "absolute necessity is a necessity that is to be found in thought alone." (A 617 = B 645) This claim is in line with his view of logical principles. He believes that logical principles can govern only the relations of thoughts and never the relations of things. Since absolute necessity and contradiction are determined by the logical principles of identity and contradiction, absolute necessity and contradiction can characterize only the conceptual relations.

The ontological argument claims that the existence of God is necessitated by the very concept of God and that the denial of his existence produces a contradiction. Here the modal terms of necessity and contradiction are used to characterize not the relation of a concept to another concept but the relation of a concept to an object. Kant maintains that this is an illegitimate extension of logical terms and principles beyond their proper domain of conceptual relations.

Kant concedes that the ontological argument can give the appearance of using the logical principles of identity and contradiction within the domain of concepts by inserting the notion of existence into the concept of God. The ontological argument can begin with the definition of God as that which necessarily exists and then go on to argue that this definition of God would be contradicted by the denial of the existence of God. But Kant says that this is an illegitimate use of the notion of existence. He holds that notion of existence cannot be used in any definition because:

(2) Existence is not a real predicate. (A 598 = B 626)

In support of this claim, Kant makes the following remark: "There is already a contradiction in introducing the concept of existence . . . into the concept of a thing which we profess to be thinking solely in reference to its possibility." (A 597 = B 625) In this rather compressed remark Kant appears to hold that the function of a concept is limited to the articulation of the possibility of an object and has nothing to do with its actuality or existence. This assertion faithfully reflects his doctrine of thought and sense. In the Postulates of Empirical Thought he has argued that only sensibility can provide the content of experience and determine the actuality of objects. Since concepts are formed by intellect and since intellect is the faculty of the possibles, he can maintain that the concepts are exclusively concerned with the domain of the possibles.

By 'a real predicate' Kant understands an entity that can become a constituent of a concept. Since every real predicate is a constituent of a concept and since every concept is an articulation of a possible object, every predicate must be an expression of a possible entity qua possible entity. Kant holds that existence cannot be a real predicate because it is not a possible entity. For this reason he maintains that it is illegitimate to insert the notion of existence into a concept of an object. Since the concept of an object is equivalent to its definition, it should be equally illegitimate to insert the notion of existence into the definition of an object.

In the proposition 'God exists,' the word 'exists' occupies the grammatical position of a predicate. Kant maintains that the ontological argument begins by mistaking this grammatical predicate for a real predicate. Since existence is mistaken for a real predicate, it is employed in the definition of God in the ontological argument. Only by this illegitimate use of existence as a constituent of a definition, Kant maintains, can the ontological argument claim that the denial of the existence of God produces a contradiction. The alleged contradiction is thus the product of misunderstanding the function of a definition or a concept.

Instead of being a real predicate, Kant means to claim, existence is the necessary precondition for predication. Since predication is the operation of ascribing attributes to a subject, predication must presuppose the *existence* of the subject. If the subject does not exist, the predication cannot accomplish its task. Thus existence is that which assures the precondition for a successful execution of predication.

(3) The assertion of existence is the synthetic function of a judgment. (A 599 = B 627)

A judgment can perform both analytical and synthetical functions. The analytical function of a judgment is to articulate the relation of concepts or the possibles, and is governed by the logical principles of identity and contradiction. Since existence cannot belong to the domain of the possibles or the real predicates, Kant argues, the relation of a concept to its object cannot be governed by the analytical function of a judgment but only by its synthetic function. Therefore every existence assertion must be a synthetic judgment and its denial cannot produce a contradiction.

We should be glad to rest the case of the ontological argument at this point, except that there have been recent attempts to revive its force. These valiant attempts have been initiated by Charles Hartshorne and resumed by Norman Malcolm.[2] Hartshorne and Malcolm accept Kant's criticism of the ontological argument, which is based on the premise that existence is not a real predicate. But they argue that the ontological argument can be formulated without assuming existence to be a real predicate. Malcolm claims that St. Anselm himself had formulated two versions of the ontological argument and that his second version did not employ existence as a real predicate.[3] For the sake of convenience, let us summarize the two versions of Anselm's ontological argument in accordance with Malcolm's meticulous exposition.

THE FIRST VERSION

(1) God is that than which no greater can be conceived.
(2) The God that exists in reality as well as in intellect is greater than the God that exists only in intellect.
(3) If God exists only in intellect and not in reality, God cannot be that than which no greater can be conceived.
(4) Therefore God must exist.

THE SECOND VERSION

(1) God is that than which no greater can be conceived.
(2) A being which cannot be conceived not to exist is greater than a being which can be conceived not to exist. (A necessary being is greater than a contingent being.)
(3) If God can be conceived not to exist, God cannot be that than which no greater can be conceived.
(4) Therefore God cannot be conceived not to exist. That is, God must exist.

Malcolm points out that the second version employs the notion of necessary existence while the first version employs the notion of existence. He maintains that necessary existence is a real predicate whereas existence is not, because the former is an attribute of perfection while the latter is not.[4] For example, he explains, necessarily existing dishes are superior to contingently existing ones. Since Kant's refutation of the ontological proof stands on the premise that existence is not a real predicate, Malcolm concludes, it can dispose of the first version but cannot affect the validity of the second. Therefore, notwithstanding Kant's criticism, Malcolm holds, St. Anselm's ontological proof still stands in its second version.

For the sake of historical accuracy, let us point out that Descartes also talks of the necessary existence of God in his version of the ontological proof. Following the medieval tradition, he argues that the existence of God must be conceived as necessary.[5] This argument later came to be formalized in in Spinoza's ontological proof, in which the second version becomes much shorter than Anselm's original, because Spinoza dispenses with Anselm's initial premise that God is that than which no greater can be conceived.[6] His simplified version can be summarized as follows:

(1) God (substance) is that which necessarily exists by its essence or nature. (The essence of God is His existence.)
(2) God cannot be conceived not to exist.
(3) Therefore God must exist.

Hartshorne also advocates this simplified version of the ontological proof based on the unity of God's essence and existence.[7] There is no need to appeal to the perfection of God in establishing his existence; the premise that God is conceived as a necessary being is sufficient to prove his existence.

Let us now see what Kant would have to say about the second version of the ontological proof.* The pivotal term in that version is 'necessary existence.' 'Necessary existence' together with 'contingent existence' has become a familiar term since the time of the medieval theologians. In spite of its familiarity, it still remains one of the most difficult terms to comprehend. Since the success of the second version depends on the function of this term, let us see what intelligible meanings it can have.

Malcolm equates 'necessary existence' with 'unlimited existence' or 'causally independent existence.'[8] This is exactly the equivalence that Kant proposed in the Fourth Antinomy. If this equivalence is correct, however, 'necessary existence' is not a strong enough predicate to sustain the ontological argument. The *nervus probandi* of its second version is the contention that a God whose existence is necessary cannot be conceived not to exist.[9] But it becomes difficult to maintain the same contention if 'necessary being' is translated into 'causally independent being,' because a God whose existence is causally independent can be conceived not to exist.

In order to illustrate this point, let us take the case of the physical universe. The universe as a whole may very well be an entity on which nothing can causally act and outside which nothing exists, but even such a universe may have come into being with a "big bang" and may go out of existence with a whimper. The existence of a causally independent universe

---

*It is exceedingly difficult to determine which version of the ontological proof Kant has in mind for criticism. He appears to take Spinoza's simplified version as the model of all ontological arguments at the outset of his criticism, where he characterizes the ontological proof as the attempt to deduce the divine existence from the concept of the absolutely necessary being. (Cf. A 592 = B 620) But the ontological proof, which he states in summary form in the course of his criticism, diverges considerably even from the Spinozan version:

may very well be contingent; there is no contradiction in the denial of the existence of such a universe. Likewise, there can be no contradiction in the denial of the existence of a God whose being is conceived as causally independent. Let us make this point clearer by restating Anselm's second version in terms of 'causally independent existence' rather than 'necessary existence':

(1) God is that than which no greater can be conceived.
(2) A being whose existence is causally independent is greater than a being whose existence is causally dependent.
(3) If God's existence is causally dependent, then God cannot be that than which no greater can be conceived.
(4) Therefore God's existence must be conceived as causally independent or rather cannot be conceived as causally dependent.

All we can extract from this restatement of the second version is the assertion that God must be conceived not as a causally dependent but as a causally independent being. Since the denial of such a being does not produce a contradiction, the second version fails to prove the existence of God insofar as 'necessary existence' is construed to be equivalent to 'causally independent being.'

---

(1) The *ens realissimum* "possesses all reality."
(2) It is justifiable to assume that the concept of the *ens realissimum* is free of self-contradiction.
(3) "All reality includes existence."
(4) "Existence is therefore contained in the concept of a thing that is possible."
(5) It is therefore self-contradictory to deny the existence of the *ens realissimum*. (A 596 = B 624)

At any rate, Kant does not seem to be aware of the possibility of using necessary existence as a divine predicate in the ontological proof.

A. G. A. Rainer construes *'ens necessarium'* to mean 'indestructible existence.'[10] Malcolm himself may very well have this meaning in mind when he equates 'necessary existence' with 'eternal existence.' But 'indestructible existence' as a divine predicate cannot fare any better than 'causally independent existence,' because God as an indestructible being can very well be conceived not to exist without contradiction.

I know of only one usage of *'ens necessarium'* which is logically strong enough to produce the kind of result Malcolm wants to extract from the second version. This usage appears in G. E. Hughes' proposal that the proposition 'God is a necessary being' be construed to mean that the proposition 'God exists' is necessary or necessarily true.[11] Professor Hartshorne in fact relies on this usage in his Ten Ontological or Modal Proofs for God's Existence.[12] If it is logically necessary that God exists, the denial of his existence must produce a contradiction. This is precisely the result that Malcolm would like to deduce in the second version.

Unfortunately, however, the proposition 'It is necessary that God exists' is not any easier to comprehend than the original 'God is a necessary existence.' Kant himself takes note of this translatability, when he examines the possibility of defining a necessary being as an entity whose existence is logically necessitated by its concept. (A 612 = B 640) But he points out that this definition of *'ens necessarium'* can apply only to the kind of entity whose existence can be proved by the ontological argument, which claims to deduce, by logical necessity, the existence of the most perfect being from the concept of it. Thus a meaning of *'ens necessarium'* that is strong enough to support the argument of the second version can be established only by a successful execution of the ontological proof in some other version. Hence the second version can be substantiated only by being transformed into a superfluous one.

The various meanings of *'ens necessarium'* we have tried out for the second version of the ontological proof can be divided into two groups: the 'ontological necessity' and the 'logical necessity.' 'Ontological necessity' means the necessity that characterizes the modality of existence or being; this 'necessary existence (or being)' means the indestructible, the independent, or the unlimited existence (or being). 'Logical necessity' means the necessity that characterizes the modality of thought or reasoning: 'It is necessary that God exists,' means that the existence of God cannot be denied without producing a contradiction.

The second version of the ontological proof stands on the convertibility of the ontological necessity into the logical or propositional necessity; that is, the proposition that God is a necessary being is convertible into, or equivalent with, the proposition that it is necessary or necessarily true that God exists. When Malcolm introduces the pivotal term *'ens necessarium'* into the second version, he gives it the meaning of an ontological necessity. But when he uses it in the development of its argument, he gives it the meaning of a logical necessity. It is this equivocation that gives the second version the appearance of being a plausible argument. But this equivocation is unjustifiable because the ontological necessity does not have the same logical strength as the logical necessity. Whereas the denial of the logical necessity produces a contradiction, the denial of the ontological necessity does not, unless the latter necessity is defined as equivalent to the former.

So far we have assumed that the concept of the ontological necessity is a valid one. But we should remember that Kant would never grant this assumption. In Chapters 1 and 6, we have seen that Kant repudiates the traditional alethic modal concepts on the ground that the modal concepts can have nothing to do with the content of knowledge. The ontological modes are the main target of Kant's criticism of the traditional modal logic precisely because they are, par excellence, the modes meant to characterize the content of knowledge. He believes that the traditional alethic modes are illegitimate usages of modal concepts and that the epistemic modes are their only legitimate usages. Thus, within Kant's epistemic modal doctrine, the very notion of the ontological modes is illegitimate, and the second version of the ontological proof can not even get off the ground.*

Let us now take note of one important criticism of the ontological proof that is applicable to both its first and second versions. This may be called Kant's overlooked criticism, because it can be formulated within the framework of his ontology, although he overlooked it.

Kant never questioned the first premise of the ontological proof: "God is that than which no greater can be conceived." But it could not escape Leibniz' astute mind that the proof would be incomplete until the concept of the infinitely perfect being is itself demonstrated to be free of self-contradiction. He tried to demonstrate this on the premise that all perfections are compatible with each other.[13] Since one perfection (a positive predicate) cannot conflict with another perfection (another positive predicate), he argues, an infinite number of perfections can be combined in the divine essence.

Leibniz' thesis that all perfections are compatible with each other reflects his ontological principle that there can be no real conflict in reality. In the Amphiboly Kant has already criticized this naïve ontological principle as the error of confusing the impossibility of logical conflict with the impossibility of real conflict. (A 264 f. = B 320 f.; A 273 = B 329) The rejection of

*Charles Hartshorne once told me that Kant's rejection of the traditional modal logic goes hand in hand with his rejection of rationalistic metaphysics. This is surely an acute observation. The logic of the ontological modalities is the foundation for the entire edifice of rationalistic metaphysics—that is, rationalistic metaphysics is meant to be the science of the transcendent truths that can be authenticated by the logic of the ontological modes. As long as this logic is not invalidated, the positivistic demand that the metaphysical assertions meet the requirement of the verification principle is entirely misplaced.

the ontological principle itself does not amount to showing the self-contradiction of the concept of the infinitely perfect being; it can only show that Leibniz' attempt to prove the possibility of God is ill-founded.

Even if we grant Leibniz' ontological principle, we have one good reason to suspect that the concept of the infinite perfection is invalid. If God is the infinitely perfect being, his existence is the existence of an actual infinite. But we have a good reason to doubt the existence of an actual infinite. Even Leibniz did not question this feature in the conception of God, perhaps because the notion of the actual infinite had become one of the favorite notions of the seventeenth century. Spinoza had propounded the infinite nature of substance (God has infinite number of attributes each of which is infinite); Leibniz had extolled the infinite nature of his creation (the world consists of an infinite number of monads). Even Pascal, whose sensitive heart had nothing but distaste for metaphysical speculations, took delight in characterizing the human predicament as an intersection of two infinite abysses.[14] Theirs is the century which gave birth to analytical geometry (the geometry of infinite analysis) and the infinitesimal calculus (the calculus of infinitesimals). The century of genius was indeed the century of the actual infinite.

Kant saw the difficulty in accepting the actual infinite at least in the domain of human experience. We have seen this in the last chapter. In the domain of human experience, he was willing to admit only the potential infinite (the indefinitely extensible) and never the actual infinite. But he did not have the audacity to deny the possibility of an actual infinite per se because he believed that the impossibility of apprehending an actual infinite only reflects the nature of the finite human intellect, which is limited by sensibility. He was willing to admit the possibility of an actual infinite for the divine intellect, which is not limited by sensibility. He must have thought that Zeno's paradoxes can arise only for the sense-bound intellect. This assumption was partly justifiable because Zeno's paradoxes and Kant's antinomies were presented in the context of the sensible world. Kant would probably have changed this view had he known Cantor's theory of transfinite sets. The paradoxes and antinomies which arise in Cantor's set theory have no inherent connection with the sensible world; they simply reflect conceptual difficulties in forming the notions of infinite sets. If Kant had known this, he would have rejected the possibility of an actual infinite not only for human experience but in and for itself.

If Kant had rejected the very possibility of an actual infinite, he would have said that God as defined in the first premise of the ontological argument is precisely the kind of entity that cannot possibly exist. Thus he could have disposed of the ontological proof by demonstrating the unacceptability of its first premise.*

Before leaving the ontological proof, let us stress the significant bearing which Kant's criticism of it has on the nature of inference. By extending the distinction between the analytical and the synthetical judgments to the domain of inference, let us distinguish between the analytical and the synthetical inferences. By the former are meant inferences whose conclusion cannot be denied without contradicting their premises; by the latter are meant inferences whose conclusion can be denied without contradicting their premises. A deductive inference is always analytical, while an inductive inference is always synthetical.

In the *Analytic* Kant argues the thesis that the human intellect cannot substantiate synthetic judgments without the aid of sensible intuition. In the *Dialectic* he extends this thesis to

*When I privately voiced this objection to the ontological proof to Charles Hartshorne, he gracefully acknowledged its unusual cogency. He also told me that he had always conceived God as a finite actuality because he was certain that the concept of an actual infinity is absurd.

the domain of inference: The human intellect cannot all by itself sustain synthetic inferences. This is a central theme throughout his criticisms of dialectical inferences, because the rationalists claimed to have produced synthetic inferences by using only the logical principle of contradiction. The ontological proof stands as the supreme example of this claim.

The ontological proof clearly violates the general principle of analytical inference: The conclusion can never contain more than its premises. This is so, because God's existence appears in its conclusion although it is not contained in any of its premises. This point has apparently provoked the following criticism by Paul Henle:

> If he [Malcolm] stated his claims using "all gods" or "whatever deities there are" in place of the proper name I do not believe he would arrive at the existence of anything. If he argued that there must be a being having necessary existence—whatever necessary existence may be—I do not believe he could conclude the existence of any specific being. The mere introduction of a proper name seems to be the sole basis for drawing his conclusion. This confusion is rendered easier because "God" functions sometimes as a proper name and sometimes as a generic term as in "There is no God."[15]

Henle is holding that a conclusion containing a proper name cannot be deduced from premises containing only general names. I believe that the distinction between proper and general names is made in terms of the denotative function of names—proper names denote individuals while general names do not. The propositions containing proper names are existential assertions, while propositions containing only general names are nonexistential ones. Henle is arguing that an analytical inference whose premise contains no existential assertions can never produce a conclusion which makes an existential claim. He believes that the ontological proof pretends to perform the miracle of deducing an existential conclusion from nonexistential premises by using the pivotal term 'God' as a general name in the latter and as a proper name in the former.

Since the human intellect is discursive, it can neither confront concrete entities nor produce proper names. Left to itself, it can never get out of the domain of general names or abstract entities. In contrast with the discursive human intellect, Kant recognizes the possibility of an intuitive intellect that would have a direct access to the domain of existence, would need no general names but use only proper names, and would think in concrete essences rather than in abstract concepts. Even St. Thomas admits the feasibility of the ontological proof for such an intuitive intellect, by saying that the necessity of God's existence cannot be denied by those who see his essence because his essence is his existence.[16] Spinoza adopts this form of the ontological proof; the premise of his proof is not the concept of God but God's essence.[17]

The Spinozistic form of the ontological proof is not really an inference but an intuition, because the intuitive intellect which can see the essence of God and its identity with his existence does not infer but intuit the divine existence. This intellectual intuition is what Kant calls the knowledge from principles or the apprehension of the particular in the universal. (A 300 = B 357) Only the intuitive intellect can see the absolute or logical necessity of the divine existence, because it is logically impossible for it to see the essence of God and yet deny His existence. Kant means to say that the human intellect does not see the essence of God but only has a concept of God and that no discursive concept can necessitate any existence. The contention of the ontological proof ("The notion of God necessarily entails his existence") can be accepted only as an assertion of the intuitive intellectual insight, but can never be substantiated as an inference of the discursive human intellect.

Whereas the ontological proof makes the apparently implausible claim of deducing the existence of God from a concept, Kant says, the cosmological proof (A 603 ff. = B 631 ff.) makes the apparently plausible claim of deducing the existence of the absolutely necessary being from contingent existences. (A 604 = B 632) He goes on to say that the cosmological proof appears to be a much more natural line of inference than the ontological proof because the cosmological proof is not wholly a priori and has some existential basis. (A 605 = B 633) In spite of this apparent plausibility, he argues that the cosmological proof is bound to commit precisely the same error that is committed by the ontological proof.

Kant maintains that the cosmological proof cannot be completed without adopting the ontological proof in toto. The cosmological proof argues for the existence of God as the absolutely necessary cause of all contingent existences. The necessary cause in question must be a necessary being, because no contingent being can be accepted as such a cause. But what is a necessary being, and how can its existence be proved? Kant claims a necessary existence to be that "which follows of necessity from its concept." (A 612 = B 640) He points out that this is the kind of entity whose existence can be proved only by a successful execution of the ontological proof. Thus, he maintains, the cosmological proof can establish the existence of the necessary cause of all the contingent existences only by adopting the contention of the ontological proof. For this reason, he charges the second proof of the divine existence with the error of *ignoratio elenchi:* "It professes to lead us by a new path, but after a short circuit brings us back to the very path which we had deserted at its bidding." (A 609 = B 637)

Let us note that St. Thomas does not share Kant's contention that the cosmological proof is inseparable from the ontological proof.* Although the Angelic Doctor rejects Anselm's onto-logical proof, he respectfully accepts Aristotle's arguments for the First Cause in his well-known five ways of proving the divine existence.[19] The second and the third of these five ways are combined into one in Kant's cosmological proof.

The disagreement between St. Thomas and Kant is really only terminological; it simply reflects their different concep-tions of *'ens necessarium.'*† When St. Thomas tries to prove the existence of God as the necessary cause of all the contingent existences, he conceives God as the causally independent being. In this he clearly assumes that 'contingent being' is equivalent to 'causally dependent being' and that 'necessary being' is equivalent to 'causally independent being.' The necessity of his necessary being is an ontological necessity. In contrast to this, the necessity of the necessary being in Kant's cosmological proof is a logical necessity, that is, its existence is logically necessitated by its concept. This sort of necessary being is what Kant calls the absolutely or unconditionally necessary being. (A 612 = B 640)

The two necessary beings differ in the scope of the causal explanations they can render. The Angelic Doctor's ontologi-cally necessary being is meant to explain the existence of all contingent beings but not its own existence; Kant's logically necessary being is meant to explain not only the existence of all contingent beings but also its own existence. The former's necessary being is not meant to explain its own existence any more than Aristotle's Prime Mover is meant to explain its own existence.* Kant's cosmological proof is thus a much stronger

*Locke also adopts the Thomistic position of rejecting the onto-logical proof and retaining the cosmological proof.[18]

†Some Thomists have tried to defend their master against Kant on the mistaken assumption that there is a substantive disagreement be-tween St. Thomas and Kant on the cosmological proof.[20]

*Some Thomists may argue that the First Cause of Aristotle and Thomas can render a causal account of itself because the unrestricted

argument than St. Thomas', or rather the cosmological proof in Kant's reformulation is much stronger than it is in its traditional form.

Kant may justify his reformulation on the ground that the cosmological proof in its traditional form cannot fulfill its initial aim of explaining the existence of every entity. If the proof ends only with the existence of the ontologically necessary being, he may say, it would fail to explain the existence of the most important entity. Only by proving the existence of the logically (or absolutely) necessary being, which can explain its own existence, he may maintain, can the cosmological proof complete its entire program.

Thus Kant appears to have understood the cosmological proof to be much stronger than it had been, as originally conceived by Aristotle and Thomas. In this stronger form, the cosmological proof cannot be completed without incorporating the entire ontological proof.

THE PHYSICO-THEOLOGICAL PROOF

The aim of this proof (A 620 ff. = B 648 ff.) is to deduce the existence of God as the absolutely necessary teleological cause of the world. The proof begins with the premise that the world is beautiful and purposeful and then argues for the cause of this teleologically ordered world. Kant admits that the physico-theological proof can take two forms. In one of the two forms, this proof will take the analogy of human art and argue for the artificer of the world. (A 627 = B 655) In this form the proof can explain only the order of the world but not its existence and matter. In order to explain the very existence of the world as well as its teleological order, Kant maintains,

---

application of the causal principle in the cosmological proof must show the First Cause to be the cause of itself. But I am not certain that Aristotle and Thomas would approve of the self-reflexive application of the causal principle or accept the notion of *causa sui*.

the physico-theological proof must incorporate the cosmological proof. (A 629 = B 657) This is the second of the two forms which the proof can take. Once the physico-theological proof incorporates the cosmological proof, Kant holds, the physico-theological proof must incorporate the ontological proof, without which the cosmological proof cannot be completed. (A 630 = B 658)

Just as we have distinguished Kant's cosmological proof from the second and third ways of Thomas, we must distinguish Kant's physico-theological proof from Thomas' fifth way. While St. Thomas is seeking the ultimate final cause that can explain the teleological order of the world, Kant is seeking the logically (or absolutely) necessary being that can explain not only the world's teleological order but also its existence and even the existence of the necessary being itself. If the physico-theological proof is conceived as such a comprehensive program of explanation as this, it must incorporate the cosmological and the ontological proof and fall into the transcendental illusion of deducing necessary existence from a concept.

Before concluding our review of Kant's criticism of rational theology, let us consider one unique feature of the concept of the *ens realissimum*. Unlike the concepts of the self and the world that provide the ultimate conceptual framework for the construction of the phenomenal world, the concept of the *ens realissimum* is too transcendent to perform any function for the constitution of experience. This difference between the ideal of pure reason and its ideas is reflected in the different attitudes that Kant takes in his criticism of the three rational pseudo-sciences. In his criticism of rational psychology and rational cosmology, Kant has tried to reformulate the rationalists' doctrines of the subject and the object in terms of his own transcendental idealism. In his criticism of rational theology, Kant has tried simply to repudiate the rationalists' position altogether. Whereas he is constructive in the former criticism, he is destructive in the latter.

Kant's thesis that the concepts of pure reason can play a regulative function is really needed to carve out some constructive function for the concept of the *ens realissimum*. It is not really necessary to invoke this thesis to provide some constructive functions for the concepts of the self and the world. Kant's contention that the idea of the self can perform a regulative function for the science of psychology must be only an architectonic afterthought. The concept of the subject cannot be consigned to any particular science (e.g. psychology) because it is an idea necessary for the constitution of the entire phenomenal world. There is no need to find a regulative function for the idea of the world. The idea of the world as completed may find no reference in the phenomenal world, but the idea of the world itself though incomplete can be given objective reference. The concept of the ens realissimum is the only concept of pure reason that can be given no objective reference in the domain of experience. Hence it is the only concept that needs to be given a regulative function.

The regulative function of the concept of the ens realissimum is to encourage the ever extensive and intensive application of the three logical principles of *homogeneity, variety,* and *affinity.* (A 657 = B 685) The function of these three logical principles is to establish as thorough a classificatory system as possible among all the objects of experience. Kant claims that the concept of ens realissimum can play a regulative function in the application of these logical principles because their application stands on the presupposition that all nature is an intelligible system *as if* it were a work of the supreme intelligence. (A 686 = B 714)

The function of the concept of God is to lead us to assume that the world of nature is an intelligible system amenable to scientific investigation. I do not believe that to regard all nature as the work of the supreme intelligence is the only thought which will lead us to assume the intelligibility of the phenomenal world. In support of the regulative function of the concept of God, some may argue that the inception and the emergence of the natural sciences were prompted by the medieval theological doctrine that nature was created by the supreme intelligence.* Perhaps we have not yet accumulated enough historical evidences to settle this point. But the Greeks did not need the idea of the divine creation to encourage their scientific outlook. Kant himself in the *Critique of Judgment* does not appeal to the idea of the divine creation to account for the systematic unity of nature. In the third *Critique* he says that nature can be regarded as an *analogue of life,* which can organize itself instead of having its organization as an imposition from some external agent.[21] This view of nature is much like Anaxagoras' conceptions, which can well sustain any scientific inquiry.

If Kant's ens realissimum is conceived as an immanent self-organizing nature rather than a transcendent deity, his concept of God would be much more like Spinoza's than Leibniz'. Spinoza says, "God is the immanent and not the transient cause of all things."[22] In the *Critique of Pure Reason* Kant might have been led to adopt the Leibnizian conception of God by his religious considerations. By the time he wrote the *Critique of Judgment,* he might have been compelled to adopt the Spinozistic conception of God by his own epistemological considerations. Whereas the concept of the transcendent God must be consigned to the domain of the unintelligible, the concept of the immanent God can be accepted into the domain of meaningful discourse. Unlike the former concept, the latter can be given the same kind of contextual reference within the phenomenal world as the concepts of the self and the world.

*Quite a few historians have recently argued that the medieval conception of nature as a book *(liber naturae)* was a crucial inspiration for the emergence of natural sciences during the Renaissance. That is, the scientific method was conceived as a method to decipher the book of nature. For details, see Marshall McLuhan, *The Gutenberg Galaxy* (Toronto, University of Toronto Press, 1962), pp. 183 ff.

To be sure, within the framework of the *Inaugural Dissertation,* Kant can meaningfully talk of the transcendent God because there the transcendent world is held to be the only intelligible world. But in the *Critique of Pure Reason* he had to reject the intelligibility of the noumenal world, at least for human beings, because he rejected the possibility of intellectual intuition for the human discursive intellect. So the concept of the transcendent God is a legacy of the *Dissertation,* a concept that could not be consistently accommodated within the framework of the *Critique.*

One may be tempted to say that the concept of the transcendent God is required by the doctrine of Kant's Critical period —that the world of nature is only the world of appearances. But we have seen in the last chapter how weak is one of the chief reasons Kant offers in support of this doctrine. I do not believe that the other arguments Kant offers in support of this doctrine have any better foundation than the one based on his doctrine of the antinomies of pure reason.

The concept of the transcendent God even in its regulative function is thus neither required nor can it be accommodated within Kant's fully Critical doctrine of experience, that is, the experience of the sensible world. If Kant still wants God to have a place within his philosophical system, he must introduce Him in some other context than that of the experience of the sensible world.

Kant's contention that the systematization of nature requires only the application of logical principles, expresses his inadequate understanding of scientific systematization. Its aim is not simply to establish a complete classificatory system of natural objects, as Kant claims. Whitehead is surely right in saying that classification is not the end but only the beginning of science. The important function of scientific systematization is to provide a unified system of explanation. Kant himself comes very close to recognizing this explanatory function of systematization when he says that the search for *fundamental power* is the search for the force underlying all the various manifestations of power. (A 649 = B 677)

If the function of systematization is not merely to classify but to explain natural objects and phenomena, this function cannot be discharged merely by the application of logical principles. When Kant conceives systematization in such a simple fashion, he assumes that pure reason can produce no synthetic judgments in the regulative use of its ideas because it is not supported by the faculty of sensibility. That is, the regulative function of reason can provide only an analytical unity because it relies only on its logical principles. But it is a naïve assumption to believe that even the classification of natural objects can be accomplished by the application of logical principles. The classification of natural objects also requires the aid of sensibility and cannot be accomplished by the analytical function of reason alone. Since the function of explanation is much more a material function than is the function of classification, the function of pure reason cannot be any less synthetic than the function of understanding.

A Kantian need not be disturbed to learn that the function of reason is synthetic. If this synthetic function of reason is understood to transcend the domain of experience, he would indeed have cause to be disturbed. The synthetic function of reason can be conceived as immanent as long as its explanatory system is postulated in the context of the phenomenal world. If reason can play as legitimate a synthetic function as understanding, we can no longer see any functional difference between the two intellectual faculties. The most important reason Kant has for claiming the distinction between the two intellectual faculties is his assumption that one of them is destined for a transcendent function and the other for an immanent function and that only the immanent faculty can produce synthetic judgments. In Chapter 9 we have seen that there can be only a difference of degree between understanding and reason in their functions of forming concepts. We can say precisely the same thing about their function of forming judgments. So we have fairly conclusive reasons for abolishing in toto the distinction between understanding and reason.

If the function of pure reason is to seek an ever more comprehensive system of explanation within the field of experience, the formation of the concept of the ens realissimum should be understood to be a part of this explanatory enterprise. That is, the concept of the ens realissimum is formed as the limiting concept of the ultimate explanans for the entire phenomenal world. Kant himself understands the concept of the ens realissimum as such a limiting concept when he conceives the ens realissimum as the ground of all realities. This concept functions as the concept of the ultimate explanans of all realities in the cosmological and the physico-theological proofs. Because the concept of ens realissimum has such an explanatory function, it must be not only used but also formed in the context of the real, that is, the phenomenal world. The concept of the ultimate explanans will be given a transcendent reference only when we lose sight of its immanent explanatory function and misconstrue its existential significance. If we keep the concept of the ultimate explanans within the framework of the phenomenal world, we are bound to regard the whole of nature as a self-organizing system rather than as an artifact of some external agent.

In the course of explaining the regulative function of pure reason, Kant does say something worthwhile from which we can adopt some fundamental maxims of the dialogical method. He says that the concepts and propositions employed in the regulative function of reason are never apodeictic but always problematic. (A 646 = B 674) This is precisely the point we stressed in the last chapter: Every proposition proposed by the dialogical method is open to revision and refutation, and no proposition can be accepted without examining the merit of all its competitors. The same principle applies to the dialogical contest for the formation of concepts. No concept can be accepted as the ultimate concept for any objects, and the adequacy of a concept can never be proved without comparing its merit with the merits of its competitors. We are always under the obligation to seek more adequate concepts than those we now have. In our enterprise of seeking explanatory systems, we should never regard any system as the final one, but always try to seek a more comprehensive system. If we borrow Kant's expression, we should say that every explanatory system is only problematic. This is the spirit of the dialogical method.

Before ending this chapter, let us clarify Kant's conception of the relation between human intellect and existence; this relation is the pervasive theme that underlies his doctrine of dialectical inferences in general and his refutation of the ontological proof in particular. Kant has said that the ontological proof is invalid because it attempts to settle a question of existence with the principle of contradiction. He has maintained that no existence question can be settled by a logical principle because a logical principle can determine only analytical relations and because the relation of concepts and objects is a synthetic one.

For Kant, all existential assertions are synthetic. The converse of this thesis is that no analytical assertions can make existential claims. If any analytical proposition can settle a question of existence, it cannot be a product of a discursive intellect like ours which has no direct contact with the domain of existence. Since analytical propositions can make no existential claims, they are always explications of conceptual relations. For example, the analytical proposition 'All men are mortal' simply spells out the relation between the concept of man and the concept of being mortal.

Kant admits that the intuitive intellect can all by itself settle existence questions that can be settled by the discursive intellect only with the aid of sensibility. He appears to have thought that the intuitive intellect requires no concepts or universals because it can know individuals without the mediation of universals. That is to say, the intuitive intellect can know the particulars by intellectual intuition. That human intellect must rely on universals simply reflects its inability to intuit.

There can be no epistemic gap between the knowledge by intuitive intellect and its object because their relation is established by immediate intuition. In contrast to this, there must always be some epistemic distance between the knowledge by discursive intellect and its object because their relation is established by the mediation of universals. The knowledge of intuitive intellect can perfectly reflect the nature of its objects; the knowledge of discursive intellect can only approximately represent the nature of its objects. The former knowledge is bound to be analytical, while the latter is bound to be synthetic. The analytical knowledge is one which has no epistemic gap, while the synthetic knowledge is one which has.

The ever-present epistemic discrepancy between human knowledge and its object is probably what constitutes the ground for Peirce's fallibilism. It is also this inevitable epistemic distance that dictates the dialogical method as the ultimate method of inquiry for the discursive intellect. Only because there is bound to be some epistemic gap between every proposition and its object, every proposition is bound to provoke some propositions which contradict it. Thus the force of a proposition can never be determined without examining the force of each of its competitors.

We can now point out that Kant's doctrine of pure intuitions cannot accommodate the dialogical method. Like the knowledge of intellectual intuition, Kant's a priori knowledge of pure intuitions cannot leave any epistemic gap between itself and its object. It is this impossibility of an epistemic gap that accounts for the axiomatic necessity of the a priori knowledge of pure intuitions. We have seen in Chapter 6 that all a priori synthetic propositions produced in the axiomatic program turn out to be analytical propositions when we fully spell out the underlying a priori knowledge of pure intuitions. Thus the axiomatic program can leave no room for doubt and hence no basis for the dialogical method. In order to make room for the dialogical method, the postulational program must repudiate the a priori intuitive knowledge of pure intuitions. Thus we confirm the claim that was made in Chapters 7 and 8.

Let us now consider Kant's doctrine of the intuitive intellect. He shows two different ways of conceiving it: One can be called the eidetic conception of the intuitive intellect, the other the poesetic conception. By 'the eidetic conception' I mean the Platonic conception of intellect as the agent to intuit the eternal forms. By 'the poesetic conception' I mean the medieval theologicans' conception of the divine intellect as the agent of creation *ex nihilo*.*

In the *Inaugural Dissertation* and in the first edition of the *Critique of Pure Reason,* Kant entertains the eidetic conception of the intuitive intellect as a correlative of his doctrine of the intelligible entities in the noumenal world. In the *Critique* he conceives the ideal of pure reason as an individual as well as a universal precisely because it is supposed to be an intelligible object of the intuitive intellect. He expresses the poesetic conception of the intuitive intellect only in the second edition of the *Critique,* where he says that the intuitive intellect not only represents given objects but creates objects by its representations. (B 72, 135, 139)

I suspect that Kant changed his conception of the intuitive intellect in accordance with the change in his conception of the human intellect. In Part II of this volume we have argued that he tried to carry out two programs of a priori knowledge,

---

*Instead of the unfamiliar expression 'the poesetic intellect' I could have used the more familiar 'the creative intellect.' But I have decided to avoid this familiar expression because it has been well assimilated into common parlance to express the creative function of human intellect. I have coined the expression 'the poesetic intellect' using the Greek word 'poesis,' which means 'to make' or 'to create.'

namely, the axiomatic and the postulational programs. There we have also argued that the human intellect plays two different roles in these two programs. In the realm of concepts, the human understanding is assumed to have innate concepts in one program and to form all its material concepts in the other. In the realm of propositions, the human understanding is assumed to have propositions of axiomatic certainty in one program and propositions of postulational necessity in the other. It is these two different conceptions of human intellect that appear to be reflected in Kant's two conceptions of the intuitive intellect.

The eidetic intuitive intellect appears to have been conceived as an analogon of the human intellect in the axiomatic program. The former must have axiomatic certainty in its intuition of the eternal forms of verities, just as the latter has it in its a priori synthetic judgments. The ideas of the eidetic intellect are archetypes to which every existent must conform just as the transcendent categories of the human understanding are the archetypes to which every object of experience must conform. The former ideas are eternal entities, which are not subject to generation and destruction; the latter categories are innate concepts, which are not subject to formation and revision.

The poesetic intuitive intellect appears to have been conceived as an analogon of the human intellect in the postulational program. The poesetic intellect creates its objects; the human intellect forms its phenomenal categories. The former are not eternal objects; the latter are not innate ideas. Both entities are subject to the decision of their makers.

The eidetic intellect is the intellect of vision; the poesetic intellect is the intellect of decision. The conception of the eidetic intellect is a Hellenic legacy; the conception of the poesetic intellect is a Judaic legacy. There is one important difference between these two views of intuitive intellect within Kant's cosmology. The eidetic intellect can have no intuition of the phenomenal world because it can intuit only intelligible entities and not sensory entities. But the poesetic intellect can intuit even the objects of the phenomenal world because its intuition is simply its creation.

I have elaborated these two views of intuitive intellect in order to elucidate what significance the ontological argument might have for the intuitive intellect. The contention of the ontological proof is that there must be at least one entity whose existence is necessitated by its concept. Kant has argued that this assertion is void of any significance for the human intellect because its concepts have no control over existence. But he is willing to concede the possibility that the same assertion can have significance for the intuitive intellect. Since the intuitive intellect can be conceived in two ways, Kant should have added, the contention of the ontological proof can be given two different interpretations in the domain of intellectual intuition.

The eidetic intellect can be certain of the existence of its object by intuition. Although intuition can be distinguished from conception in the human intellect, the same distinction cannot be made in the eidetic intellect. The conception of the eidetic intellect must always be its intuition of some existent. For this reason, the conception of the eidetic intellect can be said to necessitate the existence of its object.

The poesetic intellect can be certain of the existence of its object by creation. Since every conception of the poesetic intellect means the creation of its object, this intellect can be said to necessitate the existence of the object. The existence of the objects are therefore dependent on the intuitions of the poesetic intellect. This is the crucial difference between the two kinds of intuitive intellect. Unlike the objects of the poesetic intellect, the objects of the eidetic intellect are not dependent for their existence on intellectual intuitions.

Having spelled out these two ways for the intuitive intellect to construe the contention of the ontological proof ("the existence of an object is necessitated by its very concept"), let us call these two ways the two forms of ontological intuition. We cannot call them two forms of the intuitive ontological *proof* because intuitive intellect stands in no need of proofs and arguments. The existence of God as the primordial entity can be established only by the eidetic intuition and never by the poesetic intuition. Every entity whose existence can be established by the poesetic intuition is bound to be a creaturely entity rather than a primordial one, so the counterpart of the ontological proof for the intuitive intellect, which we have called the ontological intuition of God, can succeed only for the eidetic intellect.

We have not engaged ourselves in the foregoing observations for the sake of speculative delight, but rather with the hope of illuminating the hidden premises the human intellect must assume for executing the ontological proof. The ontological proof must have been conceived as an analogon of the ontological intuition, which is the unique prerogative of the eidetic intuitive intellect. That is, the ontological proof must have been conceived as an operation which the human intellect can perform by acting in some manner like the eidetic intuitive intellect. We will show that this resemblance between the discursive and the intuitive intellect can be justified by assuming one ontological and one epistemological principle.

That the ontological intuition of God should be admissible not for the poesetic intellect but only for the eidetic intellect, should bring out one ontological implication of the ontological proof: that it can be accepted only within the ontological framework which assures the primacy of essences over existences. For the contention of the ontological argument that an existence is necessitated by an essence in the case of God can be accepted on the general principle that all existences conform to their eternal essences. This general principle proclaims the primacy of essence over existence.

This ontological principle cannot all by itself guarantee the efficacy of the ontological proof that the human intellect can construct; it can do so only on the assumption that the human intellect thinks with ideas that resemble the eternal essences. That is, the discursive human intellect resembles or imitates the eidetic intuitive intellect. To assume this is to assume one epistemological principle about the nature of our intellect.

Thus it requires one ontological and one epistemological assumption to show even the apparent feasibility of the ontological proof. It is important to stress this point, because this proof is usually understood to be a self-contained argument which needs no external support. St. Anselm himself claims to have hit upon it in the course of searching for one self-contained argument for the existence of God:

> After I had published . . . a brief work [the *Monologium*] as an example of meditation on the grounds of faith . . . considering that this book was knit together by the linking of many arguments, I began to ask myself whether there might be found a single argument which would require no other for its proof than itself alone; and alone would suffice to demonstrate that God truly exists.[23]

Anselm believed that the entire ontological argument is contained in the concept of God. But this belief simply reflected his philosophical naïveté. The ontological intuition of God would surely be self-contained, but the ontological proof cannot be so. But St. Anselm's naïve belief has been shared by most of those who have accepted his ontological proof from Descartes and Spinoza down to Charles Hartshorne and Norman Malcolm.*

---

*Leibniz appears to have been the only exception to this. He clearly assumes the primacy of essence over existence in his ontological thesis that all possible (essences) worlds are prior to the actual (existences) world. As we have seen in Chapter 7, he also advocates the epistemological thesis that the human intellect imitates the intuitive divine intellect. Although he does not explicitly introduce these ontological and

Not only the proponents of the ontological proof but also its opponents have usually taken it for a self-contained argument. Even Kant appears to be no exception to this; he seems to treat it as a self-contained inference in his criticism. Let us suppose that he were confronted with the two assumptions in support of the ontological proof and see what he would say in sustaining his original criticism of it. He would probably make different responses, depending on whether he was operating within the axiomatic or the postulational program.

Standing within the framework of the axiomatic program, which demands the conformity of objects to concepts, Kant would not hesitate to accept the primacy of essences over existences, for the conformity of objects to concepts is analogous to the conformity of existences to essences. He would, however, reject the ontological proof because he could not accept its epistemological assumption. He would say that, without the intellectual intuition of the transcendent realm, there is no reasonable ground to assume that our ideas reflect the eternal essences or that the discursive human intellect imitates the intuitive divine intellect.

Standing within the framework of the postulational program, which demands the conformity of concepts to objects, Kant would advocate the primacy of existence over essence rather than the primacy of essence over existence, for the conformity of concepts to objects presupposes the priority of objects to concepts, which is analogous to the priority of existences to essences. Thus he would reject the ontological proof, because he could accept neither its epistemological nor its ontological assumption.

Thus the postulational program reflects Kant's adamant position on the primacy of existence over essence, while the

---

epistemological principles in defense of the ontological proof, he formulates and presents his proof in the context of a philosophical system that can provide such a defense or a support for it.

axiomatic program retains the Leibnizian priority of essence to existence. It is this Kantian primacy of existence that is proclaimed in his various transcendental maxims:

Existence cannot be a real predicate.
Existence cannot be necessitated by concepts.
Existence cannot be established by logical principles.
Existence cannot be intuited by human intellect.
Existence cannot be asserted in analytical propositions.

Now we can see why Kierkegaard said: "Kant is my philosopher."

Chapter 13

The Dialogues of Transcendence

Perhaps today we cannot really feel the full impact of Kant's refutation of the ontological argument because we may not have adequate knowledge of the philosophical settings in which it was delivered. Bred in an ametaphysical age, disdainful of flimsy metaphysical speculations, we are likely to take Kant's refutation as no more than a simple reaffirmation of plain common sense. But we should remember that the ontological proof that Kant demolished had been adopted as the unshakable foundation for the construction of metaphysical systems since Descartes' *Meditations*. In order to appreciate properly the significance of Kant's refutation, we must gain a correct understanding of the function the ontological proof performed in the pre-Kantian days.

Let us begin by stressing the fact that in Descartes' hands this proof was meant to serve a function quite different from the one it served for Anselm. Both Anselm and Descartes had seized upon the ontological proof as a device to help themselves out of certain uncomfortable situations. But their predicaments were quite different. Anselm describes his predicament in the following confessional prayer:

> O wretched lot of man, when he hath lost that for which he was made! O hard and terrible fate! Alas, what has he lost, and what has he found? What has departed, and what remains? He has lost the blessedness for which he was made, and has found the misery for which he was not made. . . .
>
> But alas! wretched that I am, one of the sons of Eve, far removed from God! What have I undertaken? What

have I accomplished? Whither was I striving? How far have I come? To what did I aspire? Amid what thoughts am I sighing? I sought blessings, and lo! confusion. I strove toward God, and I stumbled on myself. I sought calm in privacy, and I found tribulation and grief, in my inmost thoughts. . . .

And thou too, O Lord, how long? How long, O Lord, dost thou forget us; how long dost thou turn thy face from us? When wilt thou look upon us, and hear us? When wilt thou enlighten our eyes, and show thy face? When wilt thou restore thyself to us? Look upon us, Lord; hear us, enlighten us, reveal thyself to us. Restore thyself to us, that it may be well with us,—thyself, without whom it is so ill with us.[1]

St. Anselm believes that his predicament stems from his loss of innocence and that he can regain his lost bliss only through the mystery of the revealed truth. It is in his devout affirmation of the revealed truth that he invokes the ontological argument:

> I do not endeavor, O Lord, to penetrate thy sublimity, for in no wise do I compare my understanding with that; but I long to understand in some degree thy truth, which my heart believes and loves. For I do not seek to understand that I may believe, but I believe in order to understand. For this also I believe,—that unless I believed, I should not understand.[2]

Descartes' misery is due not to the loss of his religious innocence, but to the loss of his philosophical naïveté. The lost naïveté was the natural belief that the cognitive subject is in immediate contact with the objective world and that this immediate contact is established by his senses. Descartes has lost this blissful assurance of naïve realism:

So disquieting are the doubts in which yesterday's meditation has involved me that it is no longer in my power to forget them. Nor do I yet see how they are to be resolved. It is as if I had all of a sudden fallen into very deep water, and am so disconcerted that I can neither plant my feet securely on the bottom nor maintain myself by swimming on the surface. . . .

I am supposing, then, that all things I see are false; that of all the happenings my memory has ever suggested to me, none has ever so existed; that I have no senses; that body, shape, extension, movement and location are but mental fictions. What is there, then, which can be esteemed true? Perhaps this only, that nothing whatsoever is certain.[3]

Just as the Anselmian sinner has lost communion with the Creator, who alone has the power to fulfill his longings and strivings, the Cartesian subject has lost communion with the objective world, which alone has the power of providing objective references to his thoughts and senses. Just as the former is exiled to the misery of impotent privacy ("I stumble on myself"), the latter is condemned into the egocentric predicament. It is in his struggle to rescue himself from this predicament that Descartes invokes the ontological argument:

And when I consider that I doubt, that is to say that I am an incomplete and dependent thing, the idea of a being complete and independent, that is to say, of God, then presents itself to my mind with such clearness and distinctness that I can be confident that nothing more evident or more certain can be known by way of our human faculties. I am so confident, owing to this alone, that the idea of God is in me, i.e., that I exist and have the idea, that I can conclude with certainty that God exists, and that my existence depends entirely on Him at every moment of my life. Already, therefore, I here seem to find a path that will lead us from this contemplation of the true God, in whom all the treasures of the sciences and of wisdom are contained, to the knowledge of the other things in the universe.[4]

Enclosed in his egocentric world, Descartes looks upon the idea of the most perfect being as the only medium of intellectual liberation. He believes that the idea of God has such a unique eminence as to authenticate its own formal reality. By virtue of the eminence of the idea of God he tries to establish the existence of at least one external object and thereby break out of the domain of his exclusively private thought. Thus he has come to seize upon the idea of the most perfect being as his only medium of transcendence. Let us call this the Cartesian program of transcendence.

Descartes makes two different attempts to execute his program of transcendence, which we may call the causal and the ontological executions. In the causal execution he appeals to the causal principle that "there must be at least as much reality in the efficient and total cause as in its effect."[5] In an alleged reliance on this causal principle, he argues that the idea of the most perfect being could not have come from anything but the most perfect being itself. Hence, he argues, the most perfect being must exist. In the ontological execution he tries to deduce the existence of God from the idea of God. He simply adopts the ontological argument; he does not have to appeal to the causal principle.

The ontological execution is far more Cartesian in spirit than the causal execution. The causal principle, which is invoked in the latter execution, would, if true, mean that every reality whether formal or objective stands in a universal causal communion. Since such a principle would not leave any room for Cartesian privacy, its acceptance does not really resolve the Cartesian problem but rather eliminates it. In contrast to the causal principle, as we pointed out in the last chapter, the ontological proof was assumed by its proponents to require no presuppositions on the nature of reality, because it was believed to be a self-contained argument. Since only the onto-logical execution can be, if successful, accepted as valid, this proof is thus bound to take on a unique role in the Cartesian program.

To establish the existence of God and to determine His essence is not the entire aim of the Cartesian program of transcendence. The problem of God constitutes only the first half of that program; its second half is to settle the question of material objects. While the first half of the Cartesian pro-gram begins with the idea of God, its second half begins with the idea of the material object. The two parts share one com-mon feature: Both of them are anchored in ideas alone. But Descartes finds immense difference in eminence between the idea of God and the idea of the material object. Unlike the idea of the most perfect being, Descartes believes, the idea of the extended object is not so eminent as to authenticate its formal reality. He believes that the idea of the material object can at best vindicate only the possibility of existence.[6]

The first half of the Cartesian program may be called the intellectual phase and its second half the sensory phase. The intellectual phase is concerned with the objects of pure intel-lect; the sensory phase is concerned with the objects of the senses.

The sensory phase of the Cartesian program turns out to be less successful than its intellectual phase. While the latter has allegedly born the fruit of necessary knowledge, the former admittedly bears only the fruit of probable knowledge. Des-cartes allows the two phases to retain their relative autonomy; he is content to see only a negative link between them. Since God is all perfect, he argues, He must have the grace of leaving us alone in our perception of material objects.[7] He assumes that God's interference in our perception would amount to his deception of our mortal souls. He is convinced that the most perfect being cannot be a deceiver. Thus Descartes comes to conclude that material objects do probably exist although they may not be exactly what they appear to be in our obscure and confused perceptions.[8] As far as the world of material objects is concerned, Descartes ends his Last Meditation with the same disquieting doubts with which he began his First Meditation.

Pascal is said to have felt indignation with Descartes' proof of God because it has little existential significance.[9] His indignation is not well placed because Descartes' proof is not intended to answer an existential question. But Pascal could have very well lodged his complaint in the epistemic context because Descartes' proof of God has little epistemic significance in securing the intellectual communion with the sensory world. After all the elaborate arguments about the nature and existence of God, the Cartesian subject must rely on his instinct or what Pascal calls the logic of heart when he comes to face the sensory world. Thus the problem of the material world has already become the scandal in the Cartesian logic of deductive reason.

This problem was a matter of such overriding concern among the followers of Descartes that post-Cartesian developments can be viewed as a series of attempts to liberate the Cartesian subject from his instinctual acceptance of the perceptual world. Most of these post-Cartesian attempts took the form of seeking the method of elevating the sensory phase of the Cartesian program to the same august level of necessity that had been allegedly attained by its intellectual phase. We will now see some of the salient samples of these efforts.

When Malebranche comes to tackle the sensory phase of the Cartesian program, he begins by accentuating Descartes' doubt about the possibility of a real communion between the extended and the nonextended substances—the possibility that had been admitted by Descartes only with considerable reservation. Malebranche categorically denies such a communion;

he is convinced that spiritual and material substances can never interact with each other.[10]

He holds that only God can truly act on finite spiritual substances as well as on material substances. He says that our soul "is united immediately and directly to God alone."[11] In his attempt to demonstrate the fallacy of the common opinion that the soul and the body are directly united with each other, he argues that what is usually taken in our instinctive belief to be the interaction between soul and body is really nothing more than their correspondence. He maintains that all finite substances can function only as occasional causes through which God, the only true cause, manifests His power. Thus he comes to propound his occasionalism.

We have seen that Descartes had made two different attempts to implement the intellectual phase of his program of transcendence—the causal and the ontological execution. Malebranche's occasionalism seeks to extend the causal execution to the sensory phase of the Cartesian program, on the ground that not only the idea of the most perfect being but also the ideas of the material objects are causally derived from the most perfect being. Hence his famous maxim: "We see all things in God." Whereas the two phases of the Cartesian program were originally meant to establish the communion of the Cartesian subject with two different kinds of existences, they are now claimed by Malebranche to be two different aspects of one communion with God. Thus the two phases of the Cartesian program coalesce into one in Malebranche's hands.

As a new implementation of the Cartesian program of transcendence, Malebranche's occasionalism has the following unsatisfactory features. First, as we have already pointed out, to invoke the causal principle is an un-Cartesian way of tackling the Cartesian problem because to do so really eliminates the root of the problem. Second, his causal doctrine forestalls the possibility of any real communion between a finite subject